Driving Force

Driving Force

Carol Madeline Smith

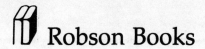 Robson Books

This book is dedicated with love to all those who kept faith.

First published in Great Britain in 1988 by Robson Books Ltd, Bolsover House, 5–6 Clipstone Street, London W1P 7EB.

Copyright © 1988 Carol Madeline Smith

British Library Cataloguing in Publication Data

Smith, Carol Madeline, *1949–*
  Driving force.
  1. Horsemanship. Smith, Carol Madeline,
  1949–. Biographies
  I. Title
798.2'092'4

ISBN 0 86051 509 5

Typeset by JCL Graphics, Bristol
Printed in Great Britain by Billing & Sons Ltd., Worcester

Contents

FOREWORD by George Bowman   6

INTRODUCTION: The Legacy   7

1   'That animal should be 'tween shafts!'   9

2   'Have you still got that nice little cob?'   18

3   The vow   51

4   'You must be prepared for the worst'   70

5   'No promises'   77

6   What appears to be the end   100

7   'Someone in this county must have space on a trailer'   109

8   'Ride? Be thankful to walk!   119

9   'Don't ever trust him again'   144

10   'I'm a vet, not a psychiatrist'   166

11   'I'm just as scared as you are, Bear'   175

12   'Nice cobs, Richard, nice cobs'   195

13   'This year the Nationals, next year the World'   210

14   New grooms and new brooms   221

15   Bad luck comes in threes   240

16   'Flag horses in front, please'   254

17   'Owners, please join your horses'   279

EPILOGUE   285

Foreword

by GEORGE BOWMAN

IT'S NOT REALLY so very long ago that most country people, at any rate, knew how to drive a horse or a pair of horses. But motor cars, buses and lorries, and tractors in the fields, have taken away nearly all the work the horses did. What then are those of us who are happiest with a fistful of reins to do?

The answer is simple. We still harness up our horses and put them to a vehicle, but instead of calling it work we call it sport — and we probably work far harder at it than ever we'd do if it was just a matter of getting from one place to another.

Britain is said to be a nation of animal lovers, and *Driving Force* is a story that will be enjoyed by everyone who likes animals. But it's more than that — Carol's enthusiastic descriptions show how what is still a minority sport can easily become a passion, one which has helped her to pull through some very rough patches in her own life. If you think 'carriage driving' sounds rather grand, don't be put off. It's a very different horsy world from that of, say, hunting or eventing — and to my mind a warmer and a friendlier one.

In her book, Carol mentions the dream she had of a horse and a cart, a well-trained animal pulling a vehicle, and that's the sport's appeal, whether you're watching or taking part. Some people drive one horse, some two, some — like the coachmen on Christmas cards, or the Wells Fargo drivers of the Wild West, or me — have four in hand, but we all want the same thing. We want *our* horses to look the smartest, to perform with the most flair in the elaborate dressage test, with the most dash and nerve in the marathon and neatly and precisely in the obstacles — to be obedient and intelligent, and to enjoy what they're doing. If they don't, we feel we've let them down.

Carol has written an exciting and moving story about her relationship to a remarkable horse, and — perhaps I should have put him first — a remarkable man. Her husband, Richard Smith, was once a miner; now he's the National Pairs Driving Champion for the second year running. The team of Carol and Richard, Bear and Blizzard (their horses) has steered its way round a difficult course and overcome many obstacles — and emerges victorious. Congratulations to them all.

Introduction

THE LEGACY

I WAS IN my middle twenties when I came into my inheritance from Great Aunt Meg.

In my late teens, she asked my father to invest her entire life savings in a trust fund for me, with the strict proviso that I couldn't touch a penny of it until I was twenty-five. Any younger, she repeatedly lectured me, and I would fritter the money away on some immature frivolity — well, 'waste aal that good money on bloody rubbish' was I think a more accurate turn of phrase. The amount invested in 1967 was somewhere just over £100, representing endless years of carefully hoarded sixpences and shillings. For herself she was left with her Co-op Insurance for her funeral expenses, and as she said, at her age what else could she want?

One day, having just been given a good tongue-scalding on my habitual wearing of trousers and 'gannin' roond lookin' like a bloody lad, wor Carol!' (I was twenty-two at the time!) I plucked up the courage to ask her just exactly what she did want me to do with the sacred trust fund when I finally reached the dizzy and mature heights of twenty-five.

She cocked a quizzical hairy eyebrow at me, paused, to my amazement smiled, and said, 'Aa wundered when the hell yu'd ask. Well, gan' on, guess!'

I frantically racked my brains for suitably mature and sound investments for her bounty.

'Towards a deposit on a house?' I ventured timidly. This suggestion received a derisory snort.

'Take an educational holiday somewhere?' A rapid shake of her head, while she peered at me from under those hairy eyebrows.

'Start a family?' I ventured, desperately thinking she might have designs on great-great-auntdom.

'No', she thundered, drawing herself up painfully to her full four feet ten inches, 'a horse, A HORSE! Aa want yer to buy a horse!''

I was utterly incapable of speech. I stood there with my mouth open. How could this sensible old Geordie woman, who had worked harder all her life than my generation could ever imagine, never known luxuries, holidays or comforts of any description, who was crippled and in agony with arthritis, who had railed at me all my life if ever I showed any inclination towards extravagance, stand there telling me she wanted me to invest her painfully scraped-together pennies and pounds on a *horse*.

'But why?' I finally managed very quietly.

'Ee, hinny,' she chuckled, 'Aa saw yer one day when yer brought that hoss down from yon riding stables, yer see daft'un, and by, Aa thowt yer looked grand. Really grand and bonny and proud. An' Aa thowt, that's what Aa want wor Carol ter dee with the money. Aye, hinny, get yersel' a horse, a grand horse.'

I took her frail bony shoulders in my arms and managed to say, 'Thank you, Aunty, oh thank you so much.'

Not for the money, which I doubted would ever be enough, nor I in a position ever to own a horse, but for the thought, for knowing what would really bring me joy.

1

'That animal should be 'tween shafts!'

BY THE TIME my twenty-fifth birthday arrived Great Aunt Meg had died, and I was in my fourth year of teaching Home Economics in a comprehensive school in Consett and had recently been promoted to Head of Department. I was also into my fourth year of marriage and my husband Michael and I had spent three of those four years, plus every spare penny we had, trying to make our home habitable. The reason that it was taking us so long was that we had chosen to buy a derelict country railway station in the upper reaches of Weardale in County Durham. When we bought it, the only water supply was a well at the side of the house and the internal plumbing was non-existent. The only running water was down the walls.

I spent most of the winter wondering how best to utilise my new-found wealth and position. To my astonishment, Great Aunt Meg's £100 — carefully invested by my father — realised just over £350. By the spring of 1976, daily sloshing through the mud in the drive, I had virtually decided Aunty really would have considered a tarmac road sound investment. Her touching wishes on the 'grand horse' project seemed more impractical than ever.

I straightened up from my battle with the brambles in the station yard one Sunday afternoon in late spring, positive I had heard the sound of horses' hooves. Strangely, for a very rural area there was a definite dearth of people riding horses. The sound was unusual though, soft and quiet. I must be hallucinating, I thought. Then, as Simon swung into the station yard, I realised why. The glorious chestnut horse with silvery flaxen mane and tail that he was riding had no shoes.

'Good Lord, Simon, that's never Barbara's little cob, is it?' My admiration was genuine.

Simon and Barbara Beckett were friends we had come to know because they too had recently renovated and modernised a derelict Weardale property. Simon's brother David was a

9

breeder of Welsh cobs and he had given Barbara the horse as a yearling. I had seen the horse when we'd visited the Becketts' the previous year (he'd put his head round the kitchen door and eaten vegetable peelings from the draining board) and, despite Barbara's enthusiasm, I'd thought him a rather scruffy, scrawny specimen — though I had made suitably polite noises at the time. She told me that his name was Blaze and I had winced, thinking it was about as subtle as calling a dog Spot or Patch.

Now the little gelding had grown, filled out, lost most of his shaggy winter coat and was doing his very best to progress in a straight line.

'Yes,' sighed Simon, rather despondently I thought, 'this is Barbara's cob.'

'But he's gorgeous, Simon.'

'I know he is. He's super — but he'll have to go.'

'Go!'

'It's Barbara's back. She hurt it years ago, you know. We had Blaze sent away, broken in and so on. Back he comes, Barbara climbs into the saddle, sets away up a hill and click; can't move for days. The bloody osteopath's cost more than the horse. He keeps putting it in, but every time she gets on the horse, click. So that's it, he says no more riding and I can't stand the flood of tears. The horse has got to go.'

There was what is usually described as a pregnant pause before I ventured, in a voice I hoped was blasé, 'How much?' Then I gulped. I couldn't believe I had just said that. I must be mad. Now Simon is a very successful private businessman who had probably got where he had by never missing a potential chink in anyone's armour. 'Of course the main considerations are a good home, and the right person.'

Frantic nods from my direction.

'But' — here my heart and pulse accelerated rapidly — 'we have just spent a fair bit on breaking him in and he is from a good line, you know.'

Less frantic nods from my direction.

'I think we'll settle for £350.'

'£350?'

Simon was obviously psychic or even more astute than I thought.

'Yes, £350, give or take.'

Operating my mouth before putting my brain into gear has always been one of my most obvious failings. What on earth was I doing? I appeared to be in the middle of negotiations to buy a horse. A horse that I barely knew, and for whom I had neither field nor stable, and at a time when having my own horse was currently in the bottom ten per cent of the 'hopes, dreams and aspirations' department of my life. It was impractical, impossible. Ridiculous. And yet . . . there was something.

Common sense surfaced not a moment too soon.

'Well, it's worth thinking over, anyway. He really looks a lovely animal, but I'm not actually looking for a horse at the present, you know.' I thought I sounded wonderfully off-hand.

'No time. I must have him off the place in the next day or two or we'll all go mad. I know a dealer who'll take him straightaway, so there's no problem,' Simon added reassuringly.

I didn't feel reassured. I felt completely unbalanced.

'Anyway, I only popped in on the off-chance that you were interested. Tell you what, I can leave it till tomorrow if you do need some time.'

'Tomorrow?' Tomorrow!'

'Give me a ring about tea-time and let me know. Come and ride him if you like. Must get back, no shoes you know.'

Tomorrow. I sank on to the grass and tried to re-organise a mind that had been calm and unruffled minutes before, but now felt like a spin-dryer in motion.

Did I want a horse? Well of course I wanted a horse — I'd always wanted a horse. Did I want a horse now? It had been the furthest thing from my mind till a few minutes ago, but the summer holidays were coming up, along with the lighter evenings. I did deserve some relaxation, some hobby in my life other than battling with derelict stations. Could I afford it? I was sure I could. After all, there was Great Aunt Meg's money to use, and my recent increase in salary would surely accommodate his needs. Talking of accommodation, had I considered where I would keep a horse? Obvious answer — in the field next to the house. It was simply a question of persuading the farmer to rent me some grazing. Stabling? Fortunately, the garage had been built for two cars, but only contained one. I quickly convinced myself that a few simple adjustments would create a marvellous loose box and anyway, I reassured myself, from what little I knew of Welsh cobs they were a hardy lot that wintered out well. I hedged carefully round the final but all-important question. If I did want a horse, did I want this particular horse?

'Yes.'

'Why?'

'I don't know.'

'Coward. Why?'

'Oh, because. Because there is something striking about him, something that made my tummy turn over when he came in the yard. His copper coat, his silver tail, the look in his eye, his presence. Something special. I don't know.'' And at that point I gave up the struggle to pit common sense against gut reaction.

By the next morning, after a most unpeaceful night, I had struck a bargain with myself. I would go and see the farmer, and if he was agreeable to me renting grazing, I would go and ride Blaze, and if, only if, I found the experience thoroughly enjoyable I would thrash Simon down to a much lower price and buy the animal. And if, I continued to convince myself with firm practicality, it didn't work out I could sell the animal and perhaps even make a profit.

Knowing the clannishness of the Dales farmer and his dislike for 'incomers' who bought the local properties, I had assumed my carefully orchestrated plan would all be hypothetical anyway as there was no way I would be rented grazing. But the farmer beamed benignly at my request, pointed out three fields I could use, told me how much better the old station was looking and how he liked to see a horse or two around the place.

Was this a sign, I asked myself? I am a firm believer in signs, and there were altogether too many of them pointing towards this little horse for me to be able to make a carefully considered independent decision about him. First of all the timing of the legacy and the exact amount, and now accommodation and grazing literally on my doorstep.

I had just about convinced myself I was unwell, unhinged or both, when the time came to go for my trial ride. I felt very apprehensive: I hadn't ridden in several years and this animal was newly broken, I mightn't be able to control him. What if I couldn't even get on? The days of my weekly pilgrimage to the local riding school were long past. Where once every spare minute and penny of pocket or birthday money had been spent on lessons and scraping together a set of riding clothes, first college and then work and marriage seemed somehow to have got in the way. The height of my equestrian activities, I realised in a moment of pure panic, had in fact taken place a solid decade ago. It was the image of a teenage girl astride a flashy, long-legged black mare that had so impressed itself on Great Aunt Meg's mind. It was a grown-up woman who now stood in trepidation at the side of a little chestnut gelding.

Somehow I clambered into the saddle without disgracing myself and, fearing the worst despite cheerful waves from Simon, set off down the lane. It wasn't a particularly eventful ride but I quickly learned several things.

Blaze liked gates. He turned hopefully into every single one we passed, stuck his head over and looked longingly at the grass. Blaze did not like drain covers and shot sideways about three feet at every one we passed. Both these tendencies made for a somewhat erratic journey down the lane. In the short intervals between gates and drains where it was possible to go in a straight line, we still did not have a great deal of success. On the plus side, he didn't seem to mind the occasional traffic passing; luckily none of it coincided with the critical moment of passing a drain. Also he was comfortable and had a lovely bouncy trot, especially when turned around and pointed homewards. Above all he was kind, light and responsive to his bit and, green as he was and as inexpert with young horses as I was, I felt happy and safe on him.

Running my hands through his luxuriant silvery mane I said quietly, 'Well, little Welsh cob, how about it? Shall we have a go and see what we can do for each other?' I can't honestly say I got any sort of response!

That left one nettle to grasp — money. I had never had dealings with buying a horse but understood that you didn't just accept the selling price straight off. One was expected to haggle. Trouble was, how did you do it? I felt embarrassed and slightly sick at the very thought.

Simon stuck his head out of the door the moment I arrived back in the yard. 'About the price . . . '

I nearly fell off. This man really must be telepathic!

'Barbara and I had a talk.'

'Oh God,' I thought, 'the price is going up. I know it.'

'Once Blaze is gone, it's stupid having his tack lying around. More use to you. It's not the best, but it's adequate, so if you'll agree to the £350, you can have his tack thrown in.'

'Done.'

'Well,' beamed Simon, 'it would appear you own a horse.'

Later that sweet and poignant early summer evening I rode Blaze home in a sort of dream state. Even when I turned him out into the field by the house I felt a vague sensation that I would wake in the morning to find him gone. But he was there when I appeared apprehensively from the back door, still in my nightie, at some unearthly hour of the morning.

Once Michael had recovered from the shock of my rash decision, he was very decent about the whole thing. After all, the mud on the drive wasn't *that* bad and it was my legacy and I had finally managed to fulfil Great Aunt Meg's wish.

In the days and weeks that followed Blaze was there morning and evening looking in a hopeful way for any scraps or vegetable peelings. His early association with Barbara's draining board left him with an acquired taste for an amazing range of culinary scraps!

Looking back now, I realise just how blessed I was with my first equine purchase. An impulse buy, especially of the unvetted, inexperienced four-legged kind, can so easily lead to disaster. Yet as the summer evenings obligingly lengthened to accommodate our lengthening rides, Blaze never once made me regret my decision to buy him. I ached in places I had forgotten I had and blew my remaining savings on jodhpurs, boots, hat and a ridiculously large grooming kit. I found myself clock-watching at school all afternoon, waiting for the blessed moment when I could head for home and my horse.

One of my favourite exercise routes took us three miles up a small valley off the Dale to the village of Rookhope and three miles back again. I soon got to know the lane and its cottages and inhabitants well, and some would poke their heads out of doors and windows and greet us as we passed. I had found the majority of the Dales people to be warm and genuine, friendly but very straight, so I soon began to wonder what on earth I had done to offend the old man who lived in the cottage on the bend. Most evenings when I rode past he would be there, working in his garden. The first time or two he nodded and stared hard. The next few times he shook his head sadly and clenched his teeth round his pipe and muttered to himself. Thinking perhaps the fault lay with me and my riding, the next time I passed I got the little cob going into his very best trot, fast and straight, just as we rounded the bend. He straightened from his digging, removed his pipe and stared very hard. He moved to the gate to watch us the more carefully.

'I've cracked it,' I thought smugly. 'Lovely evening,' I said to him as we flew past. I received no reciprocal greeting. In fact, the last glimpse I had from the corner of my eye was of him stomping and cursing round his vegetable plot.

I was very perplexed and not a little hurt. What on earth had I done wrong? How was I offending this old man? I ventured to raise the subject with the landlord when next in my local. I had rapidly discovered him to be an invaluable source of who, what and why in the Dale.

'Ah yes,' he chuckled when I explained my dilemma, 'he never could stand to see a good animal not doing a useful job, wasted like.'

'Wasted!' I spluttered. 'What do you mean?'

'Why don't you ask him,' was the only reply I got.

I became almost paranoid after that and for a while avoided the ride altogether. Then I told myself firmly I was being stupid and set off resolutely for Rookhope again.

'Perhaps he'll not be around,' I told myself cheerily. He was. I walked Blaze slowly up to him, knowing I had been spotted, and stopped. I felt I had to say something.

'I hope I don't disturb your gardening, riding past this way in an evening,' I said politely.

'Mmm' he growled.

'Do you not . . . well . . . like horses?' I ventured timidly.

'Like 'em? Like 'em?' He went slightly purplish. 'I've worked wi' 'em all my life.'

'This is my first horse,' I admitted, 'he's a Welsh cob, you know.'

That seemed to do it. The poor man obviously couldn't contain his anger and indignation any longer.

'Aye,' he spluttered. 'Aye, that he is and a bloody good 'un. You're wasting him traipsing up and down here, lass.'

He removed his pipe, leaned over the gate and wagging his finger at me like an Old Testament prophet he pronounced: 'That animal, that animal should be 'tween shafts,' and with a final grunt, his opinion finally aired, he walked majestically into his cottage.

That marvellous period in my life was marred by only one thing. Although I had been pushing the fact into the least accessible corner of my mind, my personal life in general — my marriage in particular — was in trouble. I had thought that buying a horse and getting involved with it would keep me so busy physically and mentally that my other problems would be blotted from my consciousness. To my surprise, and indeed dismay, I found the opposite to be true. Ambling peacefully along country lanes, alone with my horse and my thoughts, seemed to sharpen my awareness to everything: to the sounds and smells of early summer, to the glorious countryside of Upper Weardale, to the joy of a willing response and increasing fitness and stamina from my new friend. And to an insistent internal voice telling me that all was not well with my life and something drastic had to be done and soon.

As the school summer holidays approached, things reached a crisis, and I came to my decision. It was probably the most fateful decision of my life — to date anyway — and one I was to regret and mourn over for many years until I met Richard.

Maria, my oldest school friend, and her husband, John, lived some fifteen miles away in Allendale where they were also doing up a derelict property. It was a bleak and barely habitable farmhouse with a little land and, in a melodramatic way, was a fitting setting for my state of mind at the time. So I headed towards Allendale one July evening, travelling slowly on what was a long journey for my young, unmuscled horse. I carried a bag on the saddle with me with what basic requirements I thought I would need for the foreseeable future. The whole trouble, though, was that the future was so unforeseeable. However, my most precious possession was safely underneath me and that seemed to be all that mattered at the time. The desolate countryside above Rookhope with its worked-out lead mines and long-deserted cottages reflected my mood perfectly as we plodded stoically along. I had badly underestimated the time it would take to make the long climb over that moorland road, and as the light began to fade I felt very alone and very vulnerable.

Weary and numb, we finally plodded the last mile across a rough track to the house in near-total darkness. Outside lights came on, welcoming hands helped me down.

'Good God, where have you been? We've been worried sick. You feel frozen, come in and get warm. John's made a place in the barn for your horse, he'll see to him.'

Maria continued with her gently chiding, anxious chatter till I was in the house.

'Are you sure you're all right?' she asked me with a penetrating look.

'I'm all right,' I said slowly, 'but I can't say I'm sure.'

It was indeed a fateful decision. The end of my journey that day marked the end of my life as I had known it. At one stroke I turned my back on my husband, my home and my job for ever. It was cowardice — pure and simple. Everything felt wrong in my life and I hadn't the courage to try and put matters right. I simply wanted everything to be as it had, happy and uncomplicated and certain, without any more effort or agony going into discovering who I was, where I wanted to be and who I wanted to spend my life with. And so I ran away.

It took me just over a month to discover I had been incredibly stupid and totally, agonisingly wrong to do what I did. But by then it was all too late. I had resigned from my job, begun divorce proceedings agreeing to accept all blame, and the beloved home into which so much of our love and dreams had been built had been snapped up by the first couple who saw it.

I had run away. The shock waves and agony that I had caused were making ripples that spread and touched everyone and everything I had ever known and loved.

There was nothing left to do but keep on running.

2

'Have you still got that nice little cob?'

I ONLY RETURNED once to my home in Weardale, to collect some of my possessions, but by then it wasn't a home, merely an empty shell around some dead dreams. I launched myself determinedly into a new life, a new job and even a new husband, Ian. But happiness, in the naïve uncomplicated form I had once known it, continued to elude me. The longing for that now lost era of my life was bound up with places as well as people. I was not physically exiled from the Dale, I still lived within half an hour of it, but returning to look only emphasised that I no longer belonged.

When I had left in such a dramatic and final fashion, disappearing over the moors on my horse never to return, my friends and acquaintances had rapidly fallen into two camps: those who stood by me, despite being at a loss to understand, and those who simply did not want to see or speak to me again. Perhaps not surprisingly, ninety per cent had fallen into the latter category. Those good friends I did have, however, stood by me through the tough early months, found a cottage for me to live in and a field for my horse, saw me settled into a new teaching post and supported me through my divorce. My decision to re-marry less than twelve months after my divorce lost me a few more peripheral friends and even the die-hards uttered fatalistic warnings about doing things 'on the rebound'. But I was determined that only in making a good second marriage could I in some way atone for my past failures.

Ian and I sank our combined resources into a vast mausoleum of a red-brick farmhouse. It was square and ugly and had no architectural merit whatsoever. In fact there were only two things that attracted us to it; it had a one-acre paddock at the front and it was cheap. It was cheap because it had been rented out by Ushaw College, the Catholic seminary which owned land and farms in the neighbourhood, to a succession of tenants for years without any repairs or modernisation whatsoever being

18

done, and it was in a considerable state of dilapidation, though not actual collapse. When the final tenants did a moonlight flit, owing money in every direction, the Ushaw College Estate discovered that the tenants had been using the inside of the house as a dog farm, breeding Alsatians to sell as guard dogs. The resultant mess and smell was so appalling that the Estate decided to cut its losses, put the house on the market and sell it quick and cheap. It took a wheelbarrow and shovel, gallons of strong disinfectant, several pairs of rubber gloves and a determination not to throw up before I deemed the house in any way fit for human habitation.

I had given up teaching after re-marrying. Not only was there so much renovation, redecoration and plain hard graft still to do on the house but the property was also large enough to double as an office for Ian's newly-launched business as a chartered surveyor. It was cheaper to employ my ear for the phone than anyone else's so now I found myself for the first time in my life technically a 'housewife'. However decorator/landscape gardener/cook/cleaner/receptionist/kennel maid/groom would have been a more definitive description. At least my new life allowed a far more flexible use of my time and I was certainly never, ever bored. Exhausted yes, but never bored.

I could, and did, choose to spend as much time as I could with the horse I now called Bear.

When I bought him he was Blaze, and I called him that — though I was never keen on it. He had acquired his peculiarly different name tag during the first winter I had him. I had no stabling for him, but a kind farmer allowed me the use of a field about a mile from the cottage where I was living. It had a good hedge around it and was nicely in the lee of the hill behind, so I'd hoped it would give some shelter and protection and that his breeding would do the rest. I need not have had any fears on that score. By late autumn his coat was coming thick and fast. Just how thick and fast wasn't brought home to me until I introduced him to Lizzie.

I had met Lizzie at a village function, liked her at once and we chatted all evening. It didn't take long to find out she was horse-mad, rode regularly, even had some British Horse Society qualifications (something all recognised riding instructors have to possess) but despaired of ever having her own horse. Knowing only too well how she felt, I was quick to leap in with offers to come and ride my marvellous young Welsh cob whenever she wanted. I confessed that he and I were both very green and he probably needed a lot of education that I couldn't possibly provide but she was thrilled to accept.

I don't know what sort of mental picture of a large and hot-blooded steed she had built up from my enthusiastic rantings, but the first time she laid eyes upon him she burst into fits of giggles.

'Is anything wrong?' I enquired, trying to keep my bruised ego under control.

'Oh no, no,' she giggled, 'it's just . . . ' she was desperately trying to keep her face straight. Then seeing my crestfallen expression she cleared her throat and started again.

'It's just . . . he's not . . . well, quite what I expected from what you said.'

'Well, he's got his winter coat in, you know.' I bristled to his defence.

'Coat? Oh, he's got a coat all right! A coat and a half. He looks more like a woolly Welsh bear than a horse! By the way, is he a horse or a pony?'

That really rattled me. 'He's fourteen hands three inches, so he's a horse. Only by an inch I admit, but he's a horse. And he's only three and I'm told Welsh cobs mature late.'

They say love is blind and it took Lizzie's amused astonishment to make me look again, this time objectively, at my pride and joy. It hurt, to be honest, but he resembled nothing more or less than a shaggy, woolly overgrown pony from a Thelwell cartoon. But I needn't have worried. Tail trailing on the ground, mane nearly ditto, and buried beneath two-inch thick orange fur, my little horse had made a friend.

'He's lovely,' she said, quite serious now, 'and he'll need all this . . . this thermal underwear if he's living out all winter. Let's just leave him alone until the spring and then we'll see if we can tidy him up a bit.'

And that's what we did. Though at least once a week I would get a phone call enquiring how 'the Bear' was and whether it was convenient to come and ride. By the spring the 'the' had gone but Bear was here to stay.

My husband Ian came from a family with great hunting traditions, his father had been master of a pack of beagles as well as whipper-in for a pack of foxhounds, and my husband had continued the tradition as whipper-in and then huntsman of the beagles. Though I did my very best to live up to the family honour and all that, I had rapidly discovered that neither my lungs, legs nor general constitution were really designed for beagling. Gasping, sweating and plodging over mile after mile of usually wet, cold and hilly Northumbrian moorland, I desperately tried to keep at least in visual touch with a merry little pack of tireless dogs and their equally tireless hunt staff. Without fail, as I managed to push my exhausted aching body to the crest of the desired hill, the whole joyous band would change course and with a blur of green jackets and twinkling legs would disappear over the horizon. Those who petition and demonstrate for the abolition of cruel sports perhaps have a point — beagling definitely is inhuman, and I am prepared to testify, as one who has suffered.

I therefore viewed Lizzie's persuasive chatter on the subject of hunting with grave suspicion.

'But Bear would love it!' she persisted.

'Mmm!'

'It would do him a great deal of good. There's nothing like a season's hunting for a young horse to develop lung capacity and stamina, you know.'

That was a sneaky one. She had me interested now. We had both had a great deal of fun with Bear over the spring and summer months. He had certainly changed beyond recognition from the shaggy little creature Lizzie first saw. His mane and tail were shorter and neater. His copper-coloured summer coat was fine and sleek. With regular work and feeding he had muscled up, filled out and grown. He was now a respectable fifteen hands high and apparently hadn't stopped growing. (He was in fact to be in his sixth year before he levelled out at fifteen hands one inch.) In July we had even entered him at the local village Show in the 'Mountain and Moorland' class. He hadn't been placed anywhere but it was great fun, and my first-ever Show.

With autumn now approaching once more, Lizzie was determined Bear wasn't going to go to seed over the winter. For a start, we had acquired a stable. Although my new home didn't boast any farm buildings of its own, there was a full range of nearly derelict buildings to the rear of it. These, and all the land that had once gone with the farmhouse, were rented by Ushaw College to Mr Suddess, a farmer in the nearby village. As he rarely used them except to store a bit of straw or the odd farm implement, he was delighted, for 'a bit in his hand', to sublet one to us; we used it as a garage at one end and a stable at the other. The hunting debate continued with Lizzie and I played my trump card.

'Aha, what about clothes? I haven't got all that fancy gear and I don't see me lashing out on it on the off-chance I might enjoy it.'

'If you start with the cub-hunting, that's when they train the young hounds early in the season, you don't need any. An ordinary hacking jacket is quite acceptable and you've got one of those.'

'Aren't you forgetting two things?'

'Such as?'

'Firstly, people jump things out hunting — you know, hedges, stone walls, ditches, little things like that — and I've never jumped anything in my life and neither has Bear.'

'And secondly?' She certainly wasn't to be put off easily.

'Secondly, transport. People who go hunting usually arrive in things called horseboxes. We don't have one.'

'Okay.' Her smile was confident. 'Firstly, you don't jump when you're cub-hunting. So you'd have a couple of months to get used to the whole idea and see if you like it without being at a disadvantage. As for Bear, well he's just built to jump, isn't he? Look at the quarters on him. Oh, we'll have him jumping in a crack!'

'What about me? I'm not entirely sure about my quarters.' She ignored that one completely.

'And, secondly, you live in the middle of the Braes of Derwent's Wednesday country.'

'The what?'

I got a very long-suffering look.

'Every hunt works different areas on different days. They all have a Saturday country and a Wednesday country; some packs that hunt three days a week even have a Monday country. Now the Braes of Derwent, our local hunt, has its Saturday country over the Northumberland border, but the Wednesday country is round here. So you'd probably not have far to hack to the Wednesday meets — ten miles at the very most.'

It didn't sound much when she said it quickly.

'Well, if you're so sure it will do him good, I'll give it a try. There's one thing for sure: following foxhounds on a horse can't be as exhausting as following beagles on foot!'

Oh how wrong you can be, how wrong you can be.

When the alarm went off at an unearthly hour of the morning, I groaned and turned over. I felt a great deal less enthusiastic about the whole subject of hunting in the chilly semi-darkness of a very early October morning. The temptation to snuggle back down under my quilt was overwhelming. Then I thought of all the preparation the day before for today's debut. My saddle and bridle, my riding boots and, of course, Bear had been cleaned and polished until my arm ached. I had clear and explicit instructions from Lizzie where to go and what to do. If I backed out now she would never forgive me. So I rolled out of bed and staggered down the stairs.

By the time I'd had a cup of tea and got dressed in front of my beloved ever-warm, ever-comforting Aga, I felt much better; in fact I began to view the day ahead with some enthusiasm. I couldn't face the thought of breakfast at that hour but mindful that there was a long and energetic morning ahead, I made some marmalade sandwiches, wrapped them up and popped them into the capacious pocket of my hacking jacket.

Bear blinked at me with grave suspicion when I switched the stable light on. He had obligingly kept himself quite clean overnight and it didn't take long to whisk a brush over him and tack him up. Hounds were meeting only about three miles away, which is why it had been deemed a good day for a first outing. Once the season proper started on the first of November, the hounds always met at 11 a.m. and the whole affair became more formal. Cub-hunting, however, commenced much earlier in the day, didn't last as long as a proper meet and was quite informal. In fact the only rules Lizzie had drummed into my head were to say 'Good morning' to the master, never to overtake the hunt staff and to avoid trampling on the hounds. Breaking any of these rules could lead to instant ex-communication.

Everyone has a favourite season. For a lot of people it is the spring, for others summer. I love autumn. There is a smell of autumn, misty and aromatic, and a quality of the sunlight, a golden precious quality as the days shorten towards the long winter ahead. As Bear and I hacked gently down the lane, the morning gave every indication of developing into just such a jewel of an autumn day. The morning sun made the hedgerows sparkle as it reflected from the damp cobwebs, and a thin, low mist still hung in some of the fields.

We arrived at the appointed time and place to find about eight other horses and a small pack of hounds milling around. I only recognised one or two faces and then very vaguely, but I smiled and said 'Good morning' to everyone and everyone smiled back, so I soon felt more at ease. With no ceremony or warning, everyone started moving off down the side of the wood and, mindful of keeping Bear in his place, we tagged along near the rear. One nice lady enquired whether this was my first time out — was it so blatantly obvious I wondered? — and took me under her wing.

We had a marvellous morning. As Lizzie had explained, the main purpose of the exercise was to give experience to young hounds, and to get unfit, grass-fat horses back into condition for the hunting season to come. There was no jumping, no fast galloping, but plenty of long and exhilarating canters which we both thoroughly enjoyed. In fact, as the morning wore on, Bear got increasingly enthusiastic about the whole idea and began to pull more and more strongly, though thankfully at no point did he quite gain the upper hand and tank off with me. The young hounds also thoroughly enjoyed themselves, galloping around in a frenzy of lolling tongues and tails. They only once got on to the scent of a fox, giving tongue to a joyous chorus of babbling excitement, and I understood for the first time why people found that noise a glorious music. Then they lost the scent and the noise subsided.

After a few more draws the huntsmen decided to call it a morning and we all split up, some setting off together back to their horseboxes at the meet, others to hack their various ways home. With slightly aching arms and legs, but otherwise unscathed, I was trotting triumphantly up the drive by lunchtime. Ian was very approving of my exploits.

Having been deprived of his breakfast, Bear was ravenous and began angrily nosing his manger the moment he was in his stable. My own rumbling stomach suddenly reminded me that, with all the excitement of the morning, I had completely forgotten about breakfast. I put my hand in my pocket and extracted a package of sticky, battered marmalade sandwiches. They didn't look particularly appetising any more but Bear's ears pricked up hopefully when he saw them. It seemed a small reward for giving me such a glorious morning but he munched the sticky slices with great relish then looked at me hopefully for more. I suddenly began to giggle uncontrollably and he eyed me suspiciously. Had all this early-morning lark gone to my head?

'It's all right, Bear,' I assured him, 'it's just that . . . ' another wave of giggles hit me, 'with tastes like that perhaps we should change your name to Paddington!'

For the rest of the month it needed no encouragement to get me up and out early on Wednesday mornings. I was thoroughly enjoying myself and so was Bear. Each week saw him fitter and more keen — and harder to hold back.

But this pleasant interlude was inevitably short-lived as November drew ever nearer. I was in a quandary over what to do; the cub-hunting had been fun but now we were talking about the real thing.

Lizzie bulldozed through all my doubts. Cost? Apparently you could hunt up to three times a season just paying a small 'cap' (a nominal subscription for a day's hunting) so there was no need to lay out a hunt subscription straight away. Clothes? I had everything I needed except a black jacket, and Lizzie just happened to have a friend who just happened to be my size but who no longer rode. Jumping? Bit of a problem admittedly, but there was often an alternative route or gate and for all we knew Bear might be a 'natural'. Getting lost? Making a social gaffe? Never fear; Lizzie would hire a horse from her regular riding establishment and come with me to the opening meet. It appeared I had small grounds left for objection.

The opening Wednesday meet of the season was held at the Queen's Head at Lanchester about three or four miles away, mostly downhill, from home. As Bear and I turned the corner into the car park I realised to my horror that this was going to be very different from cub-hunting. Very different indeed.

Instead of the small casual gathering that had assembled for cub-hunting, upwards of thirty horses were milling around. Most of them were large and fine-bred animals with long, haughty faces, their fine sleek coats gleaming and their manes all either short and neatly pulled, lying effortlessly flat to one side or else plaited at neat regular intervals along their neck. There were some less smart types but they all looked hardened campaigners, tough and workmanlike.

One or two curious glances came in my direction and I began to feel very out of place and to wonder whose bright idea this all was. Although I had brushed Bear until my arm ached and carefully plastered his mane down with water, he still stood out as hairy and positively unkempt. Though he hadn't yet acquired all his winter woollies, it was November and Bear's coat was making its usual abundant seasonal appearance. And his mane. Well, his mane was a constant trial. It was incredibly bushy and thick and halfway up his neck there was a parting of the ways where one half laid naturally to the left and the other half to the right. No amount of brushing and coaxing could persuade it to do otherwise. It would consent to be laid to one side when saturated with water, but as soon as it dried, it would spring back with a vengeance. Our three-mile hack that morning had made his unruly mane sprout and spread from his neck at all angles, the road dust and puddles had totally removed the sheen from his carefully cleaned and oiled feet, and the novelty and excitement of the occasion was already making him break out in damp, dark patches of sweat. He must have looked, I thought to myself in anguish, more than ever like a Thelwell cartoon.

A great temptation to sneak quietly out of the car park and away home was foiled when a familiar figure detached itself from a group of horses, waved, and rode in my direction. It was Lizzie. Her hired mount, I saw at once, was tall and leggy, its main in perfect little plaits and its fine dark coat spotless after its journey in the horsebox. Her real leather boots were polished to perfection. Mine were rubber. 'Oh, the swine!' I thought, 'The swine — how could she do this to me!' But her greeting was warm and very genuine.

'Oh good, you've made it in plenty of time. I had a nasty feeling you might chicken out!'

I gave her a watery smile. A lady with a tray suddenly appeared at my side and I thankfully took the proffered drink and downed it in two gulps. When I could breathe again I felt much better. I felt more secure now that Lizzie was with me and I began to take note of what was going on.

As well as all the mounted riders there were a good many people wandering about and others just standing watching the scene. There was a couple of men in knarly boots and flat caps with battle-scarred little dogs yapping round their ankles. These were the terrier men, Lizzie explained; they would employ their talents and dogs to bolt a fox that ran to earth. Then there were the hunt staff and whippers-in present in full force that morning and resplendent in their scarlet jackets. The master and field master were also distinguishable by their wearing of the pink. I had been severely warned never to refer to a huntsman's coat as red. Pink or scarlet yes, red, never. There was a much larger pack of hounds present than I had encountered out cub-hunting including, when I looked closely, some grey-muzzled old timers. Their sterns waving madly, they busied in and out of peoples' and horses' legs devouring any stray sausage rolls that came their way and returning swiftly to the huntsman when he rebuked them for wandering too far. Bridles jingled, horse shoes rang on the paving stones as horses danced in impatience. There was a warm, happy buzz of chatter and the occasional excited yelp of a young hound. It was a timeless and colourful scene and very, very English.

As the village clock struck eleven, the huntsman extracted his copper horn from between the second and third buttons of his hunt coat and gave a single short sharp note. The hunt staff cracked their whip thongs to get the attention of the hounds. Horses pranced and snorted and with a great surge we were off. There was no going back. I looked longingly for the lady with the tray. I could have done with another drink!

Six hours later, as we crawled the last mile towards home, suffering was beginning to take on a whole new dimension. I had just about reached my limits a couple of hours earlier, when the huntsman, to my immense relief, had gathered his hounds together and decided that we'd had all the sport we were to see for one day. Throughout the afternoon hounds had run relentlessly on from the meet in exactly the opposite direction from home. This meant we were now a good hour's hack from where we had started and from where horseboxes awaited those lucky enough to possess them. For Bear and me, a further hour's journey home, most of it uphill, still faced us. On that long climb homeward I think we both passed through the pain barrier. I had ceased trying to ease my aching bones from one side of the saddle to the other and allowed my arms, leaden and throbbing from hours of holding Bear back, just to lie limply in front of me. Bear plodded along, head and neck down, concentrating hard on just putting one foot in front of the other. I would have loved to have got off and eased his back by walking alongside him but I knew I just didn't have the walk home in me and, once off, I could never have climbed back in the saddle unaided. So he had to carry me.

We had both had a great time, it had been exciting and great fun mostly, but we had both over-reached our mutual reserves of energy and muscular power and I had completely overlooked leaving something in reserve for the journey home.

The biggest lesson of the day had been to discover that neither Bear nor I were, as Lizzie has optimistically predicted, natural jumpers. Just looking at some of the stone walls and huge drops that most of the hunt went sailing effortlessly over made me break out in cold sweat and when, every now and then a horse and rider parted company in mid-air I felt positively unwell. I did canter resolutely up to one or two small inviting fences once everyone had leapt contemptuously over them but at the last moment, usually the exact micro-second that my courage waved the white flag, Bear would switch off the revs and do a nose-dive into the bottom of the fence. Lizzie had stayed with me and encouraged and even bullied — to no avail. In the end I insisted she leave me to manage as best I could and not spoil her own day's sport. She was finally persuaded and popped over a wall and was away.

However I was not left completely alone, for I was not the only non-jumper. There were a couple of elderly ladies on elderly mounts who had long since abandoned the lunacy of trying to get a horse air-borne. They looked after me very well but their way of keeping in contact with the day's sport across country was to prove twice as exhausting as the regular method. They were wiry and wily old birds and they knew every lane and field gate in the vicinity. So when hounds and followers set off across terrain they knew involved jumping, they would head off with great alacrity on one of their 'alternative routes'. I soon found this inevitably meant a two-or-more mile detour at a flat-out canter across fields and a spine-juddering trot along lanes until we joined forces with the main body once more. By mid-afternoon I was wondering where on earth the old dears and their mounts got their stamina from and whether Bear and I could keep up. But it was keep up or be alone and completely lost, so we kept up. Every one of their detours clocked up more mileage.

For the first couple of hours Bear pulled like a Saturn rocket. Not wishing to be expelled from the fields for overtaking hounds on my first venture out, I hung grimly on to him but my arms and neck were on fire with the effort by midday. I cursed him and hollered at him, and in the end even pleaded with him, but he just ploughed relentlessly on. Indeed he seemed to gain new reserves of energy to pit against me. It did not matter how much rein I hauled in or how short they got, he would just bury his chin deeper on his chest, open his mouth slightly to evade his bit and tank off. The miles and the hours finally took the edge off him, and at last he steadied and became responsive again. But then the damage was done as far as my shoulders and neck muscles were concerned. I felt as though I'd been on the rack.

Purists would not consider my activities to be associated with the main business of the day at all, fox-hunting. I must admit I never caught a glimpse of a fox all day, rarely got within sight of the hounds and hadn't a clue what they were doing when I did. But when they did run and give tongue to their babbling music it stirred the blood of horse and rider in some ancient, un-fathomable manner. They didn't kill that day, and I was strangely glad.

At the bottom of the drive I was ready to weep with relief. I painfully extracted both feet from my stirrups only to find the weight of my unsupported legs was even more excruciating. I dropped my reins, hauled both knees up on to the front of the saddle and perched there, hugging my legs like an overgrown garden gnome, while Bear plodded the last hundred yards or so on auto-pilot. My attempt at dismounting was not elegant. As I touched *terra firma* my knees buckled, all but gave way and I was quite alarmed when my legs suddenly refused to obey orders. When I finally did make contact with the bottom half of my body I realised that, apart from a couple of prickly episodes trying to have a quick pee behind a wall, I had been in the saddle for over seven hours. That was getting on for twice my previous endurance record.

I untacked Bear and he headed with obvious urgency for his hay rack and started munching as though he hadn't seen food for a week. Remembering everything the horse management books preached about 'putting your horse's needs before your own' I saw to it that his saddle patch was washed with warm salty water; checked his legs for cuts and bumps, rugged him up with a good thatch of straw under his rug in case he broke out in sweat overnight and provided fresh water and a warm bran mash, before I finally creaked up the stairs to a longed-for hot soak and a large whisky provided by a quietly pleased husband.

The next morning, according to the book, I should have been out at the crack of dawn to attend to Bear's every need. Alas, frail flesh! Just getting out of bed, which I finally accomplished by about nine o'clock, was a major achievement. Getting my clothes on was a near-miracle. Everything hurt, really ached and thumped and hurt. Only some bits hurt more than others. My sore tailbone made sitting down on a hard kitchen chair agony, my fingers tried and almost failed to grasp the cutlery and the bits of flesh between thumb and index finger were too painful even to touch after the constant hauling on Bear's reins.

Slightly rallied by a good breakfast I waddled painfully out to the stable. Highly indignant at being neglected till mid-morning, Bear was banging on the bottom of his stable door with impatience. There was obviously not much wrong with him. As he devoured his breakfast with relish I fingered his shaggy, unkempt mane and wondered what on earth he had thought of the previous day's antics. Judging by the speed with which he had recovered, it had done him no harm and for a little horse who wasn't really hunting-fit he'd done remarkably well.

'You don't suppose,' I asked him in a conspiratorial tone, 'that we should take up something a bit less demanding and exhausting?'

The unbidden thought came back. 'Like beagling, for instance?'

I decided hunting must be a bit like child-birth; the memory of the pain soon vanishes, leaving only a rosy hue surrounding the whole event and whetting your appetite for another attempt.

By the time I'd had another couple of exhausting but enjoyable days, the main problems were very obvious. I had no transport, and neither Bear nor I could jump. This put such an extended mileage on to a day's hunting that it made the whole thing almost beyond my powers of physical endurance. I emphasise beyond *my* powers, not beyond Bear's. He, on the contrary, thrived, getting fitter and stronger every time out and, alas, hairier. By the end of November he was two inches deep in fur and his mane defied my every attempt to keep it under control. I tried plaiting it one day but the resultant cauliflower-like lumps sprang out of their restraining elastic bands by the time we'd galloped over the first field. I didn't exactly feel ashamed of Bear, as he couldn't help his winter woollies, but I did feel a bit self-conscious at times in the company of all those sleek, clean-legged animals.

The solution, Lizzie explained patiently, was very simple. Did I imagine those sleek creatures naturally stayed like that all winter? Certainly not. They were probably nearly as hairy as Bear. The difference was that they were clipped. Clipping, she enthused, not only made the horse appear neater and smarter, but also far more comfortable because it could sweat freely when doing fast work and then dry off again very quickly. A clipped horse was very much easier to groom. For me, twenty-four hours before going hunting seemed to be fully occupied with removing the previous week's thick mud and dust which clung tenaciously to Bear's shaggy coat. The twenty-four hours after hunting seemed to be spent trying to get his thick damp hair dry again so that he could go out and roll in more mud. This clipping business sounded a good idea, a very good idea in fact.

The horsy world into which Bear had plunged me was full of unexpected surprises and rituals — and most of all expenses. Little things like shoeing, feed bills, worming, vet bills, fencing, rugs and so on. I had started out with a horse, a saddle and a bridle and had thought myself totally equipped. What painful innocence! There should be a statutory declaration given with every horse or pony sold to the effect that the moment people want to do anything other than gaze at it in a field, they will require a large bank balance and probably a large whisky as well.

Clippers, I quickly discovered, were going to cost me nearly half as much as my horse had. And even if I had a pair, I wouldn't have had a clue where to start. *Nil desperandum*. In the vicinity of most hunts there operates a band of dedicated and skilled people who, with little regard for their own safety, will hire their services out to do all the nasty and time-consuming jobs that owners might shirk — like trimming and mane-pulling and clipping. For a price that is.

Reeling at the thought of how many haircuts I could get for the price of Bear's clip, I nevertheless arranged for a confident-sounding young lady called Vivienne to call. She set up her equipment with an ease of long practice that I envied. She went through a delicate and thorough ritual of dismantling and cleaning her clippers, lovingly wiping off any stray bristles clinging to the blades with a little brush before carefully adding drops of oil here and there and then re-assembling the whole lot. A few more drops of oil and she plugged them into the socket and listened to them attentively for a few moments before giving a satisfied grunt and a cheerful 'Right, let's get cracking'.

I was fascinated. There was obviously a lot more to this than I had imagined. Clippers, it transpired, were held in awesome respect by their owners. Not only did they cost a lot of money to begin with, but they needed constant loving care and attention and blades re-sharpening and engines overhauling to give a long working life. Clippers develop their own personalities and quirks known only to those who use them regularly and for this reason Vivienne and her colleagues were more likely to give you their back teeth than loan you their clippers.

As requested, Bear was clean and warm and dry in his box, his bed swept to one side, thus obeying the first law of clipping: 'thou shalt not attempt to clip a damp or dirty horse'. The second law of clipping was: 'horses and electric cables are a dangerous mixture and the results could be disastrous for all concerned', so we had arranged an extension lead from the garage to the stable and attached the socket safely near the top of the wall.

Vivienne chuckled when she saw Bear. 'Good job I haven't anyone else booked for this morning, isn't it! What sort of clip had you in mind?'

Gulp. What sort of clip? What did she mean?

'Do you want a trace clip, a blanket clip or clipped right out? Oh, and do you want his legs on or off?'

Take his legs off!

'Well — er — what do you think?'

'Depends what you want to use him for.'

Now we were getting somewhere.

'Well, it's for hunting actually — he gets so hot and sweaty and impossibly untidy.'

'Yes, I can imagine,' she chuckled again. 'First time he's been clipped, is it?'

I nodded a little apprehensively, and said, 'He'll be okay, won't he?'

'Well he looks quiet enough,' she said.

Bear hadn't even had the good manners to pause from eating his hay since she had come in.

'I'll tell you what. Why don't I clip his body and head and neck but leave his legs on, the hair that is, then you can have a look and see what you think. I think that just a trace or a blanket clip wouldn't take off enough to solve your problems out hunting, though they'd do for light work.'

Bear did lift his head from his hay and glare suspiciously at Vivienne as her clippers buzzed into action but before she started actually clipping she laid first her hand on his back, then the clippers on top of her hand, then the clippers themselves, though not the blades, to get him used to the vibrating sensation. He very quickly was and turned back to gently chewing his hay. Vivienne worked quickly and accurately, every long slice of her blades leaving a pale runway on Bear's back and tufts of chestnut hair on the floor. As the mound of discarded hair grew I realised the wisdom of putting his bed to one side.

It took far, far longer than I'd expected. I think it took longer than Vivienne expected too. She explained that Bear, rather like an eider duck, had two coats, one of long coarse top hair and a very fine fluffy under-coat. In effect she was having to clip him twice, once to remove the long hair and then again for the fuzzy bits. Indeed, it wasn't so much like clipping, she exclaimed almost in desperation at one point, it was more like sculpting in hair. By the time she had finished his head, which he didn't take too kindly to, we were ankle deep in orange fuzz. She switched off the clippers and we both stood back to look at the results.

My first reaction was shock. Bear had completely changed colour. Gone was his fox-red coat; instead a smooth pale caramel-covered body attached to four thick hairy red columns with flowing white feathers stood before me. The picture was completed by a copious thatch of long wayward flaxen mane. He looked ridiculous. I could have sat in the corner of the box and wailed, but Vivienne was quite unperturbed.

'Mmm, just as I thought. Looks bloody awful. Those legs are

like hairy tree trunks, they'll have to come off. And those feathers, well, you'll find it a lot easier to keep his heels dry and avoid cracking with that lot off. White-legged cobs are buggers for cracked heels in my experience.'

And before I had time to draw a breath of protest the clippers were flashing up and down his legs, two inches of thick red hair surrendered to the blades and his long thick white feathers fell to the ground as if from some plucked Christmas turkey.

The transformation was amazing. I am no lover of long, spindly thoroughbreds, but equally I had been a little mortified by one or two oblique references to my 'cart-horse' on the hunting field. Now, with the outline of his legs clean and defined and perfectly in proportion to his smooth muscled body, he looked super. Or nearly super. We both stared at his mane and then at each other.

'Any suggestions as to what I can do with that?'

'Yes. But I am not sure if you'd agree. It's pretty radical,' she warned.

'Try me.'

'Hog him.'

'Pardon?'

'Hog him; take it all off with the clippers. Then about nine inches off his tail so that it just falls to his hocks and bang it straight across the bottom, leaving it full and short. He'd look bloody gorgeous.'

It was all getting a bit too much for me. The more hair we took off the more it felt like sharpening and re-sharpening a pencil. Soon we'd be left with just a stump.

'Will it all grow again?' I enquired anxiously.

'Oh, his coat will need clipping again in about six weeks or so, and his tail will get long over the summer. But once you've hogged him it's pretty irreversible. The mane grows, of course, but thicker than ever and it doesn't fall to one side, just tends to grow straight up, Once hogged, you've got to keep him hogged.'

'Well, I've got to do something,' I wailed. 'Look at it! It's like a weed out of control. Do you really think he would look nice with it all off?'

'Have you never looked at old hunting prints? Cobs were always hogged because they've got such gorgeous well-muscled necks and it actually shows them off better. Lots of people just do it for convenience, but if you haven't got a horse with a decent neck it ends up looking like a camel. Look!' she said, going over to Bear and sweeping all his mane tightly over to one

side and holding it there, 'just look at that. He looks neat,
workmanlike and very macho.'

She grinned while I took a deep breath.

'All right then, do it! Quick, before I change my mind.'

As the long flaxen strands fell all around me, lumps pulsed in
my throat and tears pricked my eyes. I was like a mother
watching the long golden curls of her once baby son vanish for
ever between the barber's scissors. It took only three or four
minutes, then the clippers were finally silent.

The picture before me filled my sensory centres to the point of
briefly paralysing my vocal cords. My woolly Welsh Bear had
gone and in his place stood a mature, arrogant and very
beautiful creature in whose presence I felt strangely timid.

'Well?'

'You were quite right,' I said with a grin of Cheshire Cat
proportions. 'He looks bloody gorgeous.'

I added an extra fiver to her clipping fee that day and didn't
even flinch at having to fork out for a New Zealand rug now that
he no longer had any protection from the elements when he was
out in the field.

The effect of 'the clip' upon Bear transcended pure change in
physical appearance. He began to act differently too — nothing
drastic, just a slightly more aloof attitude to life and a more
mature and very positive attitude to work in general and to
hunting in particular. Almost too positive at times. Like an
athlete released from legwarmers and track suit, he revelled in
the freedom from his cumbersome coat. His new 'cooling
system' increased his staying power and speed in the field. The
regular fast work coupled with the long steady hacks to and
from meets filled out and hardened his muscles and increased
his lung capacity. He was seven years old now, approaching
maturity of body and mind. He was a nightmare to hold at
times. I tried and discarded umpteen bits in an attempt to find
some brakes, but he seemed to be able to arch his neck and flex
the muscles against anything my hands were doing to his
mouth. Chin just about on his chest, his high-stepping knees
powering along like tireless pistons, he would arrive at a meet,
veins bulging and flames coming from his nostrils. At one meet
he flew down the hill to the pub car park breathing fire, and I
just managed to haul him to a halt before he scattered his elders
and betters. One of the hunt grooms coldly enquired whether
'that horse' was mad.

But Bear wasn't mad, nor was he ever bad. Headstrong, yes: stubborn, yes: naughty, definitely; but he never did a wicked thing or a dangerous thing. He never bucked or kicked, nor did he set out, as a truly wicked horse will do, to dislodge his rider on purpose. And although he pulled like a steam train for the first couple of hours and gave the appearance of tanking off with me, he never did a stupid thing nor crossed treacherous ground at an unsafe speed. Most importantly, he never frightened me. My red woolly Welsh Bear had gone and in his place I rode upon a golden Welsh dragon. He didn't have the speed of the blood horses at a gallop of course, but long after they had blown up, frothy and foot-sore, Bear would go on, steady and sure-footed to the end of the day. If he did get tired or blown I would give him ten minutes and in return he would give me another half an hour.

One elderly hunting farmer rode up beside us one day, quite misty-eyed, and said, 'By, it's grand to see a reet proper cob out these days. He's a good 'un, that he is.' I glowed with love and pride.

I remained, perhaps to my shame, fairly ignorant of the tactics and manoeuvres of the hunt and rarely, if ever, saw any close-up action with the hounds. Largely this was due to our non-jumping which meant we were often busy taking devious detours rather than following the hounds. But I really didn't care. I began to know a union I'd never imagined possible with my horse; the point at which almost telepathic communication takes place over speed and direction.

The only dampener on our day's activities was the long journey home, which often meant we had to leave the rest and set back before I got outside the range of *my* 'getting back' powers — allowed to take it at his own speed Bear seemed to be able to go on indefinitely. One bright spark once commented, 'She'll kill that horse before the season's out, hacking all that distance every week.' Bear's elderly hunting farmer fan retorted sharply, 'Don't be bloody daft. It's your horses that're ower soft these days. What the 'ell d'you think we did afore horseboxes came along? Aa tell yer, the horses were better for it. Aye, better for it!'

By Christmas, an ingenious solution to my 'getting back' problem had been found. Ian hadn't ridden to hounds since he was a boy, preferring to do it the hard way on foot. In fact, when I started hunting, he viewed the whole thing with tolerant amusement. However, as Bear blossomed and matured, Ian developed a decidedly interested look. Finally with a sort of 'greater love hath no woman' attitude I let him have a day's hunting. His reaction was the same as mine; tremendous fun (if only the bloody animal would jump) but totally exhausting when coupled with perhaps twenty miles' hacking.

A wonderful compromise was arrived at. I would hack Bear to the meet one week, allowing Ian to arrive keen and fresh in the car. I would then join the rest of the hunt car followers for the day, then hack Bear home. The following week the arrangement would be reversed. Apart from throwing the hunt secretary into pink fits over how much subscription to charge one horse with two riders, the idea worked beautifully.

This continued through into February the following year when my hunting came to an abrupt end on my discovering, to my immense joy, that I was to have a baby. Now I was aware that there were horribly hearty County ladies who never let a little thing like pregnancy interfere with their sport, and hunted until they were about ready to foal. But, love my horse though I did, I was not in that league. Since adolescence I had been beset with various gynaecological problems and now, approaching thirty and expecting my first baby, I wasn't taking any chances. The season had only about another month to run anyway and was seen out by my husband. He had made friends with a hunting butcher in the next village who owned, oh joy of joys, a Rice double horse trailer and who gave him lifts to the meet. Unfortunately, his horse, an Irish Draught stallion, could jump like a stag, which meant that Bear was often out of contact by the end of the day and still had to hack home.

To overcome this, two revolutionary proposals were put forward by Ian. Firstly to sell our car and get a Land Rover and trailer; fine, super, excellent idea. Secondly, as Bear really wasn't much use out hunting if he couldn't jump, and I wasn't going to be using him for upwards of a year, yet he would still have to be fed and kept, why didn't I sell Bear, and we'd buy a horse that could jump for Ian to hunt next season. Of course, if I wanted a horse of my own at a later date, we would get one. But, he argued with the cold logic that appears to be available only to the male of the species, I should get a mare next time so that if I had another baby, it could do something useful — like have a foal — rather than stand around idle.

The ensuing cessation of all diplomatic — and other — relations, coupled with red-rimmed eyes, lasted for about four days. The second proposal was tactfully withdrawn and replaced with an amendment. I could keep Bear on condition that I lent him out to someone competent who would benefit the horse and pay for his keep: someone who might even teach him to jump; someone, for instance, like Lizzie. I agreed with frantic relief, feeling as if I'd just had an eleventh-hour remission from the death sentence.

Proposal three resulted from amendment two. Ian would still have to invest in a suitable mount for himself for next season. In fact, it just so happened he knew of a grand black Irish gelding coming on the market. But, I asked, if I couldn't look after or exercise Bear while I was pregnant or nursing, who would look after this new hunter during the week? Infallible male logic assured me it would be easy to employ a girl groom locally to help out. Well, of course; why didn't I think of that?

It was only after Bear had been dispatched for nine months to an overjoyed Lizzie that I realised that this 'horsy bit' was becoming an economic snowball taking over more and more of our budget, our energy and our lives. The little horse I'd bought with his saddle and bridle thrown in now demanded clothes for him, clothes for me, hay and straw, feed and supplements, a stable, muck heap and field. Now it appeared there was to be another four-legged mouth to feed with similar requirements, plus the odd Land Rover, trailer and girl groom. Where would it all end, I asked myself, where would it all end?

When Ian proudly showed me the plans he had drawn up for the new stable block and hay shed ('after all that old stable is totally inadequate for two horses and we'll need more storage space'), I heartily agreed with his proposals. Well, I mean it was obvious, wasn't it? We really needed them — and the increase in the mortgage wasn't that bad.

I never visited Bear during the whole of my pregnancy. Early on I missed him dreadfully, and felt frustrated that I couldn't ride when I still felt quite capable of doing so. But I decided that visiting him would only upset me and would be treading on Lizzie's toes. After all, she was paying for his keep and it was not my place to poke my nose in.

I did, of course, get regular reports. It was rather like having a beloved son away at boarding school for the first time. The reports were all very encouraging. With proper tuition and regular practice in the school, Bear soon mastered trotting poles and cavalettis, these being the first stages in teaching a horse to extend his stride by gradually widening the poles. Within a few weeks he'd moved on to bigger things and by mid-summer, to my astonishment, Lizzie was hurtling round novice cross-country courses with him. She'd also started some elementary dressage with him, and he showed a surprising aptitude in this discipline, though the words wilful and headstrong kept creeping into reports of his performance.

Without doubt, the basic education and work Lizzie did with Bear in those months laid the foundation for all his subsequent achievements. A sound basic education from a good schoolmaster is as essential to a horse as it is to a person. I remain eternally grateful for the hours of patient work and effort that Lizzie put into Bear, and from which others reaped so many and as yet unforeseeable rewards.

As the arrival of my baby grew closer I confess I rarely thought about Bear at all. I was far too preoccupied with nappies and baby baths, cradles and tiny cardigans, which wallpaper to have in the nursery, elastic stockings and how to sleep sitting up all night to avoid excruciating heartburn. However, even before the baby's arrival the household had increased.

The first new arrival was Ian's black Irish hunter whom we christened Limerick and whom I steered clear of in my vulnerable condition. He merely appeared very large and somewhat menacing.

When he came in at the end of the summer there was a stable to clean and a grass belly to work off every day so Louise, a vivacious horsy young lady with time on her hands, was engaged to take control of him. Cradling my eight-month bulge, I lumbered over to the dining room window on my grossly swollen ankles and legs to watch her schooling him in the front paddock. A tinge of envy and near-panic hit me. Would I ever really be capable of swinging up into a saddle again? I hadn't had a bad pregnancy in some ways, and I'd been spared the miseries of morning sickness altogether, thank God, but I'd put on an enormous amount of weight, a lot of it due to fluid retention. When the veins in both my legs began to bulge in protest at the strain, I was encased in heavy, thick white elastic stockings which had to be put on before I even rolled out of bed in the morning. At last, I couldn't even manage that on my own, I began to fear that I would never make physical contact with my toes again. These discomforts, minor in themselves, amalgamated to make me feel heavy, lethargic and pretty useless. I found the daily running of a twelve-room farmhouse to the standards I wanted it run a physical impossibility.

Help was found when I timidly put a postcard in the village shop saying 'Domestic help required two mornings a week'. I had hardly got back through the kitchen door and put the kettle on for a cup of tea when the phone rang.

'Are ye the woman that wants a cleaner, pet?' boomed a voice that wasn't what I'd had in mind at all.

'Well, yes, I'm looking for domestic help, not strictly a cleaner, but just someone to help out generally and do a bit of ironing. I'm expecting a baby soon you see and . . . '

'A bairn! Are ye, pet? Ee, that's lovely, Look, if ye pick us up at the Post Office at nine it'll suit fine. A can waak there tomorrow but on Friday ye can pick us up from me house. Tuesdays and Fridays it'll hef to be now and A'll hef to be back to mek me man's dinner by twelve thorty.' *Beep. Beep. Beep. Beep.* 'Oh, the bloody pips and A've ne more money! A'll see ye the morrow, pet!' The line went dead.

'Oh Lord,' I thought, 'what on earth have I done? Well, I expect I'll have to get her tomorrow and give her a try, I can always politely tell her she's not suitable and find someone else.'

I never did tell her and there never was anyone else.

Slightly plump, with merry eyes and rosy cheeks, chattering sixteen to the dozen all day, Brenda would have reminded me of a robin around the house if she hadn't sworn like a trooper and smoked like a chimney. She was, I soon discovered, marvellous at middles, not brilliant at corners, but together we made a good team. She could iron like a thing possessed and was reliable and honest as the day was long. She drank endless cups of tea but never touched the sherry, and she told us all exactly what she thought of us. She was, in short, a gem.

The official date of arrival for the baby had been set as the fourth of November. I hoped for November the fifth, thinking how easy Bonfire Night would make children's parties in years to come. The other important date in the diary for that week was the first of November, the start of the hunting season. That year it fell on a Wednesday, so the season could start on the very first day of the month. It was hard to tell whose preparations held the upper hand, mine for the arrival of the baby or Ian's for the debut of his new Irish hunter.

When my blood pressure began doing truly alarming things in the last week of October it was decided I would be safer off waiting it out in hospital. On the night of Hallowe'en I felt very unwell indeed and I was even having difficulty focusing properly. I lay awake in my little hospital room fuzzily watching the stars in a bright clear sky and balancing exhilaration against fear. On my locker, along with the obligatory half-finished matinée jacket, a pile of books and a bunch of grapes, stood a photo of Bear. It was the photo of me riding him in the local show the year before. It was an odd thing to have shoved into my suitcase at the last moment, especially as I had hardly even thought of him in the last couple of months. But there he was, the only company I had as that long, long night wore on and finally the dawn crept in on Wednesday, the first of November.

The new Irish hunter was all ready to load into the new trailer and Ian was donning his new boots and black jacket when the hospital rang to say things could wait no longer. Labour had been induced because of the risk of toxaemia to myself and the baby, and fatherhood would be sooner or later but definitely today. In the event it was later rather than sooner. Twelve hours later, to be exact, when my daughter Megan Mary made her opening meet on the first day of the season. I'd like to say her father greeted her arrival still decked in boots and breeches but I really can't remember. He was, however, excused visiting three days later to make it to the opening Saturday meet.

It was perhaps on Saturday in the brief lull in the still new and nerve-racking routines of hospital motherhood that I caught a glimpse of Bear peering out between a stockade of congratulations cards. I experienced a pang of guilt. Would it ever be the same for us now that he had a fragile, deliciously pink, scrap of life competing for my attentions? I had read plenty about sibling rivalry in baby books, even about jealous husbands, but no one had offered any advice on jealous horses.

Wouldn't it be nice, I mused, if we could all do something together. My mind conjured up an idyllic picture of rosy-cheeked children in a governess cart rolling down a leafy country lane. I sat at the reins as Bear trotted steadily along. It was a pretty but fanciful picture. Other than the odd scrapman's flat cart, generally pulled by a dejected horse, I'd never seen a horse-drawn vehicle in our part of the world. But a horse and trap would be a lovely idea. When Megan was bigger I could get Bear fit for hunting and get her out in the fresh air at the same time! And surely I'd read somewhere that Welsh cobs made good driving horses.

A little wail from beneath the pink blanket brought me sharply out of my reverie. I got up, gently lifted my daughter out of her cot and took her back into bed with me to feed.

'Yes, young lady, I just wonder what Bear's going to make of you?'

Mid-way through the proceedings, Staff Nurse came in to see that all was well.

'Yes, thanks,' I assured her, 'I think I'm getting the hang of this now, though I think I ought to christen this one "Jaws"!'

'Have you chosen a name for her yet then?' She stooped to look at the label on the cot, 'Oh yes, Megan. That's an unusual name. Welsh, isn't it?'

'Yes. You see I had this real character of a great aunt who was called Meg. Well I felt I couldn't christen the baby that, and Margaret — which was her proper name — was just too ordinary somehow. So in the end I chose Megan, as that's the Welsh form of Margaret.'

'Do you have any Welsh connections then?'

'Only my horse.'

'Sorry?'

'My horse — he's a Welsh cob.'

Full and content, Megan had fallen asleep in my arms so I leant across and extricated Bear's picture from behind the baby cards on the locker.

'That's him,' I said proudly. 'It's funny, I was just wondering how I'm going to fit exercising in to my new role as a mum. I was contemplating a horse and trap so the whole family could go out together.'

'Does your horse drive as well as ride then?'

'Heavens no, there's nothing like that goes on in this part of the world.'

'That's where you're wrong.' Staff Nurse's face lit up suddenly. 'It just so happens there's a very good driving event takes place at Beamish every spring. People come from all over the country to it, and I've been helping run it for the last three years. I don't know how I got involved really, other than living nearby, as I've never had anything to do with horses. Anyway, it's a great weekend, marvellous to see all those horses and carriages. And of course we're always in need of more helpers.' She gave a meaningful tilt of her head in my direction.

'Well . . . I er . . . I know plenty about my own horse, but not about other people's — and nothing about driving.'

'Oh, that doesn't matter. As long as you can handle a stop-watch that's all we need. Tell you what, I'll make a note of your address and when we get organised for next April I'll drop you a line. Okay?'

'Okay!' I smiled as she left my cubicle to deal with her next tiny arrival, and wondered if I would in fact ever hear from her.

The next few months went by quietly and happily. Being an only child with no experience of anyone else's babies, I had harboured many secret doubts and fears about my ability to cope with a baby of my own. But Megan was exactly the sort of baby who makes motherhood easy. She slept well, fed well and was rarely fractious without good cause. I'd seen friends red-eyed and gaunt after endless sleepless nights with their new arrivals and I realised I was blessed indeed.

As the festive season approached I was asked what I wanted for Christmas. I felt there was now only one thing missing from my life. I simply asked for Bear to come back home.

I shed the usual stupid tears when we were reunited. I was worried that he would have forgotten about home (and me) during his long months away but there was no need. He charged into his box without being asked twice, headed straight for his manger, gave a disgusted snort when he found it empty and came back to me with a plaintive look of 'What mum, no tea?' He looked in marvellous condition — clipped and neatly hogged, muscled and fit. Lizzie had done him proud and it must have been hard for her to hand him back after all the months of work she had put into him and all the pleasure they had had together. Months of work and pleasure that included regular appearances on the hunting field and, I was assured, he was now jumping boldly and confidently. There was the unspoken implication that I should not let all this effort and progress go to waste and I should carry on the good work. It was always within Bear to jump like a stag, but my ignorance (and fear) had never allowed that potential to develop. In other words, I had to get my finger out and learn to jump.

I found that everything claimed to have been achieved with Bear was true. He had become a good schoolmaster who hopped over the little fences I timidly erected in the paddock with ease and disdain. He was relaxed and balanced even if I wasn't, but as the fences in the paddock crept up in height and width, so did my confidence.

After a practice run following Limerick over some little hedges in a neighbour's field, I decided we were ready to take the plunge. Fully clipped and looking golden, fit and glorious Bear was boxed up alongside Limerick to arrive at a meet for the first time in style. I desperately wanted to look inconspicuous but it was rather difficult to miss Bear in a crowd, his full silvery tail standing out like a banner. Loads of people kept coming up and saying how nice it was to see me out again and wasn't it grand that Bear had been jumping so well for Lizzie and I ought to have a really grand day on him.

Actually I didn't feel really grand, I felt empty and panic-stricken. The proffered stirrup cup had gone down without ever touching the sides and had very little impact. In my capacious pocket I had what I'd found to be the basic emergency necessities for a long day's hunting: some lipsalve, some tissues (for noses or emergency stops behind walls), half a pound of cold fried sausage to stave off hunger pangs around 1 p.m. and my father's venerable battered silver hip-flask full of a mix of neat whisky and green ginger. On chilly days that mix could miraculously thaw out numbed hands and legs. Apart from the odd glass of wine, alcohol was something I rarely touched — except on hunting days. Was this the rocky road to ruination, I wondered? What would people think if I attacked my flask before we'd even left the meet? To hell with it. Anaesthesia was the name of the game. If I could just get over the first few fences intact I'd be fine, I knew I would. But if my courage deserted me, and we ploughed into the bottom of a fence, I would never dare show my face again. 'Throw your heart over the fence,' they had all advised me. But it wasn't really my heart I was worried about getting over, it was the rest of me.

The huntsman sounded the move off and gathered up his hounds. In the general mêlée and excitement I took a few furtive gulps from my flask and we were off.

We trotted along a pretty lane at a spanking pace, Ian keeping diplomatically out of my way. I was just beginning to relax and enjoy the noise and sights and sounds when the huntsman made a sharp left turn off the road and sent the hounds leaping over a stone wall and down into a field. As I watched first the hounds then the leading horses in the field lift and drop from sight over the wall to reappear what seemed ages after, I realised with horror that not only was the day's first obstacle a solid immovable stone wall but there was a drop of at least three feet on the other side. Sweat sprang out of every pore of my body. My hunting stock felt as if it was about to choke me. Singly and in groups the horses ahead of me moved on, took the wall and streamed their way over the field. We moved nearer and nearer the front of the queue, the horses behind me stamping and jangling impatiently for their turn. There was no escape and the anaesthetic had failed miserably. Well, if I was going to break my neck, what a glorious setting to do it in. I settled in the saddle, took a few deep breaths, tried to remember all I'd been taught about position and hands only to find my mind a total blank. Turning Bear's head towards the wall I pressed lightly with my legs and waited for the end of the world. Bear trotted for two strides, cantered for three, then his front end lifted, forelegs tucked neatly under him, and we cleared the top of the wall. He landed well out on the other side with the agility of a cat, took a firm hold of his bit and set off in pursuit of the rest of the field. I was dazed, disbelieving and overjoyed. No jockey safely negotiating the Grand National fences ever felt more proud or more thankful.

'Oh, you clever, clever lad, Bear,' I crowed giving him hearty slaps on the neck, 'you clever wonderful, fabulous horse!'

I was getting distinctly disapproving looks from some nearby riders who obviously couldn't understand what the fuss was about, so I moderated my enthusiasm. The next few jumps posed no problems at all, being no worse than fences I'd cleared at home.

By midday I was high on exhilaration and success. I was fearless. Bear was tireless. It was all so easy, I just had to point him at a jump, kick on, lean forward and we were over. How on earth could I have ever been worried over something so simple? When we cleared a four-barred timber fence with hardly a check from a gallop, I had a smug smile on my face. Even Ian was speechless with astonishment and, I hoped, admiration. One of Great Aunt Meg's favourite sayings had always been 'Pride cometh before the fall,' which I really should have remembered.

By two o'clock the pace had slackened, the field thinned out and I was getting quite blasé about the whole thing. The huntsman decided to draw a different cover a little way on. This was usually the time I would apologise, say goodnight to the master (always 'goodnight' even at two in the afternoon) and head off for my long hack home. But not today. I had a box waiting at the meet, a horse who seemed tireless and who could jump anything, and I felt no sign of flagging or fatigue and feared nothing that we had to face. The horses in front went up a rise in the road, took a sharp turn left and hopped over a little fence with a bit of a drop on the other side. Easy, I thought, as I turned Bear and lined him up. Actually, it *was* easy and he jumped it beautifully, landing nicely on the other side. What he didn't take into account of, and neither did I, was the low branch of an overhanging tree. It hit me square on the forehead with a resounding *thwack* that just about dislodged me in mid-air. I landed back on Bear, nearly in the saddle, and began a slow undignified descent down his side and was bumped un-ceremoniously along the ground for a few strides before being deposited in a cowpat. I had had it coming all day, so I suppose I got off quite lightly really.

Ian was very understanding and hardly referred to it as we jogged back towards the box. Except to remark, surveying my forehead and the large egg from which a small trickle of blood clogged up my eyebrows, 'Well, I'll say one thing: they might not have killed today, but at least you've finally been blooded.'

The remaining two months or so of the season were all too short and I had as many marvellous Wednesdays as I could. I learned to temper my initial over-confidence with judgement and only set Bear at fences that I felt were within my capabilities.

At the end of the season, I was left with a large hole in the middle of the week. I was pondering on how best to fill this vacuum when, in early April, a letter arrived from Staff Nurse. True to her word, she was recruiting volunteers to help with the Beamish Driving Trials at the end of the month and did I think I could go on 'marathon day' and time a section? Stop-watches would be provided.

Marathon? I was fascinated: I thought that was something to do with the Olympics and charity runs. Time a section? Section of what? All would be revealed, the letter continued, at the briefing early on the Sunday morning. Bring a packed lunch and how was Megan?

I wrote back immediately saying I'd love to help, would be at the appointed time and place and Megan was marvellous, thank you.

Late April in County Durham can still have a touch of Siberia in the grey air. On that appointed morning in 1979 it felt bitterly cold, with a threat of sleet. Undaunted, I donned extra socks, a sheepskin coat and dug out my hunting flask. I really didn't know what I was going to see or take part in except that there would be horse-drawn vehicles doing things in an arena and things across country.

The briefing was a revelation. Some of these volunteers had done the job before but for the first-timers everything was carefully explained. The trials would be held over two days. Most driving trials were held over three days and had a separate competition on each day. This was usually dressage on the Friday, marathon on the Saturday and the obstacle-driving or 'cones' on the Sunday. The dressage and obstacle-driving phases were done using show-standard carriages, harness and formal driving attire for the driver and groom or passengers. The marathon required a different rugged cross-country vehicle, work harness and casual dress for the competitors.

To minimise fuss at Beamish, the dressage and obstacle-driving were both held on the Saturday, followed by the

marathon on the Sunday. This meant drivers only needed their
'good' carriages on the Saturday and their cross-country
vehicles on the Sunday.

In essence, the sport was three-day eventing with a carriage
on the back. Dressage took place in a larger but otherwise
orthodox arena and was preceded by 'presentation', a little
feature unique to carriage driving where every inch of the horse,
harness, carriage and occupants was subjected to close scrutiny.

In the obstacle-driving the horses had to negotiate a series of
cones set just wider than the carriage wheels and topped with
an easily dislodged ball. As in show-jumping, the course had to
be negotiated in the right order against the clock and with
penalties for knock-downs. The obstacle-driving competition
was normally the last phase of an event so as to test a horse's
soundness, suppleness and obedience after the rigours of the
marathon.

The marathon — which could be equated to the cross-country
phase of three-day eventing — seemed to be the part of the
competition that people were getting the most excited about.
Apparently the marathon course at Beamish was credited with
being one of the toughest on the circuit, particularly as the
horses were tackling it very early in the season when they were
unlikely to be fully fit. And marathon it was indeed, being
perhaps twenty-five kilometres in length. This distance was
divided up into five sections, and there were two compulsory
ten-minute halts. The first section of some ten kilometres was to
be trotted at about fifteen kph. This was followed by a walk of a
kilometre, then the first compulsory halt and a veterinary check.
The third section was only five kilometres, but had to be gone
through at a very fast trot of twenty kph, then there was another
kilometre walk and a second halt and vet check. The final
section of some eight kilometres was done at the same speed as
the first section, but in the last few kilometres competitors had
to negotiate a series of natural and man-made hazards. These
hazards were there to test the horses' stamina, and courage —
and probably also those of the driver, who would have been
holding the reins for nearly two hours of fast and often heavy
work up hills, through streams and along rough forest tracks.
Each hazard had a twenty-metre zone marked around it and the
driver was timed from crossing the line into the hazard till he
crossed back out again. Within this zone the hazard itself was
made up of a series of gates or other elements to drive through
or around; these were lettered in alphabetical order, and all had
to be driven in the correct order. The competitor who achieved

this in the quickest time would have the fewest penalty points for doing that hazard.

Although it was all being explained very carefully, my brain began to reel a bit at this stage with the sheer effort of digesting all this new information. I began to worry in case I forgot something vital and threw a spanner in what were very obviously well-oiled works. I needn't have done because Staff Nurse came over and had a chat with me over a welcome cup of tea.

'How nice to see you again. I told you I'd find you a useful job to do.'

Somehow she looked different out of her blue starched dress and white apron.

'Er . . . yes. I only hope I do the right thing.'

'Don't worry, it's very simple really. It just sounds complicated. I've put you on to time the end of section C — that's the fast trot section — and I always put people on in pairs; can't expect them to stand there pressing a stop-watch all day. Your partner's an old hand, been helping out since this event started, so if you watch him do it for the first few you'll soon get the hang of it.'

'Will there be a lot of horses competing?' I enquired.

'Yes, there's a good entry in all the classes.'

'Classes?' I was getting lost again. 'Classes of what?'

'Well, size and number of horses I suppose. Starts with singles, then there's pairs — that's two side by side. Tandems — that's two, one in front of the other, and then there's teams — that's four. And for each of those there's a pony class and a horse class, so there's eight classes in all.'

I was very impressed. The thought of multiples of horses pulling vehicles had never crossed my mind. Somehow, I still had that image of a sweet little governess cart trotting gently along a leafy lane. Briefing over, all time-keepers were issued with a large stop-watch in the form of a box that hung round our necks on a cord.

Consulting my map, I set off to seek the end of Section C. The weather hadn't improved and the wind was bitter, but the brisk walk and the excitement both seemed to keep me warm. Section C, the fast section, ended not far from Beamish Hall itself. The horses would then walk a few yards to the start of Section D, their second walk, which took them around what had once been the gardens and brought them back into the stable yard of the old Hall for their second compulsory halt. I had half an hour or so, according to my time sheet, before the first competitor arrived and then, if they were on time, they should arrive at four-minute intervals. There was a maximum time for each section of the marathon, and penalty points would be incurred if it was exceeded. The first section also had a minimum time.

I wanted to be at my post well in advance but as the minutes ticked nearer to my first competitor coming through there was no sign of my partner. I wasn't actually panicking, but I began carefully rehearsing the procedure in case he didn't show up. Note time on clock as horse's nose passed the line, note competitor's number, write both of these on my sheet of paper. Take two green cards from competitor, fill in time on both of them and initial them, give back to competitor. Yes, surely I can manage that, I was reassuring myself when a vaguely familiar figure appeared at my elbow.

'Hello,' it said. 'Well, fancy meeting you here, as they say. Have you still got that nice little cob?'

It is an appalling habit of mine to recall a face but be unable to remember the name attached to it. I knew exactly who the person in front of me was — I'd met him several times at the house of some very good friends in Weardale when I had lived there.

'Brian Patterson?' he smiled, as if to put me out my misery.

'Of course, I'm so sorry. Hopeless with names.'

'Don't worry. It must be a few years since you left the Dale.'

'Yes, well, that's a long story,' I said uncomfortably.

'How do you come to be here today?'

I was thankful that he wasn't going to dredge any deeper into my past. 'That's a long story too. I'm remarried, you know. I've got a little girl, Megan.'

'And you've still got your horse?'

'Bear? Oh yes, I've still got Bear.' I laughed, 'You wouldn't know him now though, all grown up he is. I've been hunting him last season — he's going really well.'

'Hunting is he, mmm,' Brian mused. 'Does them good does hunting, develops their lung capacity and stamina. Have you never fancied him for this game? Always thought he'd be perfect for driving, he's the right type.'

'To be honest,' I confessed, 'I still don't know anything much about it. This is the first time I've ever been to anything like this.'

Gears ground slowly in my brain and I suddenly remembered. 'Just a minute, didn't you have something to do with horses and carts?'

'Horses and carts? Horses and carts!' Brian turned a vaguely purplish hue and I thought I'd mortally offended him but then he exploded with laughter.

The start of it all. Bear, my little Welsh cob, in 1977

Bear resembling a shaggy, woolly, overgrown pony from a Thelwell cartoon

Ian and I out hunting
on Limerick and Bear

Ian and Megan on Bear

Ken Ettridge
Bear and I negotiate the water hazard at Beamish Horse Driving Trials in 1982

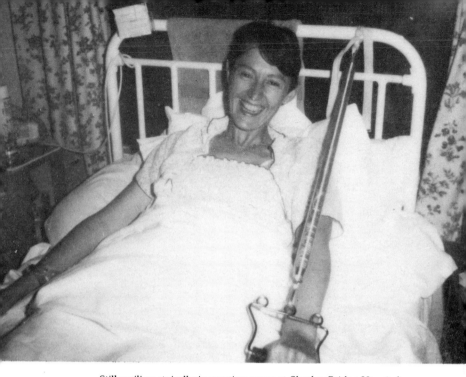

Still smiling stoically in my tiny room at Shotley Bridge Hospital

The collapsing wood and tin outbuildings of Mount Pleasant Farm, 1982

'Well I suppose I have, or had anyway. I'll have you know I was single-horse National Champion last year with my ''horse and cart''!'

I felt a complete idiot.

'I never actually saw your horse, I just remember you talking about him when we met.'

'Marvellous little horse, marvellous. Pure Dales he was and only just on the horse mark. Black Dene he was called, Blackie for short. Tireless, absolutely tireless. He won every time out with me last season.'

'Aren't you driving him here, then?'

'No. Haven't got him any more. Sold him on to go into a pair. I'm separated from my wife you see, and it's a lot of work — driving events on your own. So much cleaning and polishing and you need so much equipment. Then there's all the driving to shows and the setting up. It was just too much for me on my own. I was too tired to enjoy an event when I got there. But,' he smiled, 'I had a marvellous season with him and he's gone to a good home. Must admit though,' he finished ruefully, 'I miss it. Oh, you miss it once you're hooked. Especially on a day like today when you watch them all drive past.'

In the distance there was a rattling, bumping noise and a cacophony of hoof-beats coming towards us, very fast.

Brian consulted his clipboard.

'Stand by your stop-watch; first pair of horses.'

Then he grinned to himself. 'And look who it is!'

Around the corner two powerful dun horses swept into view, trotting faster than I had ever believed possible. Though sweated-up, they were still obviously full of life and enthusiasm and their driver was just managing to hold them back from the point of breaking into canter. The vehicle he was driving was far removed from my romantic idea of elegant carriages — it was a veritable battle-wagon, jet black with metal wheels and a step on the back on which two grooms were swaying as the whole outfit powered towards us. It was an awesome sight. Brian hit the stop-watch as the horses' noses passed him and the driver, with what appeared to be considerable difficulty and much juddering of brakes, finally succeeded in pulling up about fifty yards away. Brian followed them, also at the trot, to sign green cards and had what appeared to be quite a merry exchange with the driver before he set off at the walk to cool his horses off at the halt.

'Friend of yours?' I enquired when he returned.

'Oh, a great friend; the man I bought Black Dene from actually. He's moved from singles, you see, into pairs of horses now and I must say they are going well for him. Yes, he'll be one to watch, will Richard Smith.'

The name meant nothing; in fact the short dumpy man in the battered hat had hardly registered. But his horses, they were something else. Seeing a fit purposeful horse doing its job well never failed to move me, but to see two side by side, so visually alike and working so much in unison had positively shaken me.

'I never dreamed horses could do anything like that. I've gone quite weak at the knees,' I admitted to Brian. 'I didn't think you could do anything exciting with a horse in harness, only sitting on its back. But they — well, those horses came round there like bats out of hell. Talk about *Chariots of Fire*!'

'Exciting?' The tone was scornful. 'You call that exciting? That was nothing. Wait till you see them going through the hazards. Oh, I can see I've a lot to teach you, a lot indeed.'

And by the time I staggered home, stiff and frozen to the marrow, he most certainly had. He had pulled a few strings and got us relieved much earlier in the day than we should have been and he took me to the last part of Section E to see the horses go through the hazards. I was amazed, watching horse-drawn vehicles cover terrain and negotiate obstacles I wouldn't have believed possible, from fit, nippy little single ponies who scooted round up to the four imposing horses of a team.

'He's going so fast! They'll never get round there! I don't think I dare look,' I squealed at one point.

'Oh, but you must watch; that's the maestro, George Bowman. He'll be in and round and out of there in a crack.'

The name meant nothing of course, but watching him effort-lessly guide the whole length of his team and vehicle round some very solid timbers with little room to spare and barely a check in speed was quite an experience.

'His horses?' I said to Brian when Bowman had swept majes-tically from sight to great applause, 'they look sort of, well there's something almost familiar . . . '

'Mmm. Wondered when you'd realise, Welsh cobs, every one of them — Welsh cobs.'

The air was almost crackling with the unspoken thoughts, the images that were passing through my head. Oh yes I knew, I finally knew what I wanted to do more than anything before in my life. Next year I wouldn't be standing on the side line watching in awe, I was going to be there with my vehicle and my horse. How I was going to achieve it wasn't revealed to me in any rolling back of the heavens. I would work on little details like that later.

'Brian, did you say you haven't a horse to drive at present?'

3

The vow

OF COURSE IT wasn't as simple as that, but then it never is. But a seed was planted that day which, after a long and frustrating germination, was one day to bear undreamt-of-fruit. A year to develop and implement my plan sounded a very long time. Other commitments, however, like a young baby and a home to run, took precedence. Then there was the question of money. The inevitable equation of horses equals expense, equals even more expense came into play.

Ian was very dubious about the whole thing, calling it some momentary whim, though in the end even he came to see it was more than that, admitting 'I've never seen you so wound up, so determined about anything before.'

He made a bargain with me. The incredible degree of 'plumptiousness' I had attained by the end of my pregnancy had not, alas, departed with the arrival of Megan. I had made a few half-hearted attempts to lose weight but soon gave in, resigning myself miserably to buying size eighteen trousers and wearing baggy tops. But if Brian and I wanted to make a genuine attempt to compete Bear the next season, we would need a set of show harness and a presentation vehicle.

By early summer the deal was made. Firstly I would have to forgo any hunting the following season; that couldn't be paid for on top of this driving thing.

'Fine,' I said, 'super — can't ask the horse to work all year.' That shook him.

Secondly, I had to lose at least a stone and a half in weight. If I did, I could have a set of show harness and possibly a show vehicle, provided one could be found cheaply enough.

Throughout the summer I made the supreme effort — though with the incentive I now had it was not truly difficult. Also, borrowing Brian's work harness, the single item he had kept after selling Black Dene, and which fitted Bear like a dream (an omen! an omen!), I long-reined Bear up and down country lanes for miles and miles and miles. To begin with, it was just with the harness but later I added a swingletree and chains and a large, heavy log and we did yet more miles.

By the autumn I had lost two stone and ordered my new harness.

I then turned my attention to getting a vehicle. If ever a thing was cobbled together from a variety of unlikely sources, this was. I pleaded for hours with a man who had a pair of old wheels and an axle only to have him change his mind at the last moment when I went to collect them. Dramatically, I crumpled into a sobbing wreck outside his garage doors. Seeing that my very genuine anguish was actually having some effect, I turned the volume and the sprinklers up to the 'verging on hysteria' level. A few minutes of that and he capitulated, took my fifty quid and fled. I ordered the shafts from somewhere down south and in my ignorance didn't realise I'd have to have them 'dressed'. So what actually arrived resembled long bent fence posts and it took yet more phone calls and research to find an old firm in the next county who would dress them for me by smoothing and curving them into shape.

Oh, and did I want them plated? It would be an extra thirty quid. But plating meant attaching a metal strip along the underside to strengthen them and prevent the shafts fracturing too easily, so I agreed.

None of the vehicle would ever have become united without the talents of an astonishing man I found only six miles away (another omen!). Billy Plews took all my bits and pieces, ancient and modern, and put them together, building a body that was a reproduction Norfolk cart in record time and for modest money. He then recommended a friend who did a very respectable paint job and it only remained then to take the seat to a local furniture factory to be upholstered.

By Christmas I had my vehicle. I also discovered I was expecting another baby.

It wasn't an entire surprise, as after Megan's birth my gynaecologist had begun making rumbling noises and warnings that if I wanted another baby (oh, I did, I did; I didn't want Megan subjected to the stress of only-child-dom) then I would have to be pretty quick about it as things weren't looking too good internally.

My joy was to be short-lived however, as by February I had miscarried. I was not devastated with grief; it was far too early in the pregnancy and I had never actually experienced this baby in any real sense. Also Megan was only fifteen months old and I was so wound up in her. I took it as just one of those things and

life went on. To take my mind off it completely, we arranged for
Bear to go up the Dale to a friend of Brian's where we could
actually put him in a cart for the first time and then he would
stay with Brian for about a month for some training.

I stood back and viewed my clipping job with satisfaction,
chuckling as I thought how mystified I used to be by the art. As
it was absolutely impossible to make Bear look smart in his
woolly winter coat and anyway, lots of active work lay ahead of
him (I hoped), I had decided a haircut was the only answer.
Now he stood pale and hairless, smooth and muscular, neck
neatly hogged and looking a bit astonished. Had I gone barmy?
The hunting season was about to finish, not start. This was, I
suspected, a sore point with Bear who had watched his stable-
mate disappear for his weekly jaunt with the hounds while all
he got was gentle hacks over the fell and pulling damn logs all
over the place. He did not look amused.

'Don't look at me like that, Bear. It's not that cold. Anyway,
it's your big day tomorrow, if you did but know it, and I want
you looking beautiful, not like a scruff. And it'll be easier for
Brian to keep you clean and dry without all that hair. You know
you are ungrateful at times, Bear.'

He still did not look amused.

Next day, I trundled up the Dale with the Land Rover and
trailer. Brian met me at the farm where Bear was to stay and,
true to his word, a somewhat shabby and elderly exercise cart
was parked in the yard. I could not have been more thrilled by
the Queen's Coronation Coach awaiting us.

Four of us were assembled to do the deed.

'Don't look so nervous!'

'Sorry, Brian! Can't help it — I've done everything you told
me to do. He's done miles with logs and chains and he turns
when commanded and doesn't mind the traces wrapping themselves round his hocks, or traffic, or anything. It's just that,
well, none of that's the same as actually pulling a vehicle, is it?'

'He's going to be fine, so relax and just do what I tell you.
Okay?'

'Yes, Brian.'

After a cup of coffee while Bear settled himself into the loose
box that was to be his home for a few weeks and sampled a hay
net, we got cracking.

First Brian harnessed Bear up and long-reined him round the
paddock, using the verbal commands he'd told me to teach him:

'Walk on — come round — stand still.'

Then he quietly led him back and walked up the side of the trap and stopped just in front of the shafts. Then we aligned the vehicle straight with the horse. First law; take the vehicle to the horse, not the other way around. With two of us at Bear's head, Brian's two friends lifted the shafts up and over his back, then, talking to Bear all the time, Brian carefully fitted them into the tugs. For the first time in his life Bear was feeling the parallel rigidity of shafts against his body. The traces were attached to the back and the breeching straps buckled to the shafts. He was in.

Next Brian instructed us to fasten a lead rope to the headcollar that Bear had on under his bridle and also a long lunging line on to his bit, over his headpiece and through the bit on the other side. This would help keep him on the ground if he decided to rear. I hadn't even thought of that possibility and wished Brian hadn't mentioned it.

'Everyone ready?' he said and walked to the near side of the trap just behind Bear's rump and took up the reins. Throughout this procedure Bear had stood quite calmly, enjoying all the attention.

I had hold of the lead rope and was standing directly in front of Bear's nose to dissuade him from leaping forward. One of Brian's friends was on the lunge line and the other at the back of the cart ready to give it a push forward when Brian gave the word.

'Ready,' I answered.

'Right, Carol, stand aside. Get ready to push gently from behind . . . now! . . . Walk on, Bear! Walk on.'

Brian gave the command in a firm, authoritative voice and without hesitation, at the same moment that the cart began to move a little from behind, Bear took his first step forward.

I crooned softly and encouragingly to him, patting his neck but he didn't need my reassurance. Confident and relaxed, he walked out happily and our strange procession passed through the farm gate and down the quiet lane beyond. There were only three of us with him now, the helper from behind having been told to drop back.

'And whoa, Bear, whoa! And stand,' Brian commanded.

And he did! I was so proud; all those miles, all the 'Stop! — walk on! — stop!' routine made sense now.

Very carefully, but talking to the horse all the time, Brian climbed into the cart.

'Bear. Walk on!'

Without hesitation and this time without a shove from behind, Bear strode off once more, only his ears swinging round like Joddrell Bank radar dishes, puzzled at the change in direction of voice. All these months the commands had come from well behind him, but below ear level. Now for the first time they were above ear level. It must have seemed like a Cecil B. de Mille epic to him — The Voice From Above.

We walked a bit further and negotiated the first bend. Not a tight one, but enough to bring the pressure of the shaft gently against his side and shoulder for the first time. He didn't even seem to notice.

'I hope you two are fit enough to jog a bit! Get ready to trot. And Bear . . . trot on!'

I gave a little tug on the lead rope as Brian gave the command and, delighted to be doing something a bit more interesting, Bear trotted at once. A few hundred yards later, puffing and seeing pink mists, I was far more relieved than Bear to hear: 'And whoa, whoa and walk, just walk. Clever lad. I think you can loosen off that line now. He's not going to rear. Right, Carol, unclip your lead and fall back gently from his head and then climb up beside me. That's fine. Are you in okay?'

I could only manage a nod, partly because I was still battling to reventilate my lungs and partly because I was in one of those 'this can't really be happening, not really, actually happening' states. But it was, and after Bear had walked a little more and responded to every command and direction Brian gave him, he quietly told his friend to get up on the back step and Bear was going solo.

'Is he doing all right?' I finally managed to whisper in a strangled voice.

'All right?' Brian laughed, 'All right? There's no need to whisper, you know, it's not a funeral. You'll make him worried. Do you think most horses get this far first time out? I wouldn't have been surprised or worried if we hadn't got as far as the farm gate. The feel of the cart is often enough for many a horse the first time. But he's not put a foot wrong, he's relaxed, confident, responsive. You'd think he'd been doing this all his life.'

'He does seem quite happy,' I admitted.

'Happy! Look, this horse is a natural. And to prove it, watch — now don't worry that I'm going to do anything reckless, if he doesn't like it help can be from the back to his head in a flash.'

Choosing a widish bit of road, Brian slowed Bear's walk right down and then pulling hard on the right rein said, 'Bear, come round, come round!'

There was no way Bear could take a gentle curve at it, there wasn't the space, but he swung his head and weight to the right so hard the shaft came up right against his shoulder, pressing into him. But he just pushed against it as a person pushes against a stubborn swing door and, neatly crossing his legs, turned the trap completely around in just about its own length. Brian crowed with delight and poured praise on his head.

'This horse is a bloody marvel; did you see him shaft round there? He just about had his legs in plaits. I've known horses take weeks to learn to come round at all. I really can't wait to find out what he is capable of doing in hazards. And think of the weight he is pushing round, he's got three of us on the cart.'

All horses, wherever they are, have an inbuilt sense of when their heads are bound for home. Bear was no exception on this occasion and his step quickened further and he tugged hopefully at the bit.

'All right, clever clogs.' Brian shortened his reins. 'If you feel like a nice trot home you have one — trot on!'

Joyfully Bear sprang forward and fell almost at once into a bouncy, regular pace, full of rhythm and life. The still thin early spring air of the Dale that I knew and loved so well whipped a little more quickly against my face. I breathed in the smells of damp earth, of hillside fields awaiting the arrival of lapwings and lambs. Of all the places on earth for my horse and me to experience our first-ever drive together there was no other that could have made it quite so special.

All too quickly the farm gate awaited us. Brian's practised hands turned Bear neatly into the yard, still at the trot, and then brought him to a halt. Not until everything had been quietly and carefully removed from Bear and the cart rolled away was I allowed to hug him and cover him in an ecstasy of kisses, which embarrassed him to death, and feed him a whole tube of Polos, the little round mints he adored.

I turned to Brian, glowing with pride: 'Oh, wasn't he marvellous, wasn't he marvellous!'

'I always said he was a nice cob.'

'Oh, come on, you're not telling me all cobs are as clever as he is?'

'No. I must admit he's a natural. I wouldn't have usually dreamt of going as far as that on a first trip. But he was so happy, so willing, I just sort of forgot he'd never done it before after a while.'

'Do you think he'll be ready for Beamish?'

'Ready? He could do it next week, judging by what I've seen

today. How long have we got — six weeks or so? Well, I'll give him three weeks here and you can have him three weeks at home. Can I be serious for a moment?'

'Of course.'

'This is no ordinary horse.'

'Oh, Brian, I could have told you that!'

After driving Bear for three weeks, Brian returned him and the exercise cart to me so that work could continue from home. Bear had, he enthused, never put a foot wrong and was going like a dream. All he needed now was as much driving as possible to build up his muscles. Though already an extremely muscled and fit animal, Brian explained, he was used to carrying weight on his back and jumping — not pulling, which required somewhat different muscles.

'But how's he going to be driven except when you come?' I enquired.

'I expect you'll drive him.'

'Me!'

'Well, he's your horse, isn't he?'

'Yes, but . . . I've never driven in my life.'

'I thought that was the whole idea.'

'Oh it is, it is, eventually. I'd imagined learning, well, slowly, over the summer months.'

'Well, it looks as if you'll be learning very quickly, this weekend.'

Half an hour later Brian and I were trotting off down the lane. It was the fruition of nearly a year of dreaming and planning and hard work. When I took hold of the reins the first impression was of being a long, long way from contact with the horse's mouth. It made me want to lean forward, to stretch my arms up his back to get nearer to him. But Brian made me sit back and sit straight and I found it was possible to steer without hanging out of the front of the vehicle.

I also quickly realised how vital the spoken command was when driving. Ever since we had started breaking in Bear to drive we'd been using the same words of command whenever he performed a definite action either on the long reins or when riding. Now all it took to achieve the desired change of direction or speed was a slight movement on the reins and a clear command.

The sensation was quite unlike riding, in fact quite unlike anything I had experienced before. Like a learner driver in a car,

I found myself over-steering and crashing the gears to begin with when I changed pace, and I was tense and a bit nervous. But by my third time out the reins were lying more naturally in my hand, I could turn corners more fluently and I was much more relaxed. I was loving every minute of it.

Then Brian was gone and it was just Bear and me (and a groom on the back for safety) — our first solo flight.

I was filled with a sense of pride — not boastful pride, but pride of achievement, of what one year's hard work and determination could do. The horse, the vehicle, the harness and myself all united together at last. There was, I knew, a long way to go. I could exercise Bear but that was all. Dressage, hazards, marathons all lay ahead of me and I had an apprenticeship to serve. A season of listening and watching and feeling while Brian competed him. All year a relentless force had driven me to do things that had not come easily — like losing weight and exercising and hunting for bits of vehicle. Was this the reward, I asked myself, for all that effort? If it was, I was happy because the sensation was marvellous and well worth it. But deep inside, deep, deep inside, a voice was saying, 'This is only the beginning'.

So April 1980 found Bear and me getting ready for our first competition. Beamish Driving Trials had a reputation for two things; the severity of the marathon course and the severity of the weather. I didn't know that I was entirely ready for either, though the preparations for everything seemed to have been going on for weeks.

The first shock was just how much transport and organising it took to get to a driving event. The Land Rover and trailer took care of Bear, but Brian's car and another trailer were needed to transport the traps, and the harness and grooming kit and rugs and bandages seemed to fill the back of the Land Rover to over-flowing. And this was only a two-day local event — no staying away overnight. What would it be like at a full three-day event?

On the first day, dressage and the obstacle driving, I was in such a state of nervous tension I remembered little afterwards. I was to accompany Brian as a lady passenger, not as a groom on the back. I sat tight-lipped and grim-faced, wearing my smartest outfit of a matching camel-coloured jacket and skirt, and a new felt hat, next to Brian in his dark suit and bowler while he drove the dressage test. Not that I had a clue what he was doing. He had explained about extended trots and collected trots,

one-handed circles and serpentines but the complicated pattern
of movements he wove around the arena seemed to last an
eternity and I quaked at the thought of ever being able to
execute them in the right order from memory. The obstacles also
posed a memory problem as no two courses were ever the same
and they had to be driven in the correct order and against the
clock without any assistance from the groom or passenger. More
tight lips on my part. But even I realised he'd driven the cones
well — a clear round in the time allowed.

'What a horse!' exclaimed Brian after we'd left the arena.
'He's so straight and positive — just line him up and he flows
through; never blinked at those cones though it's the first time
he's been in an arena.'

'What about the dressage this morning?'

'Don't know yet, though it was a remarkably good test for a
first time. I think he's going to excel at dressage, he seems to
enjoy it. They're going to announce the results after the first day
at the cocktail party tonight.'

'How civilised! I think I'm going to enjoy this carriage driving
bit!'

'And the overnight leader, single horse class, is our old friend
Mr Brian Patterson driving Conwy Blaze. Well done, Brian!'

I stood absolutely speechless, my glass so limp in my hand I
almost dropped it. I hadn't heard right, it couldn't be true!

'See, told you he was a nice little cob!'

'But he can't have!'

'But he has.'

'Is he well in the lead?'

'Not well enough.'

My spirits, which had been floating around on cloud nine took
a sudden lurch.

'What do you mean?'

'Well, tomorrow is marathon day and it's tough. The
weather's been wet and the ground is heavy. It's his first time
and he's never driven real hazards before. Oh, I know I've had
him round a few trees and in and out of fence posts but these
will be big, solid hazards and I'll be taking no chances with him,
so it's the longer, safer route every time. Bear's in the lead, but
only just and there are a lot of powerful, experienced horses
right up his backside — if you'll pardon the expression.'

'Oh.' My sudden wilt in countenance said it all. I began to
view the morrow with apprehension.

'Hey! None of that. It's still fantastic what he's done today, but surely you don't expect him to win first time out?'

That put things into perspective.

'No, of course not, Brian, how silly of me. Of course you have to go steady tomorrow, there's a lot of season ahead and he doesn't want to be put off before he even starts. Well done for today, very well done.'

The weather the next day was diabolical; a Siberian wind with occasional penetrating sleet. The course was not much better in places, up vertical forest tracks, tottering along the edge of great drops and ploughing up the middle of a river bed for several hundred yards at one point. I was soaked, I was frozen and at some points I was plain petrified as the rattling vehicle hurtled through gaps in trees with slim inches to spare. I bounced and banged against the sides of the vehicle so much that I was beyond black and blue. I was green and purple.

Bear, getting thoroughly over-excited at the beginning and not knowing what was to come, could not pace himself and we had time faults on the walk section and on the fast section C. But he drove the hazards bravely and with each one seemed to learn to turn that bit quicker, that bit tighter.

By the end he was exhausted but unharmed, and I was exhausted and in considerable pain. It was a sharp, hot needle-type pain in my lower abdomen. If I hadn't already had my appendix out I would have been worried. I put in down to excitement, the extreme bumpiness of the terrain and possibly the time of month.

'Are you okay?' Brian enquired anxiously, 'You look dreadful.'

'Thanks a bundle. I've got a stitch or something, and my God, I'm not surprised after that course. I'm sure horse-drawn vehicles were never intended to cover terrain like that!'

'Did you enjoy it? That's the main thing.'

I considered that one very carefully before saying, 'On balance, yes! And with experience and once I know how to throw my weight round the cart more it'll probably be better. I was so worried about the stop-watches stopping or not giving you the right time or losing the green card, I couldn't really concentrate on what Bear was doing. I just gritted my teeth and hung in there!' I paused. 'Tell me,' I then asked quietly, 'did he do well? Only I wouldn't know, you see.'

'Carol, he was super. He tried his heart out: tried too hard, actually, to begin with, but he will learn to pace himself and he will get fitter, driving fit that is, and he's going to be elastic in hazards. I still think he is a special horse. I am proud to be the first to drive him.'

'Thank you.'

'Once he gets a few more marathons under his belt he'll be a force to reckon with in this game. And once you get a few more under your belt you'll not look so seasick and battle-shocked!'

Later that day, exhausted and still in some discomfort, but glowing with pride and satisfaction, I fell asleep on the way home in the Land Rover, clutching my green rosette which said 'Beamish Horse Driving Trials — Fourth Prize'.

Little did I dream how far off my next marathon was to be.

The pain did not go away. It niggled and rumbled despite my every attempt to ignore it and although I could hold it at bay with ordinary analgesic tablets it kept fighting back. I would, I reluctantly decided, just have to go and see the doctor at the end of the week. I hadn't time to be poorly; Bear's first full F.E.I. (Fédération Equestre Internationale, to give it its full title) event was coming up soon, and if preparing for a two-day local event had been exhausting then the preparations required to get us all away and accommodated and fed for four days were mind-bending.

It was the Thursday of the week after Beamish and the worst of my muscular aches and pains had worn off, though my bruises were just about every colour of the rainbow. On Thursday mornings a few friends, all with babies around the same age, met at each other's houses, ostensibly to start an early socialisation programme for the babes but in all honesty to have a cup of coffee and a good natter. I decided I would make the attempt to go. A restful morning would probably do me good and Megan loved company. I strapped her into the back of the Land Rover and we rumbled off.

I was seated on a very low sofa at my friend's house enjoying my tea when Megan overbalanced with a thump and began to cry. I leaned right forward, almost double, to pull myself up and off the sofa to see to her. A searing pain like a white-hot sword thrust right through my belly. My teacup and saucer rolled away with a clatter as I hit the floor. I couldn't even scream or cry out — the pain was so terrible that it was all I could do just to breathe. I was aware of Megan crying and my friends' frantic enquiries as to what was wrong but all I could manage was a barely audible moan.

The friend's house was but half a mile from Shotley Bridge

Hospital where I had had Megan and where a couple of months before I had gone for a scrape after my miscarriage. The ambulance arrived and had me back to the hospital in minutes.

After a brief examination during which I nearly passed out, I was admitted to the gynaecological ward and given a shot of pethodine to ease the pain. I watched the blue flowers on the wallpaper perform a slow intricate dance on the wall in front of me for the rest of the afternoon. At tea-time I was visited by the consultant.

'And how long have you had this pain?'

'This pain only since this morning, but a pain since last weekend.'

'Mmm. And how long since the miscarriage?'

'A couple of months ago.'

'Mmm. I believe you were warned things were not in a healthy condition after your little girl was born? In fact, you were extremely lucky to carry her to term.'

'I hadn't realised that.' Little alarms were being set off up and down my nervous system. 'But I was advised to complete my family as soon as possible as there could be problems ahead.'

'For ahead, read now.'

Without him saying any more, I knew for certain what he meant. Almost calmly I asked, 'You mean I have to have a hysterectomy, don't you?

'I think we have very little option. You have a massive and acute infection throughout the womb and into the Fallopian tubes.'

'But I'm only thirty years old.' It left my lips on a wisp of breath.

'I know that, and the only consolation I can offer you is that you have a healthy, normal little girl and many women with the internal problems you have have never managed to conceive at all. Please hang on to that fact and remember also that being thirty, fairly fit and not overweight is a distinct advantage when facing surgery.'

My mind reeled and whirled, I felt sick with fear and shock. Please God, I kept saying to myself, don't let this happen to me. I couldn't bear it. I'm not strong enough. Reading my face the consultant took my hand.

'Don't be frightened. This operation has got terrible myths surrounding it, but these days there is no need for alarm. The main point is that, when it is all over, you can't have any more children. Now you have to come to terms with that and, as I've already told you, count your blessings for the child you have.'

It all blurted out then, between bubbling, heaving sobs. 'But women who have had it done,' I gulped, 'they just go to seed, don't they? Overweight and de-feminised. Prematurely menopausal!'

'No. It won't affect your hormones. It doesn't involve the ovaries.'

'But . . . but surely your married life can never be the same afterwards!'

'I don't see why not. Listen,' he rose to leave, 'I think you need a good long talk with Sister; I'm only a man and you're not going to listen to me. I want you to rest now and I'll be back in the morning to begin treatment.'

'Treatment? I thought I was having an operation?'

'We'll talk about that in the morning.'

After a night of drug-enforced placidity I awoke to find I was still, after all, in a hospital bed. It had not been a bad dream.

It was to be a day of more shocks and hard decisions. There was no question of operating straight away. The infection was so advanced and dangerous that there was a risk of peritonitis. They wanted to get the infection as much under control as possible before they operated and that could take a long time.

'How long?'

'It could be weeks.'

They were going to attack the infection with everything they could, which meant massive doses of antibiotics — orally, by injection and by intravenous drip. Of all the events of the previous twenty-four hours, this last was the worst. I had a terror of drips, a horror of drips, it was pure torture to have one put into my vein and purgatory to lie there and watch it.

Domestic decisions had to be made. My mother was summoned and she and Brenda were to take on Megan between them. With a hollow aching heart I agreed there was no choice but to withdraw Bear from the competitions we had entered him for in the next couple of months. Louise would be able to keep him exercised, and Brian said he would come over and drive Bear now and then so he did not drop too far back. But what a shame. What a damn, crying shame.

I had plenty of time to cry and think and to try and re-adjust before the operation: four weeks, in fact, before the consultant deemed it safe enough to go ahead. I was more terrified the night before than at any other time in my life before or since but I knew in stark reality that I had no choice. And I did have Megan. Had I not, then what was to come would have been truly unbearable.

The nurses were marvellous. The first two days after surgery were the worst but, by the third, I was able to totter across the corridor to the loo grasping my drip stand in one hand and my stitches in the other to a chorus of, 'Get your back straightened up!' from every nurse that saw me.

After five days I could make it down to the day room and was off my drip. After a week my stitches came out. After ten days I was allowed to go home.

It was nearly six weeks since I'd rumbled off in the Land Rover to go for a cup of coffee. The hedgerows in the lane had been in spring bud when I left; now, as I drove home, they were a lacy white mass of cow parsley blossoms. It was early summer and every conceivable shade and hue of green vied for my attention from palest eau-de-nil to vibrant emerald. I wound down the window to drink in more fully the smell of growing things, to purge my lungs. Rounding the bend I could see in the paddock the two horses grazing and lazily swishing their tails against flies not yet numerous enough to be really troublesome. The ordeal was over. It was time to pick up the reins of my life where they'd been so suddenly dropped. It was good to be home. It was good to be alive.

It was not easy to get back into the routine I had had with Megan and the house. I tired very easily at first but every day I managed to take Megan a little further in the pushchair and do a little more in the house. Brenda, as always, was invaluable, knowing just when to leave me alone to try and do something and when to wade in and say 'You've done quite enough'.

By mid-July I had convinced everyone that I was fit and well again, and that if all the effort we had put into Bear that year was not to be wasted it was time we entered him at his first real three-day event.

Tatton Park in Cheshire was on the calendar for the end of the month. We decided we had time to get organised and that Bear was fit enough, but any suggestion that I could participate in anything but a supervisory capacity was squashed flat. I could see the sense in it, that in a tip-up or even a hard knock untold damage might be done to my newly-healed insides, but it was not easy to stand back and let Louise take my place on the vehicle.

We arrived at Tatton Park well after midnight. I had slept for hours on the journey down and was completely dislocated in time and place. We'd not been able to leave until after Brian finished work on the Thursday night and as the dressage was on the Friday morning — lateish on, thank God — everything, but everything had to be ready before we left home. Horse, harness and vehicles. Because we didn't possess a large horsebox our arrival was rather like a wagon train pulling in. First our Land Rover pulling the trailer with Bear, then Brian and Louise pulling a large caravan of Brian's in which we were all to sleep and finally some kind and good friends, who had taken the weekend off, towed the trailer carrying two carts, and had booked into a local hotel so they could be on hand.

Though totally shattered I was awake at first light and staggered out into the chill air, bleary-eyed and sticky-mouthed. An amazing sight met my eyes. In the darkness of our arrival we had just made camp as quickly and quietly as possible in the first space we'd found. I'd been aware of lumpish shapes surrounding us and heard the occasional horse cough or stamp its foot in the night. Now, in the early light, I discovered we were surrounded. We were on the edge of a vast mobile equestrian city with horseboxes from the small, much-used and very elderly up to the enormous, brand-new and palatial. All those horses? All those vehicles? All those people? All here to drive? Brian had warned me it would be very, very different from Beamish. He was right. What exactly was this sport that I was getting involved in? It was obviously bigger, much bigger than I had ever imagined.

By the end of the next three days I had a clearer idea of what carriage-driving trials were about. Hard work for a start; hard teamwork, getting and keeping horse, harness and vehicle at their best. Miles of walking — walking dressage arenas and great chunks of the marathon and over and over each hazard, looking at and thinking about approaches and turns, then doing them all just one more time to try and find a quicker route. And tension and excitement of course; the last-minute panic of getting everything just perfect for presentation. Watching the dressage test and trying to breathe at the same time. Running between hazards to try and catch a glimpse of Bear powering in and through and out just one more. The pageantry of pairs and teams with their liveried grooms and beautiful four-wheeled carriages. The amazing comradeship among the competitors; help and advice and really true sportsmanship all around us. And after the sport and work of the day, mad marvellous evenings in the competitors' marquee with food and drink and dancing till the early hours.

The noise, the smell, the spectacle of it were a whole new

world that had just been waiting for me to find it. And I loved it. I was hopelessly, totally and eternally hooked. I could think of nothing else I would ever want to spend my spare time on or put my spare money towards. This was it.

Brian and Bear won the dressage, came third on the marathon and held on to that position with a clear round in the cones; I pressed against the ringside ropes on the Sunday afternoon and clapped and clapped till my hands hurt as Brian drove Bear into the arena with the rest of the class to receive his rosette. Any disappointment I was feeling in not being in there with him was completely eclipsed by my joy and pride in my horse's achievement. Third place at his first full F.E.I. Competition.

After the presentation to the class, they trotted round and then the winner did a lap of honour and we all clapped and cheered some more. Back at our camp we were all coming reluctantly down to earth and beginning the long process of packing for the return journey. My emotional balance tipped and the euphoria of minutes before was replaced by a feeling of sad loss.

'It's all over.'

'That's the way it usually goes.'

'We've all put so much into it these last few days and you and Bear did so well, Brian. It's childish and stupid to say, but I just wanted it to go on for ever. I have never had such a marvellous weekend — I can't ever thank you enough for what you've achieved with Bear.' I fingered the yellow rosette wistfully.

'Oh, come on! You sound as if it's the end of the world. This weekend is just the start. Think of that. Think of how much talent that horse has and how far he's got to go. That rosette is his stepping-stone.'

'Stepping-stone to what?'

'This event is a qualifier,' said Brian mysteriously. 'Didn't you know?'

'Qualifier for what?'

'Dear Lord, you are new to this game, aren't you! Qualifier for the National Championships, that's what.'

I repeated the words in hushed awe. 'National Championships? I didn't know this sport had such things.'

'Well it does, and they're usually held at Royal Windsor, by kind permission of H.M. However, this September the World Team Driving Championships are being held there so they're having the National Championships at Osberton.'

'World Championships! Does this sport have World Championships as well!'

'Only teams of horses so far, but rumour has it we'll see World Championships for pairs of horses before very long.'

Oh yes, it was all bigger, much much bigger, than I had ever imagined.

The only event we could all afford the time and money to get to with Bear before the National Championships was Lowther in Cumbria. It had a fearsome reputation for a gruelling marathon in a glorious Lake District setting. I was still grounded as far as the marathon went, but I was at least allowed to sit in as lady passenger for the presentation and dressage. I made the most of the opportunity to indulge in a little dressing-up. I was getting more into the spirit and tradition of the sport and realised that the driver and passenger's dress was supposed to reflect the character and colour of the vehicle. I had a dark green Norfolk country cart with camel upholstery. Attired in a dark green long-sleeved dress with matching shawl and a beige straw hat, gloves and camel knee-rug, I hoped I presented a suitably rural picture. I also tried this time to make a little more sense of the complicated movements of the dressage test. The mysteries of driven dressage were so far beyond me that it was a grey area in my rosy dream of 'Carol the F.E.I. Driver'. But they were obviously well within Brian's grasp and to our delight Bear was yet again in the lead after this first phase. But our hopes were soon to be dashed. A single kilometre into the marathon the next day the spokes collapsed on one of the wheels of Brian's cart. He had to withdraw. It also started to rain and didn't stop again for two days. It was a salutory lesson that carriage driving was not all sunshine and roses, that it could at times be bitterly disappointing, wet, cold and uncomfortable.

September found us at Osberton. By now I felt I really was fit enough to tackle a marathon; after all, I was riding Bear and driving him regularly at home now. But Ian was adamant. No risks this season. Next season I could go on the vehicle — good God, next season I would be driving Bear myself. I thought back to the battering and bruising I had taken on the marathon at Beamish and reluctantly agreed.

An additional bonus of this sport, I was discovering, was the lovely places it took you to. Lowther had been held in the shadow of the ruins of Lowther Castle and now we were in the middle of a glorious country estate with lovely woodland all around us. The usual assemblage of horseboxes, trailers and caravans were serviced by the usual excellent eating and social facilities. All those people and all those horses, some of them there for upwards of a week, required a great deal in the way of water, daily groceries, toilet facilities, rubbish disposal and other little necessities. There were also rows of portable stabling for hire, which meant Bear could have a loose box which was much less cramped for him than the trailer. Around the arena, various trade stands sprang up, selling every item of horsy and country clothing imaginable. You could get everything from green wellies to a T-shirt printed with your horse's name.

We put that extra little bit of effort into all our preparations and polishing and I whispered extra special sweet nothings in Bear's ear. He did yet another super dressage test, which put him just a whisker in the lead. Whatever else the weekend brought, Brian pointed out, it could now be said that Bear had won the dressage on every appearance he had made in his first season's driving.

The marathon next day was very tough, the hazards demanding and the opposition very experienced. We were not therefore disappointed when he dropped to third place. And when he held that place on the final day we were mad with jubilation. My little horse — first a scraggy little hack and then my stalwart hunting friend. Now, five months and four appearances into a whole new sport, and he was the third best single horse in the country!

The year hadn't turned out the way I had planned in some respects, it was true. But that was over now; I was fit, I was well and I was watching and learning from Brian all the time. His season's work with Bear was the greatest grounding my horse could ever have had. An ex-National Champion was going to be a hard act to follow and I didn't kid myself for one moment that I would be able to step into Brian's shoes and get the results he had been getting with Bear. I had my apprenticeship to serve. But as we trotted proudly in third position around the arena to the applause of the crowd, rosettes waving in the breeze, I made a vow. I was unbelievably proud and happy. Had Bear been the overall winner I could honestly have been no happier. He had proved his worth, now I had to prove mine. I vowed silently, 'Next year, bonny lad, it's you and me. I mightn't do you the justice Brian has, but I will compete. I will compete!'

And then it was the sad ritual of packing and heading back home. Back to a well-earned rest for Bear, back to normality for the rest of us — what a horrible thought. The yearly cycle would

take up its pattern no doubt, and there would be hunters to get
fit for cub-hunting. No hunting for Bear and me this year,
though. Though he hadn't had a hard or long season he'd been
kept very fit for a long time now. Time to let down and relax,
physically and mentally. With only a one-acre paddock to our
name, we had no grass of our own to speak of and had arranged
to send Bear across the road to our neighbours Colin and Valerie
Harrison at Bell's House Farm. There he could eat and dream to
his heart's content for a few weeks. And what dreams, what
limitless endless dreams, we could now both indulge in.

4

'You must be prepared for the worst'

IT WAS A glorious October day, Megan was peacefully taking her post-lunch nap, God was in his Heaven and all was right with my world. The peace and contentment were only marred by the noise of the heavy bulldozer working on the muck mountain behind the farm buildings. I was busy in the kitchen when the phone rang.

'Hello, Colin, what can I do for you? No, Ian's not in. Can I help?'

Colin sounded very upset and very anxious not to talk to me.

'No, there's only me here. What is it, Colin?'

'It's Bear. He's fallen in the septic tank. I think you'd better come quickly.'

'Yes, yes of course.' I put the phone down gently and sank on to the hall chair. One word kept repeating over and over: no, no, no, no, *no*!

How could I go? Megan was asleep upstairs in her cot and there was no one around at all. But how could I leave Bear? Swiftly checking Megan, who was out for the count, I made a dash for the Land Rover. Bell's House Farm was only a quarter of a mile away, and I knew that Colin's wife Valerie would come straight down and look after Megan. I cursed myself for not thinking of that while on the phone.

My short journey ended and I nearly fell out of the Land Rover. I could see Colin behind a wall by the barn, just standing and apparently staring at the ground.

As I climbed over the wall, my eyes were searching everywhere for Bear.

'Where is he?' I asked, bewildered.

Colin didn't say anything. His eyes met mine briefly, then he lifted his hand and pointed. My eyes followed his hand.

'Oh my God, oh dear, dear God, oh no.'

Sunk in the midst of a mass of broken and splintered timber in a square concrete tank not much bigger than a coffin, Bear was struggling for his life. A black, stinking slurry completely

surrounded and engulfed him, his hindquarters were completely trapped under the concrete cover at the back end of the
tank. At the front end, like an obscene caricature of a hippo-
potamus, only his ears, eyeballs and widely flaring nostrils were
visible above the slurry.

I flung an accusing 'How?' at Colin.

'Someone left the field gate open and he wandered into the
stockyard. Seventeen years we've been complaining to the
landlord about that tank. Bloody timber covering it has been
rotten all that time. I knew it would be a death-trap one day.'

The horror of it seemed to have robbed Colin of his ability to
think or move and a voice in my brain was hammering that we
had to move, we had to act and we had to be quick. As yet he
had not sent for any help.

I got down beside Bear and got my hand under his chin. His
breath was coming in terrible harsh rasps as he battled to keep
his nostrils in the air.

'Bear, Bear, please hang on. I've go to go for help, but I'll be
straight back. Just hang on, Bear, I promise we'll get you out.
Don't die Bear, please don't die.'

We looked at each other; his eyes were calm but he seemed
terribly weak. I tried to shake Colin out of his trance by getting
him to come and take my place at Bear's head, his hand under
the chin to try and relieve the awful strain on Bear's neck as he
laboured to breathe.

'Talk to him, Colin, just talk to him. It will help.'

I pounded up the hill to the farmhouse. Valerie was waiting
for me distraught and tearful.

'Is there anything we can do? Oh, it's awful. What can we
do?'

'Will you go down and see if Megan is all right? I had to leave
her; there was no one at home. Can I use the phone?'

She nodded and was quickly off down the hill.

Who to phone first? I knew I was close to panic and that if I
did panic, all hope was lost. Who did we need? A vet. Definitely
a vet, and then the fire brigade, they rescued people trapped in
cars and buildings, didn't they?

The receptionist at our own vet's implored me several times to
calm down as she tried to make sense of my incoherent gabble.

'Yes, yes, I see or I think I see . . . Well, I'm afraid they're all
out on call at present . . . Now, calm down, I'll do my best to
raise one of them . . . Yes, I do understand the urgency.'

I phoned a second vet in Durham and had the distinct feeling I
was suspected of being a crank or a hoax. Perhaps that's how I

sounded, and somehow the words to describe the scene that
had met me in the yard were hard to find.

It took three attempts to hit 999 as my hands were shaking uncontrollably now. I implored the fire brigade to come and to
bring lifting gear and cutting gear and pumps. Then I realised
they thought I was talking about a person being trapped.

'No, no,' — by now I was sobbing — 'it's my horse, my horse is
drowning!'

I slammed down the phone feeling I was getting nowhere. What
if they couldn't find a vet? What if the fire brigade didn't turn out on
calls to animals? What if it took hours before they came? I needed
local help and quickly.

I dialled another number. Mr Suddess, the largest farmer in the
nearby village — who owned all the buildings and land around our
house — was definitely 'agin' horses. That was the reason we had
to send Bear up to Bell's House Farm for really good grazing,
because Mr Suddess was not going to allow grass that could be
eaten by something profitable and useful, like a sheep or cow, to be
wasted on a horse, or at least a 'pleasure horse'. I stood very much
in awe of this wiry little farmer who, together with his clan, seemed
to populate most of the village and held sway there. Margaret, his
daughter-in-law, and I were on good terms however; she had
ridden Bear a few times and was currently on a campaign to get her
own horse. When she picked up the phone my message to her was
terse and urgent.

'Margaret? It's Carol. I'm at Bell's House Farm. There's been an
accident, an awful accident. Bear's trapped in the septic tank. He's
completely trapped and he'll drown soon. Please, please send
help.'

I ran out of the farmhouse to get back to Bear, and in the peaceful
October air the only sound was that of the huge bulldozer still
eating away at the muck mountain behind our house. Of course, he
might be able to help! Instead of going into the stockyard, I made
for the Land Rover, drove recklessly down the hill, shot through
our farmyard, where an astonished Valerie was waiting for news,
and skidded to a juddering halt just beneath the giant maws of the
bulldozer. The farm lad driving it obviously thought I'd 'ta'en a fit'.

'Can you take that,' I pointed to his machine, 'up to Bell's House
Farm, straight away.'

I tried to explain why but got looks of disbelief, and also worried
mutters about having a job to do.

'Oh, it's all right,' I assured him, 'Mr Suddess knows, I've sent a
message. They're all coming.' It was a white lie at the time, but a
prophetic one.

The huge yellow giant followed surprisingly quickly, as I did awful things to the Land Rover gearbox in an attempt to get turned round and out of the farmyard. Once more, I ploughed up the hill and, fearful of finding I was too late, climbed the wall and joined Colin. As I had requested, he was sitting by Bear's head, easing his breathing by holding his muzzle and talking to him. Bear looked no different from when I had left him. Feeling very helpless again as the size of the problem hit me, I knelt down beside him and started stroking his filth-encrusted head. The smell was indescribably foul and yet so irrelevant I soon ceased to notice it.

'Help is coming, Bear. We'll get you out now.'

No sooner had I uttered the words than Colin said, 'Look!'

Up the hill a strange procession came. The car in front was followed by not one but two shiny red fire engines, and behind that clanking and groaning up the gradient came the great giant bulldozer. I had just noticed a second car pulling in at the bottom of the hill when the first one reached the top and a man and a woman I didn't know got out.

'Where's the horse?' she enquired, and added as an explanation, 'we're the vets from Durham.'

She couldn't mask her shock when she saw Bear, but immediately lay beside him and felt beneath the filth for a pulse in his neck.

'How long has he been in here?'

'We don't know,' I admitted. 'Certainly hours. It could even be part or all of the night,' I added, feeling sick at the very thought.

'His heart and pulse seem quite strong,' she reassured me. 'The amazing thing is he seems quite warm. I would have thought he would be suffering from a chill factor by now. Perhaps it's this slurry, it feels quite warm.'

'That's the washing,' Colin explained. 'Valerie's been doing a boil wash on the automatic. It'll have been pumping out into here all morning.'

'Well,' said the lady vet, 'I think it's probably kept him alive.'

Over the wall there now appeared half a dozen or so firemen, the chief of whom came forward to assess the situation. I don't think any immediate solutions presented themselves to him.

'Could you pump the slurry out?' I suggested.

Still feeling around Bear's neck, the vet said, 'Hang on, have you got any cutting gear? There's an iron girder or something down here right across his chest.'

As the firemen retreated to collect their equipment, their place was taken by the familiar face of my own vet and his young assistant. 'Oh, Mr Lowe, thank goodness you're here,' I said. He glanced down at the lady vet and I suddenly felt awkward, as if I'd committed some professional indiscretion.

'They said they couldnt get you,' I blurted out by way of explanation, 'I had to get help quickly. I had to get somebody!'

'Don't worry,' he assured me, 'I think we need all the help we can get.'

The firemen reappeared, carrying what looked suspiciously like an electric hacksaw. My heart sank; if this was their cutting gear, I felt we weren't going to get far.

'Sorry, lady,' he apologised, 'we can't get the engine any nearer on this hillside and the pumps won't reach. We'll have a go with this though.'

Ten minutes and several broken blades later, my fears were confirmed. There was no way that the little handsaw could cut through the iron bar across Bear's chest. I felt my imposed, calm facade slipping. I wanted to scream, I wanted to cry. It was hopeless, we would never get him out.

The sound of several car doors shutting and heavy feet hurrying snapped me back to practicalities. Over the wall appeared wiry old Mr Suddess, followed by his two strapping sons, all the farm workers and villagers they could have squeezed in the cars and Margaret. It took Mr Suddess all of thirty seconds to appraise the situation.

Stripping off his jacket, he growled, 'Well doon't just stand theer!' to the assembled company, then 'git buckets and straw and plenty of both!'

Margaret put her arms around me and I lost my grip. Tears poured down my face. I sobbed and heaved uncontrollably.

'Margaret, tell me it's a nightmare, tell me it's not happening,' I begged her.

'It's awful, Carol, awful. He's such a lovely animal, but we'll do all we can, you know that.' She tried to reassure me through her own tears. Her husband Jim came past with a bale of straw and looked me straight in the face.

'We *will* get him out, I promise you we will. The father's rescued more beasts than enough from old mineshafts in his time.' He hurried off.

As soon as men, buckets and straw were organised to his satisfaction, 'the father' swung into action. Totally oblivious to the stench and feel of the slurry, he started plunging a bucket down the side of Bear and passing it along the line of men who had formed up, then plunging in the next bucket he was given.

At the same time, Jim started pushing straw down the other side of Bear to replace the hauled-out slurry. It was simple, it was obvious and it quickly began to work. In a few minutes Bear didn't have to keep his neck stretched up at that impossible angle to breathe, and the dark shadow of the top of his back appeared. So did the narrow confines of his prison. The concrete tank he was trapped in was, incredibly, only about a foot wider and a foot longer than he was. It had a concrete shelf about two foot deep at the far end, beneath which his back was firmly stuck. I stood and watched disbelievingly, still numb and feeling detached from the frantic activity.

Pausing for breath, though he wouldn't consider relinquishing his place at the head of the bucket chain, Mr Suddess beckoned for his monster bulldozer to approach the tank. Following curt instructions, a rope was passed round the iron bar at the front of Bear and attached to the bulldozer, which gave a gentle, seemingly effortless tug. The concrete snapped and out came the bar. A similar procedure with a hook under the concrete slab at the back quickly removed that obstacle as well. Hope and dread chased each other around my mind. Another few minutes' work with the bucket chain and the slime-encrusted form of Bear could plainly be seen in the concrete tank, his head drooping pathetically. The vets suddenly went into a huddle, talking animatedly and then Mr Lowe came over to where I was standing. He had obviously decided on the 'take the bull by the horns' approach.

'You must be prepared for the worst,' he said to me. 'We don't know what injuries he has sustained internally or externally until we get him out of that damned hole. He could have one or more broken legs, for all we know.'

I stood, my hand across my mouth, nodding numbly. Obviously distressed and at a loss for words, Mr Lowe nodded, grunted, and rejoined his companions.

By now, most of the space formerly consisting of slurry was occupied by a thick straw soup. This had the effect of cushioning Bear from the sharp sides of the concrete, and, I suspect, of providing him with an element of warmth. Lying flat on the ground one each side of Bear, two of the Suddess men managed to get a thick piece of tractor conveyor belt under his belly to form a sling.

'Soon,' I thought, 'soon he'll be out; soon we'll know.'

I didn't want to know. For a crazy moment I felt like asking the vet to get it over with while he was still in there.

'No, no,' a firmer voice said from inside, 'there might be a chance, he might be in one piece: we must find out, we must know.'

Once more the mighty machine crawled forward to the side of the pit, and the ends of the sling were firmly attached to the jaws at the front which were positioned over Bear. Revving the engine to an ear-splitting pitch, the driver almost reluctantly put his hand to the control lever, and the great bucket began to swing upwards. No one moved, everyone watched and I suspect everyone prayed.

Grim-faced and with lethal syringe at hand, the vets stood by. Slowly, almost imperceptibly at first, the sling tightened and then began to move upwards. Then slowly and steadily the form of Bear's body also moved. A few seconds later and he was clear of the pit, just hanging there, a black and dripping mass of legs, neck and tail swinging in a grotesque, unnatural fashion several feet above the ground. I cried out and tried to go forward, but firm arms gently held me back.

'Best not,' Margaret said softly, 'they'll not want you in the way.'

The bulldozer moved gently sideways now and Bear's pathetic form was moved from over the pit to dry land. Quickly, the men formed up on either side of him as he was lowered slowly to the ground.

Everyone of us there had the same unspoken thought: 'Will he stand?'

I was biting my lip just out of the necessity to feel something, anything, when he touched the ground.

His legs splayed out and then took his weight. He stood like a cruel caricature of a new-born foal, head down, legs apart, but I kept repeating the precious words. 'He's standing, he's standing.'

The shout came: 'Nowt brokken! Nowt brokken! He's got his legs!'

Once more my composure slipped. Once more the tears came. But not despair this time, not anger, just relief.

'He's going to make it. I know he'll make it.' The voice inside was very firm this time.

5

No promises

THERE WAS A tangible release of tension in the air, people started to chat excitedly again and slap each other on the back. Half-covered with the stinking black stuff himself, Jim came past with more clean straw and grinning from ear to ear.

'See, I told you so, didn't I?'

His father was still firmly in charge of the operation and willing hands were now vigorously scraping and rubbing Bear all over with clean straw in an attempt to remove the worst of the sludge.

'Doon't mind that, doon't mind that — git him inside afore he gets chilled,' came the order.

It was beyond my comprehension just how they expected Bear to go anywhere; it was painfully obvious he was incapable of putting one foot in front of the other. It was taking all of his remaining strength just to keep standing. Before I even had time to complete the worrying process about this, a human chain formed up, linked muscular arms around him, clasped him tightly and somehow half-pushed and half-carried him the twenty yards or so into the nearest byre where a deep straw bed was awaiting him.

Groups of people began to break up and leave. The fire brigade were the first to go. The vets went into a final huddle before the lady vet and friend prepared to depart. I went over to their car.

'I don't know how to thank you enough for coming and for all your help. Everybody, I mean everybody, was wonderful.'

'I'm still amazed myself,' she smiled. 'He must be the luckiest horse in the world. To be honest I didn't think there was a hope in hell of his being in one piece.' She looked at me seriously now. 'If I'd had to get a totally unconscious horse into that . . . that thing' and she pointed at the septic tank, 'without breaking a leg, I couldn't have done it, never mind one that must have gone in fighting. No, I would say it couldn't be done. Well, goodbye.' She grinned and held her nose. 'I think a hot bath in disinfectant and clean clothes are in order before I go to my next call!'

Only Colin and Mr Lowe remained up at the byre now, the Suddess clan and neighbours having made a mass retreat down the hill. As I headed towards the byre I realised that for them the crisis was over but that for Bear, and perhaps myself, there might be a long way to go. Mr Lowe was listening and concentrating hard with his stethoscope when I went in. Was that black matted shape he was examining really Bear? For the first time since he came out of the pit I touched him on the forehead, where his white blaze was about the only recognisable feature.

Mr Lowe straightened up. 'You realise, don't you, that we're not home and dry yet? By some miracle or another there are no broken bones but what other damage there is, internally that is, it's too early to tell.'

I nodded miserably and he continued: 'The worst danger is the next eighteen hours or so: cold, shock, infection; any or all of them could hit him through the night. Now listen carefully to what I want you to do.' His instructions were clear and concise and basically very simple. Forget about trying to clean him up — any attempts at washing him would only worsen the effects of shock and chilling. He was to be blanketed and rugged up well, just as he was. His legs were to be bandaged to give them both warmth and support. He was to be given no food until we had ascertained whether his gut was still functioning and undamaged, but he needed water badly as he was possibly dehydrating by now and if I could add glucose powder, it would help him enormously in a number of ways. Quiet, warmth and sweet drinks: the classic treatment for shock.

Satisfied that I understood what was to be done and was definitely not to be done, Mr Lowe also packed up to go. 'I'll be back in the morning,' he said crisply. 'If he's still standing then and if he's passed some water and muck, then we're in with a chance but,' he warned me solemnly, 'I'm making no promises, do you understand? No promises.'

As I drove the Land Rover down the hill once more, I tried to grasp the reality of it all. A couple of hours ago I was safe and content in my kitchen and had thought Bear safe and content in a field. Surely this couldn't really be happening? Why couldn't I just stroll up the hill with the pushchair and Megan this evening and watch Bear grazing contentedly, lazily swishing flies with his tail? Why couldn't I indulge myself in my usual gloat that this beautiful and talented creature was really mine? What had he done, what had I done, to deserve this? Nothing, I told myself sternly. It would make more sense to thank God he was in one piece than to sit there snivelling.

Having rapidly organised the bare minimum of domestic requirements for my household, I piled everything I thought I might possibly need for Bear into the back of the Land Rover and headed back to him. He hadn't moved a muscle since I'd left him. Exactly as the men carried him in, he stood, legs slightly splayed out and his neck and head down. Only his eyes and ears moved when I entered the byre. After all the frantic activity it was so very good to be alone and quiet with him at last. The slurry was drying in patches on him now from the warmth of his body, with bits of straw sticking all over him where his rescuers had rubbed him down. His glorious flaxen tail hung like a frayed and knotted black rope. He looked indescribably pathetic. I followed the vet's instructions to the letter, spreading clean cream wool blankets over the stinking mess that was Bear. After I'd rugged him up I bandaged his legs with his red wool stable bandages. The effect, in some ways, was an improvement as it concealed a large part of his body. Then I mixed some glucose powder into half a bucket of water and placed it near his nose.

'Come on now, vet's orders. I know you're a stubborn thing at times, but do this for me, Bear. Please have a drink.'

With an obvious effort, he slowly lifted his neck and head enough to clear the top of the bucket and I moved it closer under his muzzle. To my delight, he lowered his head again and began to take long draughts of the water. When I could no longer hear slurping noises, I gently lifted his head back out of the bucket.

'Clever lad,' I crooned, 'clever lad. We'll try some more in a little while, eh?'

I knelt on the straw so I could stroke his head and talk gibberish to him. I found it comforting, even if he didn't. It was then that I noticed his eyes. When he tried to turn them to look at me, I realised that the surrounding flesh in the sockets was a deep, angry red and the eyeballs even appeared to be protruding in a 'pop-eyed' fashion from his head. Blinking was obviously painful and difficult. Poor Bear, the irritant fumes from the slurry had even affected the small part of him that hadn't been immersed.

The evening drew on and still he never moved. Cups of tea and anxious faces appeared at intervals.

Eventually Colin came in and said, 'I think it's time you went home.'

'I, but, I can't leave him . . . ' I began.

'And why not? You're not doing any good here, you know.'

'Yes, but the vet said . . . '

'The vet said to leave him in peace and quiet and that's what you should do. It's up to time and nature now.'

I was about to start to argue again when Bear began making a noise between a grunt and a moan and his back began to sway and his hind legs to wobble. I grabbed Colin's arm in panic.

'Oh God, Colin, he's going down! He can't go down, he'll never get up again! Don't let him. Don't let him go down!'

But Colin wasn't panicking, he was smiling. He shook me lightly to bring me back to my senses. 'Stupid woman, he's not going down; look, will you look at that!'

With a final grunt and shuffle of his hind legs, Bear began a long and, from his face, blissfully enjoyable pee. He finished off with a resounding fart.

Colin and I looked at each other and burst out laughing. We roared and hooted, which released much of the built-up tension of the previous hours. Bear looked a bit peeved and embarrassed by it all.

When the giggles had subsided, Colin said, 'Now, will you please go home and get a decent meal and a good night's sleep?'

Suddenly that sounded like a very tempting idea. 'All right,' I conceded, 'but will you try him with some more water and glucose later on?'

'Yes. Now off you go.'

'And check he's warm enough, won't you,' I added.

'Of course. Now go.'

'If you need me for any reason you will . . .'

'Go!'

Very early the next morning, Megan decided to make an official protest over her neglect of the previous day. I was relieved for an excuse to get up and do something positive. After I had settled her back down in her cot, I went downstairs and made some tea. Warming myself against the Aga, I fought back an impulse to phone Bell's House Farm. The last report I'd had just before going to bed was 'no change'. No, it was unfair to phone at his unearthly hour. I was equally tempted to pull on some clothes and sneak up the hill to check for myself but decided that would only wake up the dogs and subsequently the rest of the household. Best to wait it out until after breakfast. But despite all my efforts to put the brakes on, I was there to collect my indefatigable Brenda from the village far earlier than usual.

'By hell, yoor sharp this mornin', aren't ya!' she grumbled while taking off her slippers and putting back her fireguard.

'Sorry Brenda,' I apologised. 'I could do with you keeping an eye on Megan this morning though.'

'Well of course Aa'll mind th' bairn — is summat up like? Ya look a bit peaky.'

I tried to explain as concisely and quickly as I could what had happened.

'Bloody hell.'

She was actually at a loss for words for at least half a minute. Then, cramming the last of her breakfast in her mouth and her headscarf on her head in one synchronised movement, she propelled me to the door.

'Well howay then, there's nowt'll get dun if wa stand here gassin'.'

As I approached the byre, I knew there could be no terrible shock awaiting me. Colin would already have been in and checked Bear and he would have forewarned me if anything had happened in the night. And there Bear was. Exactly as I'd left him the night before. Exactly. The realisation brought tears to my eyes and tied knots in my breakfast. All those hours standing absolutely still. Unable or unwilling to move because of the discomfort. But the important thing, I reminded myself severely, was that he was standing.

'If he's still standing in the morning,' the vet had said. And, oh joy of joys! Never in my life before or since have I been so delighted to see horse muck! But there, sure enough, on the clean straw behind him, was a pile of muck.

'If he's passed some water and muck, then we're in with a chance,' he had said. Well he had, and we were.

'Hello, bonny lad,' I said softly.

He seemed to be managing to hold his head and neck up further off the ground which delighted me, but the slurry coating him had now dried to a hard, gritty crust.

Colin must have heard me talking and came in from the yard.

'Well, he's lasted through the night. He's got guts, has that un.'

'Yes, yes he has.'

'When's vet comin'?'

'Soon, I hope. He said he'd look in first thing. Colin,' I asked, 'would you help me change his rugs? I know we can't make him look any better, but these ones are soaked through with that stinking stuff and now they're drying on to him. At least it might make him more comfortable.'

'Aye, right. Have you clean ones in the Land Rover?'

I nodded, and he quickly fetched them in.

'Right, Bear, come on,' I said brightly, 'clean pyjamas for the doctor, you know.'

I unbuckled his rug at the front and grasping the blankets underneath gave the whole lot a good tug, as I'd done hundreds of times before. But instead of slipping cleanly off his body, the rugs came back to his rump then stopped.

'Good Lord,' I said to Colin, 'that slurry must be like glue. His rugs are actually stuck to him!'

I gave one almighty tug; Bear gave a terrible rasping groan and shuddered violently. I dropped the rugs and screamed.

'Oh my God,' said Colin, trying to steady me, for my legs had lost their feeling, the byre was reeling and I felt violently sick. Not only had I removed Bear's rugs, but about a third of the hair and skin from his rump. The whole of his backside was a mass of red and yellow weeping holes, some bleeding and some just seeping clear liquid. Some of the craters were more than a quarter of an inch deep. Some of them were larger than my hand. It was hideous.

I somehow reached the door and started gulping in the fresh morning air. My mind was trying to grasp the problem and shy away from it at the same time.

Colin said, 'Look, I'll go and get Valerie to make a cup of tea, you look as if you need it,' and was gone.

Very slowly it dawned on me what must have happened. His back end must have slipped into the tank first, scraping past the rough but very sharp edge of the concrete slab at the back. Then his front end had slid in. Once his rump was under that concrete shelf, he must have struggled and rubbed against it in an effort to free himself. All he had succeeded in doing was skinning himself and then rubbing stinking, stinging raw sewage into his wounds. For how long had he struggled? Half an hour? An hour? Many hours? I tortured myself with the thought until another wave of nausea came over me and I had to sit down.

I didn't even hear the vet's car arrive and was in a daze when he and Colin walked up. Colin must have told him for Mr Lowe announced, 'I hear we have complications. He's still on his legs, though, and he's drinking, I hear. Passed water and muck too. That's excellent, excellent,' he said in an encouraging voice.

'Shall we go and look at him?' He smiled at me kindly and I got rather shakily to my feet.

He was grim-faced while he examined him.

'Mmm,' he grunted when he'd finished. 'Well, I think those burns are the biggest worry at the moment.'

'Burns!' I gasped.

'Oh yes, they are burns, friction burns, and very deep ones: and then of course the chemical irritation from the slurry has made them worse. They will all be badly infected by now from the sewage. That's my biggest worry to be honest — infection and shock.'

'What can you do?'

'Well, I'm going to start him on a massive course of antibiotics to try and ward off the infection.'

'But what can I do with . . . with that,' I pointed hopelessly at his rear end.

'Again, to be honest, it's a problem. To reduce the risk of infection, it should all be cleaned up and kept as sterile as possible, but how do you get this lot off,' and he tapped the cement-like jacket that Bear was caked in, 'without using gallons of water and running a terrible risk of chill and shock. Yes, it's a problem.'

'Can't I put anything on to soothe it? To ease the pain?'

'Anything soothing would help, I suppose,' he said thoughtfully, 'petroleum jelly, or baby cream. Anything antiseptic is going to sting like hell and may distress him even further.'

'There must be some preparation for treating septic burns?' I asked desperately. He shook his head slowly.

'Can't think of anything specific.'

With that he packed up and prepared to go. He would call the next day to give more antibiotics and review progress.

I went home and spent the rest of the morning weary and numb beside the Aga. Brenda had allowed me to vent my anguish in a good howl before enfolding me in her more than ample bosom, giving me a motherly 'shooshing', and administering a strong cup of tea, laced with something very potent from the sideboard. In the afternoon, as if to spite my misery, the weather was so glorious, warm and golden and enticing, that I could stay in the house no longer. I put Megan in her pushchair and we set off up the hill. There was none of the usual pleasurable anticipation of seeing Bear; it felt more like visiting a loved one in hospital, but I pushed on anyhow.

He had moved! There was no doubt about it, he had definitely moved. In fact he was standing nearly at the entrance of the byre. But as I got nearer, my delight in his small progress turned once more to dismay. To begin with the smell now coming from him in the full heat of the afternoon was appalling. But more appalling were the crowds of flies which hovered all around him. Worst of all were those which were feasting, like a moving black crust on the wounds of his back. His tormented eyes said all that was necessary and I made one of my Class 1 monumental-type decisions. We set off back down the hill at a speed which soon had Megan chortling with delight.

Angels of mercy have appeared at various times in my life in some unlikely disguises. This one was a small, voluptuous long-haired blonde in green wellies. Louise was a formidable horsewoman (and a qualified nurse) who, since she'd first appeared on the scene to 'sort out' Ian's new Irish hunter while I was pregnant, had gone on to attach herself in a semi-permanent fashion to the family. Her venerable Citröen spluttered to a halt in our yard just as I was piling the last arm-load of buckets, towels and brushes into the back of the Land Rover. Word of Bear's disaster had spread far and fast and I had already spoken to her at length on the phone.

'Hello, Louise,' I grunted, struggling to shut the Land Rover door.

'How is he?'

'Being eaten alive,' I replied grimly.

'Eaten?'

'Yes, eaten, by flies. They're crawling all over his wounds and he's caked in sewage and it's quite disgusting. So I'm going to bath him.'

'Bath him?'

'Yes, bath him! Have you gone deaf or daft or what, Lou?' I snapped.

'But I thought you said the vet said on no account was he to be washed in case the shock was too much?'

'Yes, he did,' I conceded, 'but I think if shock was going to kill Bear, it would have done so by now. He's standing, even moving a little, eating hay and drinking. I honestly don't think he's in danger of shock any more. What he is in danger of is being tormented to death by those bloody flies laying their eggs in his wounds. Christ, he could be crawling with maggots in a day or two. The smell is enough to finish him off on its own,' I ended on a slightly hysterical note.

'Well, you couldn't have asked for better weather,' she said, climbing into the Land Rover. 'Come on, let's get cracking.'

It took hours. Bear tottered bravely the few steps from the byre into the sunlight of the yard and we set to with a will, trying to balance the need to work quickly and minimise the chill against the care his badly damaged skin needed. We cleaned only a portion of him at a time, trying to keep those parts which weren't being washed or that had been washed covered over. We left the worst area, his friction-burnt rump, until last. Even getting him wet was difficult, because the slurry and straw mixture had dried completely into a cement-like compound, the water simply ran off it. But eventually, after gallons of warm water, bottles of washing-up liquid and a final hose-off, we decided we'd achieved enough to make him more comfortable, less malodorous and, we hoped, less attractive to flies.

His rump was a nightmare. Never having been blessed with the strongest of stomachs when it came to dealing with wounds, it was with grateful relief that I left the worst job of the afternoon to Louise's nursing skills. Though it had been done with the best intention in the world, Bear's rescuers hadn't known when they rubbed him down so vigorously with straw that they were rubbing not his coat but, in many parts, raw, friction-burnt flesh. The result was dozens of short, sharp straws like outsized splinters embedded in the flesh of his rump. Some of them we were able to wash out; others Louise dug out with a pair of eyebrow tweezers.

'He's in a hell of a mess,' she admitted when we stood back to survey the result of our work. I could only miserably agree with her. Although the friction-burn wounds on his rump were by far the worst and the most worrying, they were not his only injuries. Now that the sludge was removed, we could see that his body was lacerated and grazed in dozens of places and that he was rubbed to the bare skin on the back of both his front legs from the knee down, and also from his chin the full length under his neck. His tail hung in a gritty, stringy grey remnant of its former glory, but there he stood in the late afternoon sunlight, blinking his still-sore eyes and munching slowly and deliberately on a small pile of hay. He was still unable to keep his neck more than a few inches off the ground for any length of time.

'What am I going to do?' I wailed, seeing once more only the black side of the situation.

'Well,' said Louise in her practical manner, 'I would say warmth, food and rest and treat those, um, wounds,' she finished less positively.

'Exactly.' Sarcasm reared its ugly head. 'Treat them with what? Tell me that, with what? Look at the size of them. He's lost about one third of his skin on his back end and the vet says they're not strictly wounds, they're burns, friction burns. How on earth do you treat a horse with severe burns in a byre? Unless you know of some Swiss clinic with a specialised equestrian burns unit?'

Ignoring my outburst, Louise's face suddenly lit up. 'That's it!' she beamed. 'We'll bring the mountain to Mohammed!' Though she had obviously been blessed with some great revelation, I was lost.

'Sorry?'

'The burns unit! My mother's the Sister in a burns unit, has been for fifteen years, and a burn's a burn, wherever and whatever it's on. We can't take Bear to the hospital, but we can find out what they would treat this lot with if we could! Come on, let's get finished here and get him back to bed.'

'Yes, nurse.' I felt a small tingle of renewed hope.

By the time I fell into bed exhausted that night, I had acquired the necessary precious scrap of paper. The long-suffering household had dined on make-do and mend for a second night running, and my long-suffering daughter had weathered another day of maternal neglect without protest.

A phone call to the burns unit had quickly procured the name of a highly recommended preparation. But it was one thing knowing what we wanted, it was another thing getting it. The preparation was only available on prescription and a GP was hardly likely to start dispensing NHS prescriptions for the benefit of my horse. By happy coincidence, however, my GP lived just along the road and was eminently approachable. Like everyone else in the vicinity, he had heard about Bear's accident. He probably thought, when I sat down wearily in his kitchen, that I'd come for some form of restorative, so my request seemed to take him a bit by surprise.

'No, you're quite right,' he admitted, when I'd finished explaining, 'I can't say I'm empowered to prescribe for a horse — much as I'd like to do it in this case. I'm not familiar with the preparation either, but then it's not something you would come across a lot in general practice.'

'Well, if I can't get it without a prescription and I can't get a prescription, then I'm stumped.' My newly aroused optimism began to fade.

'Hang on, though. Of course I can give you a prescription,' he beamed. 'I can give you a prescription, but not a National Health prescription. It would be a private one. That means you would have to meet the full cost yourself.'

I gave him a grateful smile as he went off to find a pen.

The next morning, I was standing on the chemist's doorstep in the village before he even opened, clutching my precious paper.

'My, you're an early bird,' said Mr Williamson, as he unlatched the door.

'Well, I have an unusual prescription for you and I would like to get it as soon as possible.' I outlined the situation as briefly as I could.

He peered at my scrap of paper. 'Never stocked this. I'm going to have to order it from our distributors. I'll give them a ring, should be someone there by now. Incidentally, how much of this stuff do you want? It comes in twenty-five gram tubes and you can apply it twice a day.'

'How big is a twenty-five gram tube?' I enquired.

He picked up some ointment on the display counter and said, 'That big.'

'Don't you mean that small!' I gasped. I visualised the area of skin needing treatment and multiplied by twice a day then by a couple of weeks. 'We're going to need dozens of those.'

'Sounds as if you need a whole large pack. You also realise you'll have to pay for it all?' he peered over his glasses at me.

'How much?' His reply made the contents of the shop blur momentarily. Doing some rapid mental calculations as to the state of my current account, I got my cheque book out in what I hoped appeared to be a blasé manner.

'Order it,' I said, fillling in the date.

The magic potion, as we came to call it, was worth every penny, or pound to be more accurate. It seemed to soothe and heal the wounds so quickly that visible progress could be seen day by day. This heartened us all, as did Bear's general condition.

Within a week of his accident, he was happily eating and drinking and going for twice-daily toddles round the farmyard. The muscles in his neck gradually eased and his head resumed its normal carriage. After ten days, we decided to attempt to get him down the hill and home. His wounds were no longer weeping and raw but were dry and clean, and — most wonderful of all — new skin, like bright pink fragile tissue paper, was beginning to form. Only the deepest and largest wound on the hump of his stifle bone stubbornly refused to heal in the middle. He managed the journey slowly with great dignity and gave a snort of pleasure and recognition when he finally walked into the comfort of his own loose box once more.

Mr Lowe had asked to see Bear again once he was home, so I duly arranged for him to call the next day.

'My, my,' he exclaimed, 'he looks more like his old self.' He ran his hands over the battlefield of Bear's rump and peered closely. 'Well, whatever that stuff was you got for these wounds, they're healing remarkably well. Yes, remarkably well. Of course,' he paused, in the manner I had learnt so often meant hard facts or bad news coming, 'you realise that he may well never grow hair on any of these areas again?'

'What! None?' I had imagined scars of course, but surely not an obscene chequer board of bright pink flesh and chestnut hair.

'Some of those abrasions were very deep. If they were so deep as to damage or remove the hair follicle layer, then I'm afraid so. No hair.'

I had been on a high all morning. I was so proud — of Bear, of myself, of all the friends who had worked so hard just to achieve this moment: Bear back in his own stable, out of pain and distress, on the road to full recovery. I had honestly thought we had cracked it, that it was just a matter of time before Bear would return to his former fitness and health. I had thought Mr Lowe's visit to be a sort of final formality, a pat on the back for a job well done. Though the news about his hair was a shock, I absorbed it, telling myself that Bear wasn't ever likely to be competing in beauty contests, and that lack of hair wouldn't in any way deter from his driving capabilities in competitions. I was quite unprepared though for what was to come next.

'Now that he's well enough to put up with my poking and prodding and listening, I'm going to give him a really good going over,' Mr Lowe explained.

It took him a long time. Over and over he listened to his heart and chest, first one side and then the other. Checking and re-checking. It took too long. Apprehension began tying its familiar knots in my stomach. Eventually, he straightened up and removed his stethoscope.

'Now you know I said to you "no promises",' he began as he shepherded me gently to the door of the box.

'But he's well!' I cried, tears already gathering in the corners of my eyes.

'Yes, yes, he's remarkably well, considering what he's been through,' he said quickly, 'but I warned you there might be damage, problems, things we couldn't see.'

Seeing the horrified look on my face he added quickly,

'Nothing life-threatening, you understand.'

'Well, what then?' It was a dull, flat question.

'Well,' poor Mr Lowe looked very uneasy, and my accusing look wasn't really directed at him, but at the world in general, 'there are two problems. He has strained his heart. Not very badly, but it's definitely damaged and the beat is quite arhythmic. And then his lungs — he has emphysema. Again not badly, but there's definitely fluid and infection at the bottom of his lungs. Now I repeat, neither of these are life-endangering symptoms. We could give antibiotics for the emphysema to try and clear it up, but nearly always afterwards there is residual damage to the lungs. Couple that with his strained heart and there is only one obvious conclusion, I'm afraid. This horse will never be able to compete again.'

'No!' It came out more as a howl of disbelief than a protest. 'No!'

'Listen,' he said, trying the voice of adult reason, 'I know how much this horse means to you. I know all this ghastly business has been an awful shock. But you are damned lucky he is alive at all, you know. It's a miracle we got him out of that hole in one piece. Now he's going to survive, he could even recover to the point where you could do some gentle hacking on him,' he finished reassuringly.

His words had the opposite effect. A tide of stubborn anger swept over me and the poor man got the brunt of the first wave.

'Survive?' I raged. 'Survive? Do you think he'd call that survival? To stand in a field like a wretched retired pit pony? To go for quiet walks around the block? He'd hate it! And he'd hate me for making him do it! This horse is a worker. He loves his work, he is intelligent and brave and if you are saying all he is fit for is to stand in a field for years on end, it would have been kinder if you'd destroyed him two weeks ago and, if there's no hope, no outlook beyond retirement, then do it now! Yes — do it now!'

Many a man would have simply fastened his bag, departed and sent a bill in the next post. But my vet didn't. He understood my attack wasn't on him personally; it was on life, fate and the universe in general. So he just said gently, 'You don't mean that.'

'I do — you don't know him. It would be a fate far worse than death. He would hate me for it and I would end up hating myself for being a coward.' Even as I said it, the courage of my convictions, born of anger, was ebbing swiftly. There was a silence during which we both regained our thoughts and I regained some composure.

'I'm so sorry, Mr Lowe, I didn't mean any offence to you.'

'Och, it's all right. No offence taken. I just wish there was something . . . of course . . . ' His pause this time had a definite hopeful sound to it that I detected instantly.

'Yes?'

'Of course, we could get a second opinion.'

'Yes!'

'Now steady, I'm not saying it would be any different to mine. Listen, leave it with me tonight and I'll discuss the case with a colleague of mine, then try and arrange for him to see the horse tomorrow. And remember,' he finished firmly, 'no promises.'

In bed that night, miserable and worried, I lay fruitlessly churning over the events of the day and raging inwardly. From the resulting mess of thoughts, one kept pushing persistently to the front. Finally I gave in and subjected myself to an internal interrogation. Whose future was the vet really threatening? Was it really Bear's happiness that was at stake or my own?

Throughout the shock and discomfort caused by my operation, I had clung to the thought that I would get over this temporary setback, I would get fit again and next year nothing would stop *me* being at the reins of my horse. I had become almost obsessed with the idea. I had grieved over the loss of a year's experience, of just having to watch from the sidelines. The only consolation had been to plan for next year. Now, suddenly, there wasn't to be a next year — for either of us.

True to Mr Lowe's word, the 'second opinion' arrived the next day, having been thoroughly briefed on the case prior to his arrival. He was a quiet, middle-aged man with a wealth of veterinary experience, particularly horses, behind him. I liked him at once, and as I led him across the farmyard to Bear's stable, I was firmly telling myself that whatever the outcome of his examination, I must try and keep my emotions under control and try, however hard it might be, to accept whatever advice as to Bear's future he could offer.

Apart from the buzzing of a few apathetic late-in-the-year flies around the stable door, there was total silence in the stable while he thoroughly examined Bear. He listened to his chest and heart for long minutes before finally removing his stethoscope.

'Aye, he's certainly been through it,' he said snapping shut his bag. 'It would have killed many a one no doubt, but he's a fine strong cob. His stamina and common sense are what have saved him — plus a great deal of luck.'

Was this the pleasant small talk preceding hard facts, unpleasant facts, I asked myself.

'And now you're wondering what on earth I'm going to say next.' He removed his glasses and smiled softly at my worried expression, 'and you wish I'd get on with it.'

'Something like that.'

'Well. Firstly, I agree totally with Mr Lowe's diagnosis with regard to both his heart and lungs. But as to what to do about it; what to do about it is the thing.' He tapped his teeth thoughtfully with the leg of his glasses.

'Anything! Anything that would help him, whatever it takes, whatever it costs!'

He smiled tolerantly at my passionate outburst. 'I think you need to think less in terms of "whatever" and more in terms of "whenever" for this horse. My two main suggestions for his treatment come very cheap but not always easily. Time and patience and a lot of both. Plus a little helping hand from the wonders of modern veterinary science.'

'I'm sorry. I'm not entirely sure what you're suggesting.' I tried to keep the disappointment out of my voice without a great deal of success. It sounded very much as if he were suggesting doing nothing. Just playing wait and see. I hadn't expected a magic wand but I had so hoped, oh so hoped, that there would be some treatment, some definite course of action to take.

Sensing my growing disappointment he said gently, 'What I'm suggesting is that we give him a chance. A good long chance. Because nothing is surer, or safer in the long run, than Mother Nature. And though we can't do much to hurry her up, we can provide the best possible conditions for her to work in. Now this is what I want you to do.'

Extracting a notebook and pencil from his pocket, he started walking towards the door shooing me gently out of the stable as he did so. Once in the sunlight again and once he was sure I was paying attention, he continued: 'For as long as the weather is like this,' he waved his hand in the general direction of the late autumnal trees and the afternoon sunlight, 'Bear is to go out in the paddock, all day, just as he is. At night, he is to be bedded up, deep, warm and dry with no draughts.' He waved his spectacles at me to emphasise the point. 'Once the weather turns, he's still to go out all day, every day, in a New Zealand rug. Don't worry about the cold, just as long as it's dry. Worry about the wet, he stays in on really wet days. Let him have all the best quality hay he wants and always give it to him damp. Don't let him drink icy cold water, take the chill off first.'

Though I was paying close attention and absorbing every word, everything he'd said so far could be found in a decent book on horse management.

'And,' he continued patiently, 'as well as that very commonsensical régime, I want you to add this to his feed.' He returned his specs to his nose and wrote down a proprietary name on his note pad. 'It is a supplement with high levels of vitamin E and selenium, both of which speed and assist cellular repair and may help his heart. Don't expect any rapid results with it, but fed regularly over the months, it could be a big help. And lastly, I will suggest to Mr Lowe an extended course of antibiotics over a period of six weeks to try and really attack that emphysema.'

'And that's it? No magic wand?'

He returned his notebook to his pocket, picked up his bag and together we walked slowly back to his car. I hadn't really been expecting him to disagree with Mr Lowe's diagnosis, nor pronounce a wonder cure, so why the desperate feeling of disappointment?

'No m'dear, no magic wand. But love, you know, love has a magic of its own and a way of defying all the rules. Now if love will heal this horse I'm sure he's well on the road to recovery already.'

The sincerity and frankness of the man encouraged me to venture, 'Do you honestly think there is a chance, however small, that he could recover, really recover?'

'Yes, I do,' he said definitely.

'How long?'

'Oh, a year — at least.'

I winced visibly but held my tongue. He raised his eyebrows a little.

'That too long, is it? Too long to wait for the chance of getting him back?'

'No, of course not. We're both going to have to learn to be patient and I'm afraid neither of us is very good at it,' I confessed. 'Will you call again to give him check-ups?'

'No need. When he's good and ready, he'll tell you. No point in me wasting my time and your money till then.' He got into his car and closed the door quietly. Quiet and unhurried seemed to be the mark of the man and of his treatment.

'Oh, and there's two more things.' He had been about to switch on the ignition but paused mid-way, 'Mr Lowe says you are concerned about the bad scarring and hair loss on his rump. Well, I've given it some thought, and as you know modern science doesn't give much credence to wonder hair restorers.'

He smiled and ran his hand ruefully through his own thinning, greying locks. 'However, though I can give you no medical justification for it doing any good, the old farmers my way swear by a paste of soot and lard rubbed into the damaged skin, once it's healed of course. Now it may just be an old wives' tale and it may do no good at all, but it would do no harm and at least would keep the skin supple if you wanted to try it. Well m' dear, that's all the advice I can offer you and I'll be on m' way.'

He switched on the ignition and his car sprang to life. As he began to reverse, I remembered something and ran up to the window.

'You said there were two things, that was just one.'

'Ah yes,' he smiled as he engaged first gear and started gliding slowly forward, 'just something Mr Lowe told me to remind you. I think it went along the lines of "no promises".' He purred quietly off down the drive.

The glorious autumn drew to its close and life resumed a pattern of normality. Bear embarked upon his new daily régime without a great deal of complaint. November came and with it, Megan's birthday and the start of the hunting season. Ian now kept two hunters: the big, black Limerick, and a younger grey, Ceilidh. Bear watched with mild interest as these two were boxed and driven away twice weekly, but did not seem greatly bothered. I felt guilt and remorse over my adamant stance about his being 'bored in a field'; on the contrary, he seemed quite content. Every morning, after a small feed, he would be rugged up and put out in the paddock with a large, damp hay net. By evening, he would be eager to get in, consume another small feed and then settle down to another hay net.

Feeling at times like a total idiot, I religiously rubbed a disgusting black gunk of soot and lard over the new skin that now covered large areas of the rump. In fact, I was becoming quite furtive about the whole idea and tried to slap it on when no one was looking. To say I was doing it on 'veterinary advice' only produced further howls of amusement. The main problem was injecting the prescribed antibiotics: conning Bear that there really *wasn't* another needle and syringe about to be implanted in his neck. He'd never been mad on needles in the first place, but after a month of thrice-weekly jabs, he was getting quite phobic and would try and climb in his manger, or up the wall, or on to my toes in an attempt to avoid it. However, we persevered, me discovering the line of 'no jab, no feed bucket' to be the most effective. By early December the course, thankfully for all concerned, was finished.

I had intended, in a world where best-laid plans of mice and men actually work, to clip Bear about this time and hunt him lightly till the beginning of the driving season. Instead, unchecked, his abundant winter coat began to come in. By the end of the year he was reverting to the overgrown native pony I had first known, except that his hogged mane, unclipped now for three months, was growing long, straight and totally upwards. He began to resemble an outsized lavatory brush, but I could not bring myself to subject him to a battle with the clippers after everything he had been through.

However, he did give me a marvellous early Christmas present. The groom Ian had taken on for the season was leading the hunters up to their boxes for the night and I was putting Bear to bed. I pulled off his New Zealand, trying to make up my mind whether to bother getting the pot of 'black stuff' from its hidey hole above the door; I had become less zealous about applying it as the only thing I seemed to have to show for persisting with its use was a lot of black, greasy rugs and blankets. I had to admit that his rear end still resembled a well-chewed coconut mat. On impulse, I ran my hands across his rump. Strangely my fingers did not glide across the newly healed skin as usual, but met with some resistance. I peered intently. It couldn't be! Yes, it was! Like the finest, shortest bright orange velvet, there was hair, real hair sprouting all over the area. I gave a whoop which caused Limerick in the adjacent box to nearly flatten the girl groom, who was trying to put the rugs on. Bear merely lifted his muzzle from the manger and peered round at me, clearly saying, 'Women!'

It was not a bad winter as winters go in our part of the world. The festive season came and went in an abundance of log fires and hot spiced punch and the weather kept open through most of January, which allowed the hunting to continue unchecked. The snow in February brought this to a stop, causing restless boredom in the stables and a blue haze in the house. For Megan there was the wonder of her first snow to roll about in and she played in the cold, white powder till her hands were blue and her nose red. She shrieked with a mixture of terror and delight as we flew down Bell's House hill on her shiny new red sledge. Bear too loved the snow and would roll and roll till he resembled a Yeti. Despite his hay net by the gate, he would spend happy hours digging large holes, pawing his way to the ground beneath and snorting around looking for a stray grass blade.

March was not exactly spring-like in the warm, green and verdant sense of the word, but the small signs of progress in the hedgerows and the longer days at least gave a feeling of hope that the worst was over.

I had not hunted that winter. Not only did I doubt my capability to stay safely aboard those big, headstrong Irish creatures when in full flight, but it would somehow have been an act of treachery to Bear. I realised what I was missing was not hunting as such, but the exhilaration and union I had experienced with Bear as we flew over fields, hedges and ditches. I did, however, still get some riding in, partly to get and keep fit after my operation and partly to help out with the hunters' exercise. I usually rode Limerick and the groom took the younger Ceilidh. As we rode out, Bear got into the habit of following us down the side of the field, walking step for step until we reached the end of the drive and he the end of his paddock. Then he would stand, head over the fence, and watch us disappear up the lane. I used to try to ignore him, but frequently imagined that I could feel his eyes burning into my back.

One day in early March I was going out in this fashion but, unusually, I was on my own on Limerick. It was a better sort of day, quite mild and calm — in fact I had put Bear out without a rug for the first time that year. Bear lifted his head from his hay as soon as he heard us approach and stalked over to the gate ready to begin his ritual of shadowing us down the drive.

'I wish you wouldn't do that, Bear,' I flung at him. 'You enjoy making me feel guilty, don't you. And you damn well know I'd rather be taking you, so don't rub it in.'

He eyed me with what I always call his 'piggy' look a little longer, then stopped, gave a huge snort and set off down the field at a spanking trot. I reined back Limerick, and watched amazed. Although Bear had trotted a little bit in the field since his accident, he'd never attempted anything like this. He meant business. Faster and faster he trotted round and round the perimeter of the paddock, tail raised, neck arched and flinging his feet in front of him as if he had just found them for the first time. When he could trot no further, he dipped his neck, kicked out his back legs and began to buck. He would have defied a hardened rodeo rider. With flattened ears and flaring nostrils he pounded round the field, head between his knees, giving tremendous, powerful bucks that flung his whole body in the air. Having made every attempt to turn himself inside out, Bear landed momentarily on all fours, gave another resounding snort, then, as if he had been released from the starting gate at a race, he was off at full gallop. It was not a large paddock — just over an acre in size — and it was sheer lunacy on Bear's part to be careering around it at the speed he was. At every corner he defied gravity as he swung round at the last possible second before crashing through the fence. Finally, after several circuits, his pace slackened and on the next lap he drew up at an abrupt halt facing us head on. His flanks and ribs were heaving and his nostrils flaring widely as he stood there defying me.

I wanted to laugh and cry together for I knew what this meant: the vet had said he would tell me when he was good and ready, and short of spelling it out on the ground with his hoof, I don't think the message of his astonishing display could have been clearer. 'All right, bonny lad. You'd better be sure!'

An astounded and indignant Limerick was wheeled round and trotted sharply back to his stable.

'Now m' dear, what's all the fuss about?' my 'second opinion', as I'd come to think of him, enquired as he climbed out of his car. When I phoned Mr Lowe, I wouldn't go into details in case I thought I had hallucinated the whole incident through continual wishful thinking. I simply kept on insisting I urgently needed his colleague's advice on a new development with Bear and eventually he capitulated. Now I towed the poor man down to the stable in my excitement.

'He's ready to start work again.'

He shook his head sadly, apparently reflecting that all his good advice on patience had been for nought.

'I hardly think it. It's only been, what is it, six months?'

'Yes, six months, but he's well and sound. He's ready to work again. He told me; you said he would and he did.'

Further solemn shakings of the head occurred.

A sharp poke in the back of my mind said, 'If you continue in this excitable, ridiculous fashion, he'll decide it's you who needs medical attention and not the horse. Now calm down and try to be lucid, for Heaven's sake!'

I stood still, cleared my throat, dropped my voice an octave and said slowly and clearly, 'Two days ago, that horse put on a display of fireworks that nearly terrified me. He bucked round that paddock like a thing possessed and then did a passable impression of a Derby winner. And at the end he was merely slightly out of breath. Now then, if his heart or lungs, or both, are irreparably damaged, he would have dropped down, stone dead.'

'Where is he?'

'This way please.' And I led him to Bear.

'Aha, now turn him the other way so I can listen to the other side.' A further minute or so elapsed while I continued to work on being cool and composed and very mature.

'Aha, now take him out please, trot him down the drive and back again. Gently please,' he emphasised.

I was decidedly far more out of breath than Bear at the end of that one. Once more he listened to Bear intently.

'Mmm. Have you a lunge?' I nodded. 'Good, well pop him on it in the paddock.

I fetched the long webbing rope, attached it to Bear's headcollar, and waited for instructions.

'Now just let him circle round you in his own time — don't push him.' His voice indicated he had grave misgivings about subjecting a fairly recent invalid to such exertions. However his eyebrows raised in frank astonishment when Bear's 'own time' turned out to be a mad hurtle at full extended trot. After about five minutes, he calmed down to a more normal lunging pace and looked as if he was quite able and happy to keep trotting around for the rest of the afternoon.

'I think that'll do.' He smiled encouragingly at me. 'Just hold his head while I have a wee listen.'

I knew this examination after fast work would be the most critical and said a swift prayer.

'Right, just walk him round the field to slow him down a bit, will you?'

We lapped the paddock once to give his breathing a chance to slow down. I knew that this test — of his pulse and respiration recovery rate — was also critical. After many long minutes during which my mind kept going blank, he seemed satisfied and removed his stethoscope.

'You did right to call me in.' His face revealed nothing.

'I did? Oh God — he didn't do more damage to himself the other day, did he?'

'Indeed not. I simply mean that by getting me out as quickly as you have, you may now have time to get him fit for this season. When was it you said they start this driving lark? May, isn't it?' He still sounded solemn but was unable to keep the merriment out of his eyes.

Very quietly, because I felt as if all the breath had gone out of my body, I managed to say, 'Do you mean that?'

'I do.'

'Then he's recovered? Completely back to normal?'

'Ah well,' he mused tolerantly, 'what's normal, eh? This

horse appears to be far from normal. I'm sure you already think that but I mean it in a different sense, a veterinary sense. Take his blood, for example. We sent samples away after the accident. Fascinating, fascinating. He has an incredibly high level of haemoglobin — red blood cells, you know — way above what I would call 'normal', but it's obviously normal for him. I wish my blood were in the same condition.' He chuckled and patted Bear who condescended to stand still and be admired.

'And his heart and lungs?'

'Well, the lungs. They're simple: they've cleared up, not a trace of anything wrong, and from the way he got his wind back, functioning at full efficiency again. Now it is truly rare for emphysema to clear without residual damage. But his heart, that's a different matter, not so simple. You see,' he cast his eyes over Bear again thoughtfully, 'it's still not what I would call "normal", it is somewhat arhythmic, has a "double" beat almost. However, I didn't get to listen to it before his accident. Again, that beat might be "normal" for him. All that matters though is that the beat is constant and unchanging and hard exercise has no detrimental effect on his heart at all. Aye, he's unusual to say the least. Amazing might be a better word.'

'So what you're saying is that he has weird blood and a peculiar heart, but otherwise he's normal?' I persisted.

'Oh, I don't think this horse could ever be described as normal, do you?'

I turned and buried my face in Bear's neck and made little damp patches on his long hair. For once he tolerated this sentimental outburst. Normally, he can't bear anyone being sloppy.

Snivelling and laughing at the same time I replied, 'Well, I've never considered him normal, but it's good to have a second opinion.'

Bear was growing bored with all the fuss, and fidgeting around, so I put him in his stable and the vet packed his case and returned to his car.

'Can he start work straight away?'

'No reason why not. Don't go overboard, though. Take at least eight weeks to get him fit and only walk for the first two.'

I put my hand through the open window on top of his arm and said, 'Thank you, thank you from the bottom of my heart for all you've done.' What I really wanted to do was to kiss him.

'But I've done nothing m' dear, nothing at all. Time and Mother Nature, that's all. Though,' he peered over the top of his specs, 'she would appear to have been working overtime on this occasion.'

'But you gave us hope when nothing else did.'

'Och, you didn't need a vet for that surely?'

'And his hair — what about his hair?' I insisted. 'Did you not see, it's nearly all grown back? You told me about the paste.'

'Oh, just an old wives' tale, no medical justification at all.' Even his teasing was quiet and calm.

'But,' I was getting exasperated, 'it worked. All the hair has grown in.'

'Then the hair follicles mustn't have been damaged as much as we feared, eh? Mind you . . . '

'Yes?'

'His extra rich blood supply being pumped extra-efficiently by his double heart beat might have helped, I suppose.'

'You're teasing me,' I accused.

'Perhaps m' dear, perhaps. Now, there are other less complicated patients awaiting me. I must go. Good luck to you m' dear, good luck to you both.'

6

What appears to be the end

I SAT LESS than patiently at the tail end of a long queue in the surgery. Was this going to take all morning? I'd things to do. I wished I hadn't bothered coming.

I must have overdone it. Yes, that was it, I must have overdone it. Ever since the vet had given the go-ahead for Bear, I had pushed him, and myself, relentlessly further and further each day. Not gentle, idle, dawdling rides but miles of roadwork to harden his legs, miles of steady trotting and hill work to build up his stamina. After all, we only had a couple of months before the 1981 season began.

I had it all planned — which events I could get to, how I was going to transport everything, a new cross-country vehicle that was to be Christmas, birthday and anniversary presents for the next decade. So it wasn't really surprising if I'd torn a muscle or over-stretched wounds of less than a year old. That would explain the nagging pain that I had banished to the furthest recesses of my mind for several days. So today I was doing the sensible thing, giving riding a miss and seeing the doctor. He'd probably tell me to take things easy for a few days, tell me not to ride for a while, though that was a problem as Bear had to be kept in work. Perhaps I could get round it by driving Bear — that mightn't be so uncomfortable and he was certainly fit enough to begin driving again. In fact it was high time he was back in the trap, so it might be a good idea to lay off riding for a little while.

My GP poked and prodded at my tummy very thoroughly.

'When did you have your hysterectomy?'

'May 1980, nearly a year ago now.'

'And no trouble since?'

'No, nothing. I've been absolutely great up until these last few days.'

There was a heavy pause. I don't like pauses, they make me suspicious.

'What have I done? Have I torn a muscle or something?'

Another pause.

'I'm not entirely sure that you have "done" anything, but I'm
going to phone the hospital and ask if they could see you this
afternoon.'

'What?'

'I'm not happy about what's going on around your ovaries.
I'd like it checked out as soon as possible.'

I sat stunned with disbelief while he made the arrangements.

Was I going mad? This could not, could not in my worst
nightmares, be happening to me again. The consultant at the
hospital was telling me that I had developed large cysts on both
ovaries. Similar cysts had been removed when I had my
hysterectomy and now he feared I had a condition called
endometriosis which meant that these cysts would keep
recurring unless he took drastic measures, very drastic
measures. I would probably have to lose both ovaries. From
there on I would have to rely on replacement therapy for my
female hormones.

My world caved in. It was not fear; it was total despair. I could
not be comforted, I would not be comforted. My whole life had
been sucked to the very edge of a bottomless black hole and I
didn't very much care if it totally engulfed me.

I was home again and I didn't very much care about anything.
Not about the house, not about my husband, not about Megan,
not even about Bear. I withdrew deeper and deeper into myself,
lying curled for endless hours in bed where it was warm, where
it was dark, where I could seek oblivion. Megan would toddle
across my room to cuddle me with her warm, pink little arms
and I could only bury her blonde head into me and cry the more
bitterly.

Then the panic attacks began. I dreaded waking up. The
mornings filled me with terror. At first light I would awaken to
waves of nausea and a feeling as though a hand with long,
sharp talons had a firm and merciless grip on my heart. My
insides churned and turned to water and I would have to fly to
the bathroom where, for the next twenty minutes or so, I would
have violent diarrhoea and retch endlessly on and on till I was
shaking with cold and misery and exhaustion. I would then
crawl back to bed and tremble with the impossibilities that the
day held in store for me: getting dressed, thinking about food,
seeing to Megan. Filling the endless hours till I could retreat

back to bed. To restless sleep, to the nightmares.

Day and night there was no release for me. The simplest task, the smallest job, required a superhuman effort — I felt as if I waded waist deep in thick, black treacle. My world functioned on a different gravitational and time scale from the rest of humanity.

I was prescribed pills, all sorts of pills. Pills to take before bed which enforced a heavy, dreamless, black sleep. Pills to take in the morning when the terror of the forthcoming day would hit me. Pills which did not cure but which helped obscure everything.

Some people have an awful fear of blood, others a revulsion of sickness of any kind. Some people can accept perfectly well the effects of a broken leg but cannot accept the effects of a broken mind. Some people have an inability to cope with even the concept of emotional illness. My husband was such a person. As the long weeks dragged by without a glimmer of hope that the depression was lifting, that the well-oiled wheels of our life and home would function once more, that some resemblance of my old personality would be restored, it became obvious that he found the whole situation unbearable. He did all the right things, all the practical things: got Brenda to do more in the house, got a local girl in during the day to look after Megan, even got private doctors to see me. But on the emotional front the gulf between us was widening.

The irony was that it was my pathetic need for reassurance, my constant leech-like demands for support, for affirmation that I was not a neutered, de-feminised husk that drove him further and further away.

A psychiatrist strongly recommended a short break totally away from all the pressures of home and family, in surroundings where my grief and anger and bewilderment would not be considered unusual. So I spent ten days at Winterton, the largest psychiatric hospital in County Durham. The name is a sort of 'bogey' to those who know nothing about the place — but there were no straitjackets or bars, no electric shocks or white coats. At the entrance to the ward, a sign read 'What appears to be the end could really be a new beginning.'

I took my medication, tried to begin eating regularly again, strolled around the gardens and was left a lot of the time to my thoughts. Thoughts which began painfully slowly to turn towards that which was good in my life, and to the future.

There was no miracle cure, no great transformation but I was able to rouse myself sufficiently to put on a pretty dress and do my hair and make-up on the day I was to go home. It was my fourth wedding anniversary. But I had the indelible, the unforgivable stigma upon me; I had been in a mental hospital. The gulf between us was unbridgeable.

A full-time nanny for Megan had been acquired in my absence, and other radical decisions had been made. To begin with, Ian had decided that Bear was to compete the season after all, with Louise driving him. It made perfect sense, I agreed miserably. A lot of money had been spent on a new trap and entry fees and so on, the horse was fit and well and she was competent to drive him. It could only be good experience for him and it was out of the question that I could do anything that year, so why waste him?

I had by now a fragile hold on normality. As long as there was not too much pressure or responsibility or decision-making put on me, I could cope. But I was very fearful of much that had formed the normal fabric of my life; of socialising, or entertaining, even of driving a car, and certainly of the horses. There was no physical reason at all why I shouldn't be up in the saddle and away on Bear — I had been riding him in a far shorter time after my hysterectomy. But the very thought filled me with sheer terror. So I would avoid his gaze when I went past the field, make myself scarce when others rode or drove him.

Suddenly it was Lowther again. Bear and his entourage went ahead to the event. On dressage day the nanny drove Megan and me over to watch. (I wondered which of us she was really looking after.) It was all there, the sights, the sounds, the excitement. All that I had strived and longed to be a part of. But I was not part of this, no part at all. Fighting back the tears and growing, gnawing panic I watched Ian and Louise prepare Bear for the event; watched their hugs and kisses and back-slapping when he did a presentable seventh place test. Watched the reporter from the local paper ask to interview Louise, the driver of the horse. I fled back to the car and completely broke down. Murderous jealousy filled me. It was as if I were already dead and gone and not even a ghost remained to remind anyone that this had all been mine. My husband, my horse, my dreams — and yet I was too pathetic, too impotent to stand up and claim them. I wished very strongly, for the first time, that I was dead.

The sobbing subsided, as sobbing inevitably will, leaving me drained, red-eyed and bloated. People made clucking noises that ranged from condescending to embarrassed. Made excuses for me. Perhaps I should take a rest? Take a pill? Go home early with Megan and nanny? I fled thankfully.

The inertia, the nothingness of my life went on. There were

few crises now, few scenes. I found a routine of sorts; narrow, restricted and safe. Everything functioned perfectly well without me contributing much. What energy and enthusiasm I did have, I tried to reserve for Megan. I gave up a great deal of my medication. I had made a brave and foolish attempt to just stop the tranquillizers dead. 'No more,' I said, 'no more damn pills.' But sweating, trembling and vomiting, I crawled back to them. It was Catch-22: I was caught in the late-twentieth-century tranquilliser trap. Now, on top of all my other problems, I could ostensibly add drug addiction. I actually slept with my morning 'fix' ready on the table beside me, devouring it as I fled to the bathroom for my morning purging, then hiding back under the dark blankets till I could feel the chemical brakes coming on in my body and I could get up, with an effort, and begin another day. By the afternoons I was really feeling much better and could do a little shopping or play with Megan. In the evenings I was positively normal and could cook and actually eat a meal. But no matter how well and full of determination I went to bed, my peace of mind would have vanished by morning and the whole cycle would start again. I called it 'the thief that comes in the night'.

And I think that cycle could have well gone on uninterrupted but for two things. Firstly, I had a letter from America: it came from my dear friend Judy, whom I'd known since college days. Alarmed by the news of the summer's turn of events and reading between the lines of my sketchy letters, she begged and implored me to go and spend a few weeks in Maine with her and her husband at their family 'summer home'. I'd been there once before. It was a log cabin on the edge of a calm and unpolluted lake, fringed with quiet pine and maple woods that rejoiced in the name of 'Green Pond'. It was the nearest place to paradise I had ever visited. Secondly, I received a visit one late August afternoon from my friend Fiona, a remarkable lady who had a true vocation for her work in a school for severely mentally handicapped children. I was in front of the house, enjoying the sun and playing with Megan when she arrived. After the niceties of 'Tea?' and 'You're looking better', she came to the point.

'When are you going to get off your backside and do something?'

'Well I'm doing the best I can.'

'Rubbish. You're doing nothing and you're just letting your life drift by you. It's high time now that you really did something, something new, something challenging instead of just sitting here wallowing in your misery.'

I lowered my eyes uncomfortably under her gaze.

'Carol, for God's sake, you'll convince yourself you are a neurotic invalid for the rest of your life before long. Look what you're capable of — you've got a teaching qualification and a brain. Why don't you use them for a change!'

I blanched. 'Teach? Oh I couldn't ever teach again; I feel sick at the very thought. Anyway, I couldn't possibly go back to work.'

'I didn't say go back to work, not yet anyway. I just mean do something. Anything! Take a course!'

She stuck a leaflet under my nose.

'What's that?'

'It's a list of courses at colleges and Durham University this autumn. There are some really interesting ones. Only one day a week — surely you can affort to invest that amount of time in yourself.'

'Courses at college! But I wouldn't know . . . I mean what sort of course could I possibly take!'

'Carol,' she said firmly, 'I will call back next week and if you haven't made enquiries about one of those courses, you're letting us both down.' She rose to go pausing only to say, 'You know, you can be what you want to be, do anything you want to do — if you set your mind to it. See you next week.'

And she was gone leaving me totally astonished and clutching the leaflet. There was a large red star next to something marked 'N.O.W. Course — New Opportunities for Women: all day Tuesdays. For those women who have been out of work a long time or have never worked and who need to re-build their self-confidence and job-finding abilities.' It also gave a Durham phone number.

I was equally astonished a week later to find myself booked on a flight to New York to see Judy and enrolled for the N.O.W. Course at Durham University on my return.

It was three weeks in a different world! Three weeks of peace, tranquillity, good food and loving kindness. It was early Fall in Maine; beside the lake the maples were aflame with gold and crimson and the evenings chilly enough to warrant lighting the wood-burning stove after supper. The days were brilliant and blue, and to my English tastes gloriously warm. The natives had all but abandoned the shallow, sweet lake for swimming. It was too late in the year, too cold. Used to the chill North Sea, I found it just perfect and took long leisurely swims the length and breadth of the lake at least twice a day. Far from tiring me, it relaxed and re-vitalised me. My weight was well below eight stone by now and my rib cage corrugated my T-shirts.

To remedy this, incredibly delicious and tempting food appeared at frequent and regular intervals; pancakes and maple syrup for breakfast, barbeques on the lakeside, succulent Maine lobster with ear of sweetcorn picked that afternoon and eaten on the front porch in the early evening mist. Bill, Judy's father, who had assumed the role of second father, would survey me critically throughout the day.

'Little girl, you look tired, take a nap.' This after lunch.

'Little girl, it's time you were in bed.' This at 9 p.m. and out would go all the lights and we were all left with very little option.

When I wasn't napping, swimming or eating, I would paddle the canoe Indian-style with Judy around the lake, poke around local flea markets or just sit by the lake and drink in the peace, the beauty and the harmony of it all. I began cautiously at first and gradually more firmly to draw up guidelines for my life — about what really mattered, what was truly to be valued and held on to and what was unacceptable and to be changed.

'God grant us Serenity to accept the things we cannot change, Courage to change the things we can, and Wisdom to know the difference.' I bought this text to take back for my mother but the message was more about me than from me. On my return to England, I gave myself six months. I would do everything, everything I possibly could to restore my dignity and sense of self-worth. To restore my role as responsible carer for my child, my horse and my home. To return to a relationship with my husband that in some way resembled a marriage. After six months I would try and evaluate what progress I had made, and given the wisdom and courage, make any necessary changes. As I was about to leave America, Bill slipped away and rang Ian for me, telling him that my plane was running way off schedule — I was going to be stuck at Manchester Airport without a connection at some unearthly hour of the morning. He filled in the deadly waiting time by telling Charlotte, his wife, and me what he'd said: 'It ain't going to do this little girl any good heaving cases around and sitting there like a piece of lost luggage. What? Oh sure, sure she's fine: hell, you sent her here to get better, didn't you? Well, she's better! I've made sure of that. But not so better that it wouldn't be kinda nice if *you* were there at the airport to meet her. You will? Okay.'

Charlotte and I sat and snivelled uncontrollably as the

minutes ticked by, and Bill paced the departure lounge. 'Charlotte, I can't stand wailing women, you know that! For heaven's sake stop snivelling.'

At the gate, tears rolling down his cheeks, he held me in his arms briefly. 'Goodbye, little girl. Take care.' He propelled me down the long empty tunnel to the waiting plane, towards the real world.

It was a hunting day. Nanny was waiting with the car at the other end.

The six months were nearly over, and with it, my self-imposed trial period on the rest of my life. I had to admit I'd made progress, real progress. The nanny was gone and the house and Megan were back under my control — with a little help from Brenda, of course. I was riding Bear again and had even had a few days' hunting. Megan went to a crèche on a Tuesday while I attended my course.

By the spring I had realised I was enjoying using my semi-retired brain and also that I wanted to be working towards, however gradually, returning to a career again. I knew quite definitely I did not want to teach cookery again in schools. I had a far more personal crusade: I wanted to teach health education, and in particular shed a little light for those women who were still mystified or condemned by their ignorance of the workings of their own bodies. When N.O.W. finished, I was accepted on a day-a-week, one year's Certificate Course in Health Education and found myself doing working research by running a Feminine Health Course at the prison.

My self-confidence, it would appear, had been restored.

I had cut down gradually, over a long period of time, on the tranquillisers. Apart from my ritual morning tablet, I was off them completely. The mornings were still rough at times, though, and I clung tenaciously to that one last pill, the one last step.

Yes, I had made real progress in many ways. But not in my marriage. From separate rooms we led separate lives that crossed only perfunctorily, and then usually on the middle ground of Megan. We had no personal common ground at all — our relationship was polite, distant and very, very dead.

It was a hard decision to make. Leaving. I had little certainty about the future, whether I would complete my course, find a job, eventually make myself financially independent. But what-ever the future held, I could not go on living on memories of a past life now dead and gone and mourning it forever. And my present sterile vacuum of an emotional life was becoming repugnant, immoral somehow: sharing a roof, sharing a child, sharing a bank account but sharing nothing of each other.

When the cottage came up for rent in the village I gave it a great deal of thought. When I found I could rent the old stable at the back of the pub, I made up my mind. Ian and I discussed it all thoroughly, made financial arrangements and even divided the furniture amicably. We agreed not to embark on any tug-of-love over Megan. She would go with me to the cottage, but we lived so near to each other that joint custody was realistically practical. Once again I left my home on Bear, this time to follow the furniture van to the cottage. But this time I wasn't in turmoil; excited yes, relieved yes, scared, definitely. For the first, the very first time in my life, I was truly out on my own.

7

'Someone in this county must have space on a trailer'

LOOKING BACK, I can see I had a very strange set of priorities. I had very little money and I should have cut my budget to the bone, dispensing with all unnecessary expenses. But not only was it unthinkable that I should part with Bear, even on a temporary 'out on loan' basis, but I was more determined than ever that he and I would drive together that season.

There was a matter of weeks between our moving into the cottage and the 1982 Beamish Horse Driving Trials. Defiantly I filled in the entry forms, putting my name in capital letters for the first time in the 'name of driver' space.

I had my horse, all his harness, both traps and an estate car with a tow-bar. I could easily borrow or hire a trailer for the weekend. Yes, I thought, I could do it, I would do it. Nudging round the edges of my enthusiasm came a sobering thought. I had overlooked one small detail: I had no way at all to get my traps to the event. Another car, another trailer, I did not have. Momentary panic gave way to a sensible solution. I couldn't be the only person from County Durham competing at Beamish. Someone, somewhere relatively nearby, must have space on a trailer or in a horse box. Just enough space for one small two-wheeled vehicle, surely.

I phoned Brian Patterson. He asked very kindly after Bear and was delighted that I was going to finally drive him myself. Three years had passed since, through Brian, I had set off on that particular, long path.

'The only person I can think of,' he suggested, 'is Richard Smith in Crook. You know — friend of mine — drives a pair of dun horses.'

Yes, I knew very well who he meant. Brian had introduced me to Richard and I'd seen him at most events I'd been to. He'd even been a guest at a party I'd given for horsy acquaintances who lived nearby. He'd admired Bear. If I'd had to describe Richard in four words they would have been — short, fat, bald and middle-aged. Indeed, there was something positively Pickwickian about him.

'He's back in Crook, at the moment anyway. Having another go at patching up marital differences, I think. He and his wife have split up a couple of times already. He was debating about whether to pack in his pair, but last time I saw him he was going to give it all one more go and I'm sure he's going to Beamish. Do you want his phone number?'

'No thanks, I've already got it.'

It was all arranged quite easily. It would be no bother, no trouble at all, glad to help.

I was just about on my knees with exhaustion by the time Beamish was due. It was all much, much harder on your own. I saw clearly why Brian had given up. Had I had a full-time job I don't see how it could have been done. As it was, between a day at college and a day at the prison, ferrying Megan back and forth from crèche and nursery, mucking out at an unearthly hour every morning and exercising Bear at least once a day, the days were bursting at the seams. In the evenings, no matter how tired I was, I had my course work to do and the laundry, cooking and housework at the cottage. It wasn't a cottage in the single-storey detached sense of the word, it was actually a little Georgian-windowed, white-washed mid-terrace house. It had a lovely big kitchen with a coal fire, a front room downstairs and a nice bathroom and three tiny bedrooms upstairs. I loved it. It had all just been modernised whilst retaining its rustic character and it was big enough for Megan and me and small enough to run cheaply and easily.

Not having any grazing for Bear was my worst problem. I had to get him out of that stable twice a day if just to stretch his legs. I know people take a dog and a child for a walk, but we made a strange trio every teatime, me in the middle, three-year-old trotting along on one side and Welsh cob ambling along on the other.

In those first weeks I found myself several times on the verge of pure panic again. Of admitting that I could not cope with the role I had set myself. Of admitting defeat. There were, I knew, only too many people waiting with smug satisfaction for just such a defeat to occur.

Beamish was everything I'd expected it to be: cold, wet and frightening. I got through the first day, the dressage and cones, no better and no worse than I had feared. I didn't forget the test so we were not eliminated, but my driving was tense and erratic and so therefore was Bear. Knowing what he'd been capable of doing with Brian, I found it a travesty of his potential that we should be near the bottom of the class. He'd been overnight leader two years before. But there was no backing out; I had to drive the marathon. The weather was absolutely diabolical. The freezing sleet drove into us till we were totally numb. My passenger was a girl I knew, not very well, who kindly agreed to do the event but who was as green as I was.

When I hit the railway sleeper in the first hazard, she bounced out of the cart with such force that she actually left her shoes behind. Mercifully we didn't tip up and she wasn't hurt. White as a sheet and with sopping, freezing feet she clambered back in the trap. Poor bewildered soul, all I could do was growl, 'Damn, that's twenty penalties for the groom dismounting!'

Our marathon actually inched us up a slot or two but even so, we finished in the bottom third of the class.

All in all, I told myself, I was still reasonably satisfied with the weekend. I'd set out only to prove that I could get my horse and myself round unscathed and without elimination. That I could drive it. Having got Bear safely unloaded and stabled and my harness unpacked and Megan seen to, I collapsed into bed to sleep the sleep of the just. Richard Smith brought my trap back the next evening.

'Where do you want it putting? You don't keep it on this apology for a lawn, do you?'

'No, no,' I laughed. 'I keep the vehicles down the road, actually. I rent the old stable building at the pub. I have to share with a couple of goats and the odd hen but otherwise it's fine. I'll get Megan's wellies on and we'll come and help you unload.'

When we'd done that and he'd had a good look at Bear and pronounced him fit and well after his previous days' exertions, Richard accepted an invitation for a cup of tea. I built the fire up and produced some scones and, settling my weary aching bones into an armchair, started a conversation which was soon deep into events and hazards and dressage tests. It was Megan's quite justified whining that made me realise it was past both her teatime and her bedtime.

'Look, I'm sorry, I'll have to see to Megan. She had a late night last night and she's about out on her feet.'

'That's fine,' he said. 'Carry on.' And he settled himself deeper into the chair by the fire. I remember we all had boiled eggs for supper.

After Megan was bathed and read to and sung to, I closed up the rail on her cot. I really would have to find the money from somewhere to buy her a single bed. She was three and a half after all. I remembered my guest downstairs. I did hope he wasn't going to stay too long, I needed an early night myself.

'Did you enjoy your first event then? You look absolutely knackered, if you don't mind me saying so,' he said.

'Thanks a million and yes, I did, and yes, I am.'

'Grand horse that, grand horse. Brian raved on about him all the time a couple of years back, and I can see why.'

'Yes, Bear is a grand horse.'

'You are on your own now, are you?'

'Yes.' I felt, quite unnecessarily, the need to justify myself.

'I've had a lot of problems, well, medical problems, over the last couple of years and when I finally came out the other end I wasn't the same person as when I went in. It was just gone, dead — the relationship. It seemed so futile to carry on. Anyway, I need to prove a lot of things to myself, so here I am. Rightly or wrongly.'

'Oh, no, no you're right, I'm sure of that. Once you see clearly you're on the wrong track, get off, that's what I say. Get off and find a better way.'

I began yawning uncontrollably.

'I can see you need your bed as much as the bairn did, so I'll be off.'

He picked a battered and very ancient hat off the chair and made for the door. 'What are you planning next for that horse of yours?'

'Well, I want to go to Holker Hall with him. That would be my first F.E.I. event, but it's a while off yet so I just have to keep him fit and try and get some practice in.'

'If you don't mind me asking, having you any idea what you're doing in that dressage arena?'

The remark was so honest I had to laugh.

'No, not really!'

'Could you do with a bit of advice?'

'That's an understatement.'

'I'll be round for my tea tomorrow. The scones were lovely. Goodnight.'

And so he was. Not just the next night, but for many of the subsequent early May evenings. We would take Bear and the trap over to a large open piece of waste ground and I would drive in an imaginary dressage area, practising my collected trots, my extensions, my one-handed circles and my rein-backs.

Richard would produce a pile of 'lost' road cones from the back of his Land Cruiser and suddenly I had a makeshift obstacle course. I quickly made some real progress. Megan would watch us while she played in the capacious back of his vehicle. She loved Uncle Richard's Land Cruiser. How had he suddenly become Uncle Richard? Sometimes he would take both of us in the trap and drive us out for an hour or so in the sweet May air. Megan loved that too.

There was a small one-day event coming up in Northumberland that a friend of his ran. It was to be held at a place with the unlikely name of Shortflat Towers. But it was a good little event and would be good experience for me. Richard was far from convinced that I was ready for a full F.E.I. event. Stubbornly, I put my entries in for Holker Hall.

'Are you competing at Shortflat?' I enquired.

'No.'

'Are you saving your pair for Holker?'

'No; in fact I don't have them any more.'

'You don't have them?' I gasped: I was genuinely shocked.

'I've sent them away for the summer to a friend; until I find the right buyer for them. They've got to go to the right home.'

'But why? I mean, why are you parting with them?'

'Well, one of them has had arthritis in her knee for a while now and it's unfair to keep on eventing her. And there's other reasons, other problems. Things I've got to sort out.'

'I hope I'm not one of the reasons,' I said suddenly, then wished I hadn't. What right had I to say that?

After a pause he said quietly, 'Perhaps.'

I was quite panic-stricken. Oh Lord, I didn't want to get involved, not with him, not with anyone. Not yet. Things were moving too fast. I had to find my new path, my better way. Be independent. Prove myself to myself as well as to the rest of the world.

I made all sorts of excuses for it to be inconvenient to drive Bear, to spend any time in the evenings. Richard certainly took the hint; I heard and saw nothing of him all week.

Reluctantly but undeniably I had to admit I missed Richard. Not just working with Bear, and polishing up my dressage. I missed him: missed him sitting there by the fire, missed cooking an extra bit of this and that in case he called. Missed our talks which had begun to range far beyond the confines of driving horses. I was being ridiculous. Some new-generation woman I was. Barely a month or so out of one relationship, barely embarked on a new life. Good Lord, be realistic, I hardly knew the man. He was still married, still living with his wife. He was fifteen years older than me and an ex-miner who was now an antique and second-hand furniture dealer. Educationally and socially we were a universe apart. The only common ground or interest we had appeared to be driving horses. He was shorter than me, bald as a coot on top and of very ample girth. But he was comfortable and easy to be with, he made no pretence about being any other than what he appeared. Above all, he was kind.

When towards the end of the second week of absence I heard the unmistakable sound of his engine at the back door, I flew out without even stopping to think, flew into his arms without stopping to reason why and clung there, warm and comfortable and safe.

We sat round the fire late into that night. He told me that he'd decided if he commended me for my courage in taking decisive action on the course of my life, then he was a coward if he couldn't do the same himself. He had finally and irrevocably split up with his wife and she'd gone to live with her parents for the time being. Divorce proceedings had started.

I decided it was time to bare my soul; even at the risk of him feeling differently about me. Above all, I wanted the relationship to be honest. I did not want any skeletons to come crawling out of their cupboards at a later date.

'There are things I think you should know about me.'

'Will I need to brace myself for the shock?' he asked, amused.

'No, seriously, it's not funny, or easy, but there are things I want you to know.'

'I'm listening.'

Now that I'd committed myself I was finding the words hard. I said in a rush: 'I'm thirty-two years old and I've already been married twice. That's a diabolical track record.'

Instead of shrinking back in horror he smiled and said, 'I'm so glad; because then we're even. Don't flatter yourself that you're in any way unique in that sense.'

That one floored me a bit, but I carried on:

'I had what they call a "nervous breakdown" about a year ago. I suppose I'm still coming out of it really — I get panic attacks now and then, and I still have to take a tranquilliser in the morning. Just one silly little pill. The doctor says that dosage can't make any difference but it's a big step to stop that one little pill.'

'I'm sure you'll make it when you're good and ready.'

'And,' I was almost disappointed in my inability to provoke shock and horror in this man, 'I've had fairly drastic gynaeco-logical surgery. I can't have any more children and I have to take hormone replacement therapy.'

'Does this mean,' he asked in a whisper, 'that your voice is going to break and you'll develop a beard?'

'Good God, no!'

'Well then, why are you worrying? I thought for a minute you were going to tell me something really serious.'

I kept repeating that whatever was happening between us, I didn't want to make any commitments to him or to anyone else, not for a very long while yet.

Oh, indeed, he agreed, he quite agreed.

I wanted to be free to concentrate on my course and my future, getting back to a career.

Oh, but of course, I must.

It was vital that I discovered if I could function as an independent human being.

Oh, vital, vital, absolutely vital.

The next day a van drew up and a man emerged with a large bouquet and a parcel. In the bouquet were exactly thirty-two red roses and in the parcel there was an antique vase with a card that simply said 'To The Better Way'.

I did drive at Shortflat. Arrogant and independent, I insisted on going it alone. I hired an ancient horsebox from my blacksmith which would take both Bear and the vehicle and off I went. Behind my fixed smile I was not quite so confident; I'd never driven anything bigger than a Land Rover and trailer before. But I would not hear of Richard taking me and my turnout in his big horsebox. Out of the question. My passenger from Beamish, who must have been a glutton for punishment, joined me again.

Over confident and over-fast, I came to the third hazard. I had walked it with contempt earlier. Of course I could get through that gate. Easy. Too late I tried to rein back, too late I threw my weight to the other side of the trap, but we were wedged firmly on one side and tipping on the other. We reached the point of no return and gravity did the rest.

Then we were on the ground, winded and humiliated and Bear was standing with the twisted trap, the broken shaft tip digging painfully into him. I drove home very humbled and very, very anxious. Richard was very good really, not a single 'I told you so' but I didn't need admonishing; my broken shaft and Bear's rapidly swelling shoulder was all the punishment I needed. As was having to withdraw from Holker Hall because he wasn't sound in time.

The next event on the calendar was Kelso. I took a long, hard look at myself and my horse. Since doing so brilliantly with Brian two years before Bear'd never even been placed. This could not be his fault; it had to be the driver's. Was it fair to frustrate his talent? Was it fair to risk his neck through ignorance and lack of experience? I hadn't had my so-called 'apprentice-ship' with Brian, because the surgery I'd undergone after Beamish had prohibited me from even going as a groom on the marathons. True, I had driven around Beamish myself, but that could have been good luck rather than good management; and was it truly sufficient experience to attempt a three-day F.E.I. competition? If I was really painfully honest with myself, the answer was no.

Richard did not actually leap at my suggestion that he drive Bear at Kelso, which rather surprised me.

'It'll raise a few eyebrows.'

'Why should it?'

'Oh grow up. People are people and gossip is gossip, even in this sport. What do you suppose they'll say if I drive your horse with you on the back?'

'I'd never thought of it that way,' I said, crushed. 'Perhaps you're right.'

'Of course I am — but you don't think that's going to stop me, do you?'

Richard loved giving me surprises. Big, small or simply surprising surprises. The girl on the doorstep was a surprising surprise.

'Hello, I'm Carol Herbert; I've come in reply to the advert.'

'Advert?'

'The one in the Post Office: "Help wanted in mornings with horse". You are the lady with the horse, aren't you?'

'Well, I suppose I am but — look, you'd better come in.'

She was tall, well-built and had long fair hair and a lovely, open, kind face.

'I'm not really interested in the money,' she added quickly. 'It's just something to do, anything to do, especially with horses. I used to help exercise the racehorses over in the next village but they've gone now. Your horse is the chestnut one with the lovely tail, isn't it, the one in the pub stable? You drive him too, don't you?'

I smiled. 'There doesn't seem to be much you don't know about me.'

She looked embarrassed and dropped her eyes.

'Oh, I'm sorry if I seemed — well — nosey, like, but I never miss watching a horse go by.'

She stood there expectant and hopeful. The Post Office? Advert? This had to be Richard's doing. He had been having a very serious dig at me over the last week, about doing too much, stretching myself too thinly. He'd even suggested I should choose between my horse or my course as I was doing neither justice.

'Would you like to learn the ropes tomorrow morning?'

Her face lit up.

She was a gem, was Carol Herbert, an absolute gem, who fell hopelessly and completely in love with Bear at first sight. He wallowed in the adoration and was mucked out, groomed and exercised thoroughly, meticulously and lovingly every day. I felt like a working mum who's found the perfect nanny for her child.

Carol lived with her mother and four siblings in a tiny terraced house between my cottage and the stable. Her father had died very suddenly in his early forties at the beginning of the year and the family's grief, especially that of her mother, had left Carol directionless and lost. With Bear the vacuum was filled and both our lives became happier and easier. Only her name caused problems; there was one too many Carols around. In a very uninspired moment she became simply 'Herbie' in an effort to avoid confusion.

She went to Kelso with us, did Herbie. She accompanied me in my estate car, towing Bear in a borrowed trailer while Richard followed towing the traps. It turned out she was not a good traveller: whether it was the excitement or not I don't know but the road to Scotland was punctuated with several hasty, unscheduled stops. She also had peculiar eating habits. I would have thought such a well-made girl would have a healthy appetite but she picked unenthusiastically at her food, seeming to prefer to live on a diet of fish-paste sandwiches.

We tried to behave with absolute decorum; Herbie and I sleeping in the swept-out double trailer and Richard in the dormitory accommodation at the nearby racecourse. But we could not resist jubilant kisses when, right back on form in the dressage arena, Bear finished the event in third place. I thoroughly enjoyed my trip round the marathon standing on the back step that Richard had welded on to my cross-country cart. I could balance much more safely from there and I suffered never a twinge from my insides. Actually, experiencing hazards being driven expertly again made me realise just how far I had to go. But best of all, our third place rosette meant once again that Bear was through to the National Championships at Windsor in September.

I was so delighted with our result, and so content with planning our next event at Lowther and with life in general, that I began to wonder if things weren't going *too* well. I'd even weaned myself painlessly off the morning pill.

'This isn't what I had in mind at all,' I confessed to my friend Jill, while I was enjoying a rare quiet morning with her over a cup of coffee.

'I mean I hadn't intended getting involved in any way, with anyone at all, not for a very long while yet. Richard has come as a bit of a shock to my system, to be honest.'

She viewed me sagely over the top of her coffee mug.

'Well, I must say you look well on it and, you know, you sometimes have to kiss a lot of frogs before you find your prince.'

'Yes, maybe so, but what happens if you fall in love with the frog!'

8

'Ride? Be thankful to walk!'

AS I STOWED the trunk containing my show harness into the back
of the estate car, I was terribly excited. I was actually going away
for a couple of days. Away from all the pressure and problems
and emotional conflicts that still surrounded my everyday life.
And best of all, I was taking Bear. John and Joan Sykes were
friends who lived at Boroughbridge in the North Riding of
Yorkshire. They owned the place that I coveted most on earth,
next to Green Pond in Maine. Their house was red brick and
very compact with a tall arched central window. It was quilted
with ivy and Virginia creeper, making the outside a kaleido-
scope of seasonal colour. Around the house ran a walled garden
of old-fashioned country flowers. In fact, the whole atmosphere
was so Beatrix Potter-like, I always expected to find Peter Rabbit
in a soporific stupor amongst the neat rows of lettuce in the
kitchen garden. There, amidst the culinary herbs and tangled
strawberry patch, was even a glass house in which a venerable
vine obliged for every harvest festival with bunches of luscious,
sweet, green grapes. Beyond the gardens lay the yard,
comprising rows of airy, light loose boxes, feed-room, barns and
a harness room whose atmosphere was laden with years of
saddle soap and elbow grease. In short, the place was sheer
heaven.

Ostensibly, my visit was an opportunity to drive Bear in the
local Agricultural Show at which John organised the driving
class every year. I had never entered a show class before, and
doubted very much whether Bear would do very well with his
much-scarred legs and rump. In actual fact, I think an appearance at the show was just a useful excuse to get me away for a
couple of days. John and Joan were undoubtedly among the
kindest, dearest people I had ever met. When I last popped in to
see them they had been clearly worried by the upheavals in my
life and the signs of strain I was showing, including losing
weight.

I had told John that I had decided to let Richard drive Bear for

119

the rest of the season and, whilst he agreed with my reasoning, he knew me well enough to realise that I was a little disappointed about yet another, though self-enforced, delay in competing personally. Hence, I suspect, the invite to go down for the local show. When I pointed out I could borrow a trailer and transport Bear, but could not manage to bring my trap, he quickly solved the problem by suggesting I simply brought Bear and used his show vehicle. So it was all agreed. My mother, bless her, happily volunteered to have Megan. With John and Joan's blessing, I had asked Herbie to go with me. Not that I needed any help with Bear, but I knew she too got little chance to go away and would thoroughly enjoy the occasion.

I checked carefully one last time that I had all that was necessary in the car and that the trailer was firmly and safely attached to the tow bar and the lights connected up. I had taken Megan over to my mother's early that morning and now simply had to pick up Herbie who would be waiting down at Bear's stable. He would, she said, be all ready to travel. And when I pulled up a couple of minutes later, there they were, both with their coats on and both with a grin on their faces. We loaded Bear into the trailer, or rather, stood back while he charged up the ramp, and we were all set to go.

The late July weather was perfect and there was a distinct holiday atmosphere in the car on the short journey. It was warm and sunny so I was wearing a short-sleeved shirt but Herbie steadfastly kept on her anorak, saying she wasn't warm. I really did worry about that girl's metabolism at times. At least she seemed to be travelling better and was not violently sick as on the last two occasions.

We arrived mid-afternoon to an overwhelming welcome. John had obviously been keeping a weather eye open for us as he appeared to open the gate as soon as I slowed at the bend by the house.

'Hello m' dear. Hello. This must be your little friend. Well, come in, come in. Let's get you organised. Joan's got the tea all ready.'

The picturesque little yard immediately cast its spell of charm on Herbie who could only keep muttering: 'Isn't it beautiful! Isn't it beautiful?' under her breath to me.

I felt awash with happiness and contentment. Whatever else was wrong in my world, I was blessed with good friends, good health and a marvellous horse. Well, I was going to enjoy all of them to the full in the next couple of days.

'Right now, let's have him in here.' John led the way the

the moment Bear was unloaded. 'This box ought to do him. Red Rum's stayed in this box before, you know.'

John's eyes twinkled most of the time, so it was always very difficult to tell if he was being serious or not. Whether he was or not, Herbie was clearly impressed and reverently led Bear in.

'You go into the house and I'll see to him,' she said firmly.

I protested, 'No, not at all, I didn't bring you so you could do all the work for me. I'll give you a hand.'

'Honestly,' she insisted, 'I'll enjoy settling him in and I'll unload everything out of the car and trailer and get sorted out for tomorrow.'

After a high tea which surpassed even my expectations and had Herbie's eyes boggling, we all sat around, drowsy and happy, and chatted about horses and hunting and horses and driving and horses and horses until I suddenly realised the clock was creeping round to seven.

'If you'll excuse us,' I said, groaning at the effort of getting up, 'we'd better get on. Bear wants his last feed and we've all my show harness to clean. I'd like to get everything organised for tomorrow as well as then there is no rush.'

'There'll be no rush,' said John. 'Your class is not until late morning and the showfield is only a twenty-minute gentle trot away.'

'In that case, I think I'd better get up really early and give Bear a ride to settle him. I've got him fighting fit at present, you know, because Lowther is at the end of next week — and he has not had a lot of work this morning. I would hate him to disgrace himself by getting over-enthusiastic in the showring. He's not very good at standing still at the best of times.' As an after-thought I added, 'I don't suppose you've anything Herbie could ride so she can come with me? It's glorious on the gallops in the early morning.'

It was a lovely thought, but one which in the weeks and months ahead I was to wish over and over that I had never voiced.

John thought for a moment and then said, 'Well, there's only the three-year-old Dales mare we've just had broken in. She's a nice ride, though she can be a bit sharp, so watch her. Actually, I'd be happier if you took her out, Carol. No offence to Herbie,' he added hastily, 'but I know you're a good jockey.'

When the alarm went off at 5.45 a.m. it took me a few moments to get my bearings. The sunlight was already streaming in the bedroom window and the birds were in full chorus. Herbie was billeted on the camp bed at the foot of my bed and she blinked blearily at me as I headed for the bathroom.

'Morning, least I expect it's morning. Is it going to be a good day for the show?'

'It is,' I assured her, 'the most glorious, perfect, beautiful morning, and there's two horses out there just waiting for us to enjoy it with them.'

I made a quick cup of tea but we didn't bother with food. It would make the smell of frying bacon all the more tantalising when we got back. Shortly after six, we were on the yard tacking up. My mount proved to be a typical, well-built Dales, stocky, powerful, and all muscle. I thought, 'Yes, I bet you can pull a bit; you must do if they use a curb bridle on you.' I had asked John the night before where her tack was, and he'd said to use the bridle behind the door. She didn't seem at all happy as I put her bit in. A Pelham seemed rather severe I thought to use with a young and newly broken horse, but the Dales could be very headstrong so maybe it was necessary.

When we were saddled up, we led them through the gate before mounting on the village green in front of the house.

'Are you sure you don't mind me riding Bear?' Herbie asked.

'Not at all; it feels a bit funny, but it'll do me good to ride something else for a change.'

'Talking about change, there's something different about you, something missing.' She stared at me in close scrutiny, 'I've been trying to figure it out since yesterday.'

'Missing?'

'Yes, there's something that I normally see when I look at you that I'm not seeing. I know,' she exclaimed triumphantly, 'it's that thing you always wear around your neck; I've never seen you without it before.'

'That thing' was a medallion I had bought on my last visit to America. It was in fact an Irish half-crown with an outline of a horse on its reverse side. It wasn't very valuable, but I loved it and always wore it. Always. Night and day, swimming or socialising, I always wore it. Until the day before, when I'd snapped the chain while making my bed. There was not time to have it mended before we set off, so I just left it on the dressing table. For someone who is a firm believer in omens, that was a pretty dumb thing to do.

We walked the horses through the still-sleepy village, unwilling to disturb the peace on that unbelievably beautiful morning. It was idyllic; the village green, the pub, the spreading trees, the picturesque church. All blue and green and gold in the early sun. It was so beautiful, it was almost unreal and it had the effect of subduing even the perpetually bubbly and chattery Herbie to an awed hush. As we passed the last cottage, we set away at a brisk trot down the lane towards the gallops to warm the horses up. They trotted quite happily together. The mare flattened her ears occasionally but made no move to kick Bear. We swung off the lane on to the broad track of the gallop.

As soon as he hit softer ground, Bear automatically changed up two gears, as he always did. Herbie hauled him back.

'Don't let him get away with anything,' I advised her, 'but let him have a good run while he's got the chance. He's obviously full of himself.'

'You can say that again,' she said grinning.

'I tell you what, I'll set away for a bit of a canter on the mare and you can hold back a while, then let Bear follow. Right?'

'Right!'

I squeezed gently on the mare's sides and sat down in the saddle. Whoever had broken her in had made a good job of it and she readily accelerated and changed pace to canter. We cantered steadily for a couple of hundred yards. Then I heard a shout behind, 'Will you just look at this horse of yours!'

I turned my head as far as I could, but out of the corner of my eye all I could see was a reddish golden blur approaching very quickly with forelegs doing things more normally associated with hackney horses than cobs.

'Good God,' I thought, 'he's trotting faster than I'm cantering!'

Neck arched, nose pulled in, Bear was powering up behind me and gaining ground at every stride. It was a rare glimpse of his real power. His true beauty and strength. My horse, the horse who had defied his scars and his injuries to come back to perfect fitness. My eyes misted with pride and love and happiness, my mind wandered from where I was and what I was supposed to be doing and focused only on Bear. I needed a better look, a longer look. I put both reins in my right hand and swung round in the saddle to face back the way I'd come, just as I'd done out hunting on Bear so many, many times. I've often heard it said that at critical moments there is a distortion, a lengthening in time. Certainly, it seemed as though I turned and gazed at Bear for long seconds before it happened. In reality, I had hardly finished pivoting in the saddle when the forward momentum of the mare ceased and the upward momentum started. It was as simple as that. One moment we were cantering along easily, the next she was on her hind legs and rearing, and she kept on rearing, up and still further up. I was totally unprepared, totally unbalanced, and she dislodged me effortlessly from the saddle.

I fell with a thud on my left side with a bit of wind knocked out of me, but that was all. It seemed at the time I had registered all these facts before I glanced up and saw a blackness fill the sky above me. At the time, I seemed to ponder for endless moments on what was causing this eclipse of my light before I realised it was the mare; still on her hind legs, but this time moving backwards, falling slowly to the earth where I lay. There was no question of moving. The moment seemed endless, the descent slow, so incredibly slow, like a movie film, frame by frame. Yet still I couldn't move. I knew I had no time, no real time that was. Night fell. The eclipse was total. My body registered the breaking of bones with the sensation of crunching, like a walnut and yet with no pain, only that sickening, dull crunch.

Then the slow motion was over, the grass beside my nose was very green and still damp and looked quite beautiful. The sobs certainly weren't mine, I was lying quite still and quiet. A deeply primitive voice inside was insisting on that. 'Don't move! Don't move!' No, the sobbing wasn't mine.

'Oh God, oh God. What shall I do? Please tell me what to do!' It was Herbie, Bear's rein looped over her arm, lying on the ground beside me.

A voice that certainly sounded like mine issued instructions. 'Go back and get help. You must go for help. Tell John to phone for a doctor. Quickly. I've broken something, I don't know what.'

'But I can't,' she sobbed, 'I can't just leave you here!'

'Please, Herbie, please go. There's nothing you can do here, I need help and you'll have to get it. Now go on, I'm all right. I'm in no pain and' — what a time to crack feeble jokes — 'I promise I won't go away.'

My light-hearted approach to the situation seemed to reassure her and she squeezed my hand, then disappeared from my limited field of vision. I heard the sound of her getting up into the saddle, then the rapid fading thud of galloping hooves. Then nothing. Absolutely nothing.

A deep instinct was telling me that I was hurt, badly hurt but I must not panic, and above all I must not move. My 'obscure facts' department remembered that I had read about people very badly hurt, even losing limbs, who recalled suffering no great pain at the time. Something to do with endomorphines.

What a mine of useless information I was. Around the edges of the unnatural calm, fear began to nibble. Fear of feeling great pain and a worse fear of feeling no pain at all. What if, oh my God, what if my back was broken? Panic welled up in my chest. I must know if I could move my legs, or even if I could wiggle my toes. Deep within my rubber boots something stirred and I choked on a sob of relief.

Lying as I was on my left side with my right hip in the air and my head on one side at ground level, my vision was curiously two-dimensional. Like a young child's painting, my world was flat and divided into two bands of colour, one blue and one bright green.

The quietness of the early morning was broken by the trill of a bird high above me. Lines of an old folk song ran through my head:

Oh the lark in the morning, she rises from her nest
And she rises through the air with the dew on her breast.

Silly thoughts. Irrelevant thoughts. I really was quite peaceful lying there. In a strange way, I didn't want it to end; I didn't want help to come because that would be the end of this peaceful interlude and the start of something unknown, something frightening. Why hadn't I passed out, I wondered. It would all be so much easier in a way if I were unconscious. As it was, someone, somehow was going to have to move me. The thought made me feel chill.

Then from far away I heard the unmistakable drone of John's old Land Rover. It approached rapidly, swung off the metalled lane on to the gallops and shuddered to a halt somewhere behind me. Doors slammed and feet approached. It was odd only being able to see people's feet. It made me very lonely. Kneeling beside me, John and Herbie felt nearer but I couldn't really see their faces.

'Oh my dear, whatever's happened, whatever's happened?' John's voice was pure anguish. 'Now then, doctor's coming, just hang on there, just hang on.' He gripped my hand tightly.

'I don't know what happened, John. She just came right up and over on me. I can't understand it.'

'I think I know. It was the bridle, m' dear. I caught her when she came clattering into the yard without you. God, I knew there'd been an accident when I saw her. The bridle she had on wasn't her bridle. She's never felt a curb chain on her in her life before.'

'Oh, John, what an idiot I am. I thought something was wrong. I took the wrong bridle. I'm sorry.'

'Sorry,' he choked, 'you're sorry. If I'd only checked!'

'No one's to blame.' I squeezed his hand back. Just then another car arrived.

'The doctor's here m' dear. Now just tell him everything you can. I'm sure that whatever's wrong, he'll . . . ' The unspoken worry in John's voice choked off the rest of the sentence.

'John?'

'Yes, m' dear?' The pressure on my hand increased.

'Tell him I can wiggle all my toes.'

'Oh, thank God, thank God.'

From somewhere above, a drop splashed on my hand, then another. Rain? The analytical part of my brain queried it from such a cloudless sky. Then I felt not the cold wetness of a rain drop spread over my hand, but the warmth of a tear. Dear John, poor John, how dreadful he must be feeling.

The doctor talked hurriedly with Herbie before speaking to me. At the prospect of being prodded or asked to move I began to tremble uncontrollably, but to my immense relief he never touched my legs.

'I've sent for an ambulance and it'll take a wee while to get here,' he said. 'I'm just going to give you an injection that'll make you feel a great deal more comfortable and relaxed.'

'But I'm not really in any pain,' I protested. I never was a lover of needles.

'I assure you, you'll feel better for this.'

I certainly must admit it relaxed me; before very long, the blue and green bands were wavy lines before my eyes and time had once again changed pace.

The ambulance bell was the next thing to make any real impression on my brain and it brought me back to some knowledge of reality. Ambulance? They were coming to get me, to take me away, to move me. I began to cry in sheer terror. Someone held my hand. I don't know who.

'Don't move me, please don't move me,' I sobbed.

'Now listen carefully,' a reassuring voice said, 'all I want you to do is to place this mask over your face and take some deep breaths. Can you do that for me?'

'Don't move me!'

'We've got a very special stretcher here that we're going to slide under you, but not until you're fast asleep. So come on, lass, just a few good deep breaths, you'll know nowt about it, I promise you.' The black rubber triangle was placed over my face and I inhaled the sickly sweet mixture deep into my lungs. I knew nothing more.

I was lost. Snatches of nightmares, snatches of noises, dim awareness of lights that came and went. Then for a long time, nothingness. Struggling through an oppressive fog back to consciousness, the first thing I was aware of was Richard's face bending over me. I tried to move and found to my horror I couldn't. Then I was aware that I was lying with my whole body tipped backwards at an acute angle. With a great effort I was able to lift my head a fraction off the pillow, but from the waist down nothing happened. 'Richard, I'm not . . . ' I began to stammer. 'My back. I haven't . . . ? I'm not . . . ?' I hadn't the courage to ask the question.

'No, no,' he said quickly and firmly, 'there's nothing wrong with your back. They won't tell me everything but the Sister said it's your hip and pelvis that's damaged. They've done an operation on your hip, that's what all this is for.' He pointed to the contraptions and pulleys above the bed and I began to focus attention on my surroundings.

I felt round under the bed clothes with my hands and discovered I was sprouting tubes from various places and I could see from the bottle by the bed that I had a drip in my arm. There was a cage over my legs under which they were held firm and immobile in a foam cocoon, and pulleys and ropes disappeared over the foot of the bed which was decidedly uphill. It was a small relief to realise that all this was the reason I literally couldn't move from the waist down. It was rather as an after-thought that I enquired where I was. It seemed somehow irrelevant.

'Harrogate,' Richard replied. 'It was the nearest big hospital.' There was an uncomfortable silence, then we both tried to speak at once. I won, but speaking was hard and my voice more a croak.

'How did you find out? How did you get here?' I managed to wriggle my free hand out of the bed clothes and close it on his. I felt instantly happier and reassured.

'Oh, phone calls and friends. We still have them, you know. Anyway, none of that matters now. The hardest part was getting in this ward; they would only allow husbands and next-of-kin in, but I, um, persuaded them.' His grin was boyish but his eyes were all anxiety.

'Bless you for coming,' I said. I suddenly felt very weary and

weak and very frightened again. Sensing my fatigue and
Sister's piercing looks, Richard straightened up and prepared to
leave. 'Well now, all that matters is for you to get well, do you
hear me? You rest and be a good girl and I'll be back tomorrow.'

'Richard. I . . . ' I began to cry.

'Now then, none of that sweetheart. You're going to be fine, I
promise you. Everything will be all right.'

Everything all right? What would happen to Megan? Where
was she? How would I see her? Where was Bear? How, oh dear
God how, did I go on from here? The need to slip back into the
fog was overwhelming.

'I'm sorry, Richard, I'm so very sorry,' I managed to whisper
first.

By the next morning I was far less groggy and had managed to
assemble most of the facts. My pelvis was broken in four places,
the worst break being in the middle of the pubic bone and I had
badly dislocated my right hip. They had been unable to replace
the bone manually and so they had operated the previous night
to do so. I had an eight-inch-long incision on my hip, a fifteen-
pound weight on my leg and would have to spend several
weeks on my back in traction. The consultant, I was informed,
would be round later that morning to see me and he would
answer any further questions.

The consultant's arrival was heralded by a flurry of last-
minute activity. As the nurse flattened the last micro-wrinkle in
my bedspread, she warned me he was in a foul mood. The
previous day's 'irresponsible, dangerous sports casualties', of
which I was one and the lady in the next bed, who had broken
her ankle badly parachuting for the first time, another, had
completely mucked up his operating list for scheduled cases. As
he was due to go on holiday the next day, everyone had been
going flat out to catch up. He was a severe-looking middle-aged
man who peered at me without warmth. He explained the
extent of the injuries and how he had operated on my hip, but
didn't enlighten me much more than the Sister had. I, on the
other hand, was after rather more basic facts and figures. 'How
long will I be, well, like this?'

'Mmm, well you need traction for that hip for several weeks
and as I've decided purely on bed rest for the pelvis, it could be
a bit longer. Say six weeks to a couple of months.'

'A couple of months!' The ward suddenly became swimmy,
and taking my stunned silence to be the end of my questions he

turned to leave. Just in time I found my voice.

'Doctor, excuse me, but how will it affect me afterwards? I mean, will I have a limp or anything like that? I will be able to ride again, won't I?'

It was his turn to be momentarily struck dumb, then slightly red around the neck, he spluttered, 'Ride? Ride? Is that all that's worrying you? Ride? Young lady, you be thankful to walk!'

He left the ward majestically with a flurry of white-coated acolytes at his heels.

I laid my head back on my crisp white pillow, quite shattered. For the first time the enormity of what had happened hit me and I began to think of the consequences of my accident. What did he mean 'thankful to walk'? Was there any doubt about it? Did he mean I wouldn't be able to walk unaided? Would I need a stick, or crutches, or, my God, a wheelchair? How would I manage at the cottage with the steep stairs? The bath? How would I manage Megan — and Bear? Where was Megan now; was she still at her grandmother's? And where was Bear? Still at John's?

Dear Lord, what had happened to my world, to my life? I should have been happily driving home from the show that day. Perhaps with a pretty rosette. That's all I'd wanted; a pretty rosette at a little country show. What had I done to deserve this? It was unfair, it was unjust. Hot tears slid down the sides of my eyes and trickled into my ears. Was this my new beginning? My better way? The crying made sickly dull pains shoot up my body and I tried to sob without moving. Even that soon attracted the attention of a vigilant nurse. I was overwrought, she told me, still reacting to the operation, in a state of shock. She'd see if I could have something to settle me down, something to ease the pain. I wasn't really in sharp pain, but I accepted the tablets gladly, hoping they would at least take the bite off the sharp edge of reality.

Richard returned that evening. He looked tired and worried. I wondered what I looked like: I dreaded to think. He reassured me everything was under control; he'd brought a friend with him so between them they would take Bear and my car and trailer back. Herbie was lovingly caring for Bear and had sent a message not to worry for one moment about his welfare, she would attend to his every need until I came home.

My tear ducts, which had been working over-time a lot of the day, sprang into action again. Home. I wanted to go home. I felt a stranger in a strange land. How could I hope to see Megan, or my mother, or anyone a hundred miles from home? Richard promised he would ask the Sister if anything could be done to move me.

'I'll go mad, Richard, if I have to stay here for two months.'

'No, you won't,' he said, squeezing the hand that wasn't sprouting a drip, 'you've been in hospital plenty of times before this.'

'I've never been kept in bed for more than a couple of days before. But this —' I gestured helplessly at the pulley disappearing over the edge of the bed and the cage over my legs, 'this is awful. I keep getting these feelings of panic, of being tied down against my will. I know it's stupid, but it wouldn't feel so bad if I was nearer home. Nearer you, nearer Megan.' I paused before asking the question I'd been putting off.

'Where is she?'

'Back with her father.'

'Oh.' It was an empty hollow noise. I knew it was the best thing, I knew it was the right thing. Yet it filled me with foreboding. What hurdles would I have to overcome to get her back? How long before I'd be capable of caring for her again?

Before the tears started again I implored him, 'Please, please, see if you can get me home.'

A week later, screwed into a fiendish metal brace contraption, still dangling the fifteen-pound weight on the end of my leg, I made an uncomfortable but uncomplaining journey courtesy of the Yorkshire Ambulance Service to Shotley Bridge Hospital. I was delirious with joy. I was coming home! Well nearly home. I had no idea at the time just how far 'nearly' can be.

The orthopaedic ward of Shotley Bridge Hospital was a far cry from Harrogate. For a start, it was based in one of a number of huts. There was no other word for them, for that's really what they were. And while modernisation and extension went on in the rest of the hospital, the huts clung on to their hillside where they'd been since they were put up as a temporary measure during the War. There were no wards in the hut. Inside it was divided into numerous tiny single rooms, just big enough to get a bed and a locker in and still squeeze round the edges. The faded chintz of the curtains and the venerable cream paint were far from fashionable and the iron bedstead looked as though it dated from when the place was a workhouse. No overhead pulleys and adjustable tilting beds here. But even as the porter and a nurse were trying to get me off a trolley and on to my bed, a short stout lady in a pink overall stuck her head round the door and said, 'Could you do with a cup of tea, pet?' And I knew I was at least on home ground.

Sister put her head round the door and said, 'Miss Robinson, the consultant, is on her way to see you.' 'Oh Lord,' I thought, 'another consultant, and this one's a spinster. Probably middle-aged, sour and loathes horses. I wonder if I put her waiting list all to pot.'

Miss Robinson was a revelation. She had long hair held more or less under control in a bun, open-toed flat sandals and a multi-coloured Indian cotton skirt peeping under her white coat. She immediately plonked herself on the bed beside me and took out some X-rays.

'Well, let's see what they've sent us.' Holding up the X-rays to the light from the window she squinted at them. 'Good God, Sister,' she said over her shoulder, 'I thought that these were pre-operative but they're not; they're *after* the hip surgery. Look at the state of that pelvis! Surely to God they weren't intending leaving it like that.'

I shrank miserably under the covers.

She paused a while as if pondering her words. 'The hip has been done. I'm not entirely convinced I would have done it that way, but it has been done and it should be all right. Now this pelvis.' Another pause for thought. 'You know it's broken in several places?'

I nodded.

'And they told you they intended just letting things heal with bed rest?'

I nodded again.

'Well, I don't think I go along with that. Three of the breaks yes, but the main one, the one in the pubic bone I would say not. What has happened is that it has snapped in two and the edges of the broken bone have moved apart and in opposite directions.' I was looking puzzled and worried now.

'Look, I'll show you.' She drew down the bed clothes, hitched up my nightie, and ran her fingers with light firmness over my pubic area. When she pressed a little harder I gave a gasp of pain.

'Sorry about that, but it shows what I mean. Give me your hand.'

She took my right hand in hers and pressed it across the surface of the bone. Instead of the regular flatness I'd been accustomed to all my life, the area was tilted sharply upwards on the left side, then there was almost a step down to the right side which was unbelievably painful to prod around. 'You see what I mean. One half of the pelvis is sticking up in the air, the other bone is tilting downwards into the abdomen. In fact, that'll be why,' she consulted the notes again, 'you're getting blood appearing in your urine; the bone is probably pressing right into the bladder.'

I was stunned by the news; there couldn't be any more complications, surely there couldn't. I asked her quietly, 'What are you intending doing?'

'Well normally I would operate here,' she ran her finger along the bikini scar of my previous operations, 'dig down and get that piece of bone that's disappearing into your bladder, pull it back in place, drill holes in the bone on both sides and plate and wire them back together again.'

I was white with shock by the time she'd finished her graphic description. I half expected her to produce a Black and Decker and a tool box from under the bed. Then another thought struck me.

'You said, ''normally''. Am I not normal?'

'How long is it since your accident?' I thought back and counted: 'Nine days today.'

'Mmm. Did you know there is a time limit on operating on broken bones?'

'No.'

'Well there is, and it is ten days at the very latest. Some say even that is too late so that makes it tomorrow or never. And tomorrow is Saturday and my day off.'

I lay back on the pillow drained and confused.

'Look, I'll try and sum up the options,' she continued in a suddenly gentle voice. 'I feel an operation would give a far better chance of those bones knitting together as they should and in the right place, and a far better chance of you being able to walk normally again. However, there is the risk of further surgery so soon after the hip surgery and there is the risk that it is too late and the bone won't be co-operative. But I believe,' she squeezed my hand, 'that there is a fifty-two per cent chance that it will work and on the balance of that two per cent, I am prepared to forego my morning off and have a try, if that is what you want.'

'If you were me, what would you do?' I felt enormously drawn to this strong, blunt woman. I felt I could literally put my life into her hands.

'I'd give it a try.'

'Tomorrow?'
'Tomorrow.'

There were faces, there were noises, there was pain. They all came and went in an endless slow procession. But there was one face that I longed to see — one friendly Pickwickian face that I knew would make me feel better.

After the operation, I took two days to recover consciousness fully. Miss Robinson even had to forego her Sunday as well as her Saturday on my behalf.

I lay and alternately dozed and studied the patterns on the faded curtains. How many nights would I have to lie and stare at those curtains? I pushed the thought away. I couldn't handle that one now. In between a doze and a paisley squiggle, the door quietly opened and Richard came in.

'Hello, sweetheart.'

'Richard!' It was so good to see him and look at the grin spreading across his face.

'Lots of people have been asking about you and send their regards,' he said.

'Really?' I was genuinely touched.

'Really. And I've been phoning too, did they tell you?'

'No; well, if they did, I wasn't in a fit state to take it in.'

'How are you now? Really, I mean.'

'All right. They tell me they think the operation will be a success. I'm sore, frustrated, worried. There's so much I don't know yet. Where will it all end? And when will it end — how long am I going to be here like this?' I gestured angrily at the rope pulley at the end of the bed.

'Now's not the time to deal with all that. You just get a good night's sleep.'

'How is Bear?'

'He's fine. Honest.' He leant over and kissed me lightly on the forehead. 'Now, I'll see you tomorrow.'

'You don't have to come in every day, you know.'

'Daft woman, I know I don't have to. See you tomorrow.'

'Goodnight.'

He slipped quietly out.

Next day, I took the bull by the horns — or, rather, the consultant by the stethoscope.

'How long will I be tied to this confounded contraption on my leg?'

'Six weeks.'

'Six weeks!' I did a rapid mental calculation. 'That's forty-two days; I'll never lie here tied to this bed for forty-two days. I can't sleep properly, for a start, lying on my back. I'll go mad in forty-two days.'

'No, you won't. Nobody ever has. You should think yourself extremely lucky; there are people on this ward who've been here six months, never mind six weeks. It's nothing out of your life, that. Nothing if it gives those bones a chance of healing and for you to walk properly again.'

'Then what?'

'Out on crutches, or perhaps a wheelchair, and no weight-bearing on that leg for at least three months.'

'And then?'

'Then, God willing, you walk and all this becomes a far-off dream.'

I almost didn't ask the next question, considering the reaction I'd had the last time.

'Will I ever be able to ride again?'

'Don't see why not,' she replied immediately.

'Really?' My spirits soared for the first time.

'No, I don't see that that would put any undue pressure on the hip; in fact the exercise in the saddle would probably do it good and the front of the pelvis should be OK. Not jumping, though. Jumping is definitely out; too much concussion on landing. There's two things you have to avoid if you want to keep that hip joint healthy, concussion and torque — that's twisting, you know. So no jogging, no aerobic dancing, no jumping, not ever. But plenty of walking, the more the better, and swimming too, that's excellent.'

'This forty-two days. When does it run from?'

'From the day I did the operation.'

I extracted my diary from my handbag on the locker and counted pages.

'That's two weeks before the Nationals.'

'The Nationals?' Miss Robinson look puzzled.

'The National Championships at Windsor,' I took Bear's photo off my locker and showed it to her and explained about driving and Richard and about Megan and my present circumstances and she listened carefully to it all.

'So you see it's very important to me, very, very important that Bear gets to the Nationals. Is there any chance I'd be able to go?' I ended, almost pleading.

'I'll tell you what,' she said. 'I'll make a deal with you. You behave yourself and resign yourself to six weeks in here and I see no reason why you couldn't go to Windsor. Bearing in mind, of course, that you'd be on sticks and probably have a wheelchair. If they can get you in without using your bad leg. I see no reason why you can't sit in a trap for this dressage business, but there's no way, no way at all, that you can do this cross-country thing where you stand on the back of a vehicle.'

'No, I hadn't expected to be fit enough to do that at Windsor.'

'I don't mean at Windsor, I mean ever.'

'What, never?' My new-found optimism for the future took a kick in the teeth.

'From what you say, and looking at these photos, you take far more banging around on the back of this thing than even jogging.'

'It can be very bumpy,' I admitted.

'Well, unless you want to be in here for a hip replacement, I would advise most strongly against it. Sitting in the vehicle yes, standing on the back, definitely no.'

As soon as she'd gone I found a sheet of paper and a pen and made a grid of six squares by seven. The forty-two days. Then I counted back. Could I count the actual day of the operation? I didn't see why not; it had been in the morning after all. That made four to cross off. I filled in four squares with heavy obliterating strokes and stuck the chart on the side of my locker. I felt purposeful and positive. At least I had made a start.

My good intentions, however, proved very hard to live up to. At times, I was very low and verging on despair.

Dear Richard — without his nightly visits I couldn't have hung on and wouldn't have wanted to. Every night before he left, he would implore me to 'hang on in there kid, just hang on, there's another one over.'

The main problem was the dragging of time. I had been moaning to Richard that I could have filled many of the long hours staring at the television but the reception was so bad I could never get a picture without a proper aerial.

The next afternoon I was gazing out of my window. I didn't do that too often because it looked down and into the next hut on the hillside, the men's geriatric ward. The painfully slow and colourless routine of their daily life was even more depressing to contemplate than my own. Suddenly, a slightly red face with a mischievous look on it appeared around the side of my window. It was Richard. If I could have fallen out of bed, I would have done. He grinned, extracted a screwdriver from the toolbag he was carrying and prised up my window.

'What on earth are you doing?' I hissed.

'If anyone asks, just say I'm the maintenance man.' He disappeared for a moment and then reappeared, carrying what looked like a long pole.

'Sorry I had to creep up on you,' he said, 'but I had to make sure I had the right room.'

'What's that?'

'That?' he said innocently. 'Oh that's a fifteen-foot pole with an aerial on the top. Now if I can just use your windowsill to stand on, I'll get up on the roof and have this fixed in a jiffy.'

At first I was struck dumb with disbelief, then with a nagging worry over what would happen if he fell off the roof, or — worse — got caught in the act. What finally overcame me, though, was a fit of giggles which I tried to stifle in case the unfamiliar noise attracted attention. It was the first good laugh I'd had in weeks. Only Richard could have pulled such a stunt, only Richard could have got away with it.

After a few minutes of muffled thumps and bangs from the roof, he began to descend again. His wellington-booted feet had just appeared, Father Christmas-like, in the top two panes of my window when my door opened and the stout pink ward orderly appeared with my afternoon tea.

She took one look at the feet dangling in mid-air, yelped 'Oh my God!' and nearly dropped her tray.

As she opened her mouth even wider to bellow for Fire, Police and Ambulance I quickly said, 'Shush, it's all right, honestly — it's only Richard.'

Still trembling, she came into the room. 'What the hell is he doing? Can he not come in the front door, like?'

'He's trying to fix me an aerial for my telly; I can't get a decent picture, you know.'

Richard completed his descent and beamed through the window at the lady in pink. 'Good afternoon. Tea? My word, that was good timing.' He nonchalantly stepped into the room through the lower half of my window. I was reduced to helpless giggles again, which seemed to be infectious as the tea lady was also grinning broadly.

'Ah'll go and get you a cup, pet,' she said. 'Ah think you desorve it, just for cheek.'

When Staff Nurse floated past a minute later, she glanced in at the open door as she passed, stopped and came back for another look.

'Hello, Mr Smith,' she said puzzled. 'That's funny, I don't remember seeing you come past the office.'

'Oh, it's all right Staff. I just dropped in.'

I had other visitors, of course. My mother faithfully came twice a week despite a very long bus journey. And Carol Herbert came once or twice but seemed distressed and awkward in the confines of the hospital and said she was better off at home looking after Bear. And Megan. Ian had employed a nanny to care for her and nanny brought in Megan regularly to see me. She would scamper into my room and climb on to the bed for a cuddle, having quickly learned which was Mummy's 'good' side. I kept a supply of books and goodies for her in my locker and we would spend a happy half hour reading and chatting. But always I was aware of nanny, polite and cool, waiting to whisk her off again. Although I couldn't have borne not to see Megan, it became an ordeal. Rather like visiting day at the prison. When the time was up, she would trot obediently up the corridor with the nanny and as I listened to the quick pat-pat of her little patent leather shoes fade away, I would be filled with loss and anguish and a great foreboding of future battles.

We decided that Richard and Bear should compete at Osberton to keep them both fit, and by the time they left for Osberton, two-thirds of the dreaded white squares had been obliterated and I began to feel I was on the home run. So much so that I was able to take a genuine interest in their going to the event and send them off in good spirits.

On the Saturday night I was being very stoical about not having had any visitors and trying to interest myself in something good on the telly. Half my mind was occupied with wondering how Bear had done in the dressage and on the marathon. If he'd done well in both, Richard would stand a good chance of finishing in the ribbons. I actually wasn't too stunned with surprise when the door opened and Richard walked in. It was the sort of thing I was beginning to expect of him. He'd felt lost, he explained, once the marathon was over and there was nothing else to do that night. Herbie was there to look after Bear, and it was only a couple of hours' drive so he thought he'd pop up.

I was quite overcome with happiness. My feelings were reaching the point, I realised, where without Richard there would just be a vacuum in my life. Without his loving, constant attention, I would never have got this far. Yet what right did I have to get too deeply involved? I hadn't wanted that at the outset. I had my own plans. Independence. Now I realised I had no plans. I was staring dependence in the face. That wasn't fair on him. I certainly didn't want to win him on a sympathy vote.

'Richard, it's too late for you to drive back to Osberton tonight.'

'I must admit the marathon is catching up with me a wee bit now.'

'Can't you stay up here tonight and go back in the morning?'

'Not really. The cones for our class are quite early.'

'I shall worry about you driving back dog-tired. It's unbelievably lovely to see you, but I wish you hadn't done it.'

'Tell you what,' he said. 'I'll go back to my flat and get my head down for a few hours. I could do with picking up some clean shirts anyway. If I leave at four in the morning, I'll be back in time to knock Herbie up for breakfast.'

'I think that's an excellent idea.'

It turned out to be one of the worst ones he'd ever had.

Next day, the Sunday, he reappeared far, far earlier than I'd expected. As soon as he came into the room I knew something was wrong, terribly wrong. His normal pink and cheerful face was ashen and drawn.

'Richard, what . . . '

'Carol, something awful has happened,' he said quietly.

The bottom fell out of my stomach and I stuck my fingers in my mouth and bit them, hard.

'Bear?' I gasped.

'No, no sweetheart, Bear's fine. God, don't worry about Bear.'

'Well what . . . '

'There's been a fire.'

'A fire?' Of all the things in the world I was preparing myself for him to say, it was not that.

'The police contacted me at Osberton. Early this morning, not long after I'd left, the flat went up in flames. It spread into the shop below and everything's burnt out. It's all gone, the flat, the shop, the stock — everything I had has gone.'

He collapsed into, rather than sat on, the chair by the bed. I was too stunned to know what to say, so for a long time we both sat in silence.

'Was anyone hurt?' I asked quietly.

'No, nobody's hurt. But if it had been a couple of hours earlier I'd have been barbecued. I couldn't believe it when I saw it. That fire and water could do that to a place. Do you realise,' he chuckled mirthlessly, 'I'm left with the clothes I'm wearing and the few that were down at the show.'

'Oh, Richard.'

He looked all-in, drained and beaten. And what bloody good could I be to him, helpless and immobile? He rose wearily to leave and my heart ached for him.

'I'd best get back. The police want to see me again and then I've got to meet the fire chief there and there'll be the insurance people to deal with likely.'

'Look, I know it's terrible and the shock hasn't worn off yet, but do try to thank God that you're alive and no one else was hurt. And promise me you'll go straight to the cottage, have a bath and a good night's sleep. Promise me that.'

He nodded and squeezed my hand.

'And the worst thing,' he said with a flicker of his usual humour in his eyes, 'I didn't even get to drive the cones.'

Suddenly we were both crying and trying to comfort each other at the same time.

'I know I've not led a blameless life,' I thought savagely through my tears, 'but dear God, what have I done to deserve all this? Where is it going to end? And do you have to punish Richard as well?'

For the next few days I almost dreaded Richard's visits, as each day seemed to bring him lower in spirits and nearer to total exhaustion. I had never felt so helpless in my life, though even if I'd had my mobility I'm not sure I could have helped. Still stunned and shaken, he was at times so tired that for most of his visit he just sat quietly in the chair by my bed with his eyes closed. Between them, the police and the insurance company had questioned him for hours on end. He felt, he said, like a victim of the Spanish Inquisition. Eventually the fire brigade were able to prove conclusively that it was an electrical fault and the tension, if nothing else, eased a little. Within a week he had acquired a small nucleus of stock and had set up shop from an old warehouse at the back of his shop premises. Very gradually, his natural optimism was returning.

There were seven white squares left on my chart. A new type of anxiety possessed me — what happened next? I had given little thought to what I was going to do or how I was going to cope when I did. I had wanted my relationship with Richard to

develop at its own pace, to completely regain my self-confidence
and independence before I made any long-term commitments
again. And I imagined Richard wanted to do the same.

But my accident meant that I would need help and I didn't
know how much or for how long. Saddling Richard with coping
with an invalid in a wheelchair had not been in my grand
scheme of things. He had no duty or obligation toward me and I
would have loathed him doing it out of pity. But the fire had
changed everything. Richard was literally homeless and virtually out of business; in our own way we were both crippled.

After an unusually quiet and subdued visit when we both
seemed to hedge politely around the issue, I finally waded in.
'What happens, I mean really happens, when I get out of here
next week?'

'Well, we get you back to your cottage and find out how you
can cope and where the problem areas are and what we can do
to get round them. What aids or assistance we can get you.'

'I see. And what are you going to do?'

'Well — I'm a bit stuck at this exact moment and the cottage
has been a useful base since the fire. But I'll be, er, looking for a
flat or something to rent as soon as I can.'

'Why?' I asked gently.

'I've got to have a roof over my head.'

'What's wrong with the cottage?'

'Nothing; it's lovely, a smashing little house but, well,' he
finished with great effort, 'it's yours; yours and Megan's home.'

'It's not mine.' I replied quickly. 'It's simply a rented cottage.
A way-station I took till I found where my life was going. Now
I've no idea of that any more. Look, Richard' — I wasn't doing
this as well as when I'd rehearsed it — 'in a way, for me that is,
this fire has been a blessing because it's evened up the problems
table. Without it, if you'd ended up trying to look after me I'd
have been always worried you were doing it out of the kindness
of your heart or, worse still, pity. I might have ended up
resenting that, or resenting you. Now I feel the situation is even
again. Before, I'd seen us as leading independent lives with a
mutual overlap in the middle. Now that overlap is bigger. Not
that we are now dependent on each other, but we both have
problems that could be best and most practically solved by
helping each other through a very sticky patch. When we are
out of the treacle tin we can think again, start again, become
independent again, if that's what you want.'

'I would,' he said, 'like that very much.'

'Oh come on, come on, come on,' I fumed. 'It's daylight. Where are you? God, you've been shoving things into me and under me at the crack of dawn for weeks. Why not this morning?'

One remaining square stood out from the black mass in the early light. But this one wasn't going to be blackened, this was a red letter day, this was Day Forty-two. I decided the staff were going to take a sadistic pleasure in prolonging the big moment for as long as possible. I rattled the weight at the end of my pulley wires. 'Not long now, you evil lump.'

It was well after breakfast when Sister, Staff and a student entered solemnly.

'Ready?' said Sister.

'You'd better believe it.'

'Please don't expect miracles,' she warned.

Staff Nurse had an inscrutable look on her face, and I wondered whose side she was on. I'd have thought she'd be gald to see the back of me.

The weight was removed and the pulley cords cut. The cords were attached from ankle to above the knee with heavy adhesive plaster. For over seven weeks the hairs on my leg had grown unchecked into the plaster. Staff whipped it off with scarcely-veiled relish while I gritted my teeth stoically, determined not to let her see me weaken.

'Now, you can sit up and swing your legs over the edge of the bed. Slowly,' Sister emphasised, 'very slowly, you could be a bit dizzy at first.'

This was it. The moment I'd been imagining and rehearsing for weeks. Freedom beckoned. I was scared stiff.

'Well done. Now we're going to wheel you along to the bathroom and you can have a nice soak.' Expert hands quickly slid me into a waiting chair and we were off. Oh, the exhilaration, the thrill of seeing cream corridor walls flash by. And after nearly two months a bath, a real hot, wet, bath. I felt as if I'd come into a fortune.

The bath was every bit as heavenly as I'd hoped and after I'd mastered the technique of getting in and out on one leg using a stool to their satisfaction, I was dressed in a tracksuit and trainers and taken to the physio department, where my brand new aluminium crutches awaited me. I mastered the art of covering flat ground quicker than I'd ever dared hope and delighted the physiotherapist. Years of heaving buckets and bales and Bear around the hunting field had finally paid off. There was nothing wrong with my arm muscles.

Learning to cope with stairs up and down was quite alarming, but simple once I learned the technique.

After that I was wheeled back to my room and shortly after 'walked' along to the dining room for lunch at a real table. I was high on adrenalin and determination but after lunch I returned to my room and fell into a deep sleep. I awoke late in the afternoon with a bursting bladder. I rang my bell and Staff Nurse appeared.

'I need to spend a penny,' I said, expecting a bedpan to appear in mid-air.

'What's the matter?' she chuckled. 'Can't you make it to the toilet? Too tired, are we?'

'Certainly not,' I retorted hotly. But by the time I'd hopped back to my room from the loo, I had to admit to aching muscles.

Miss Robinson arrived. 'How's it going?' she enquired non-committedly.

'Marvellous — honestly.'

'Come on then, let's see you do your stuff.'

Keeping a mask of supreme confidence firmly in place, I got my sticks, got off the bed and headed down the corridor. At least I had my back to her so I could puff if I needed to. On the return lap I ploughed determinedly on, repeating firmly behind my fixed smile 'You can, you can, you can' with each plonk of my crutches.

'Okay. You can go home.'

It was as simple as that.

'Oh that's marvellous,' I said fighting against tears.

'All I want you to do, young lady, is to take it steady, nothing stupid and don't ever be tempted to put weight on that leg, do you hear? Never. Get yourself away with your horse to this Nationals thing in a couple of weeks but don't overdo it. If your body says rest, then rest. And if you have any problems or think something's wrong, contact the hospital. And do me one more thing.'

'Yes, of course, if I can.'

'Send me a photo of the horse at this Nationals thing.' That was too much. The tears splashed down.

'Miss Robinson, I don't know how to, how to thank you. I know I've not been the easiest of patients, but . . . ' But she was gone, striding purposefully down the corridor bellowing, 'Sister, is there anything left to eat on the patients' trolley? I missed lunch again.'

Richard arrived at teatime. I gave him a hug, the first real unencumbered hug in a long time. He was glowing with delight.

'I thought they wouldn't be able to keep you in after today. Are you all packed? I'll start taking it out to the car. While I do, here's something for you; I found it on the dressing-table and I reckon it's time you had it back on. I've had it done properly like, all soldered, so it shouldn't happen again.' He handed me a small cardboard box then staggered out, television under one arm, suitcase under the other.

Inside on a piece of cotton wool lay my horse medallion, mended and polished till it shone like new. I reverently replaced it around my neck.

I thought he was a long time coming back until I heard muffled thuds from the roof area. With a quick sheepish look in at the window he was off, television aerial in hand. For weeks it had been there, fifteen foot high and no one, not a soul, at that hospital had noticed.

Then I was heading down the corridor bidding tearful goodbyes to all the nurses on the way. Worst of all was Staff Nurse who was so choked she could only clasp me to her ample bosom and hug me. The swing doors opened and I was out in the fresh air. It was a lovely, late September day. Good God, it was autumn, I realised. It had been summer when I had my accident.

Very gently Richard helped me into the car, which he had filled with cushions and pillows to pad me against any discomfort.

'OK?'

I nodded, too happy to speak.

'Shall we go home?'

I couldn't decide whether the emphasis was on the 'we' or the term 'home'.

'Richard. I love you.'

9

'Don't ever trust him again'

WE WERE ON our way. We were actually on our way. All those weeks of waiting and dreaming were over; we were on our way to Windsor. I nestled back in my nest of pillows and duvets in the front of the Land Cruiser and allowed myself the luxury of relaxing, of letting the built-up tension drain away. I was warm, comfortable and in no pain. It was heavenly.

The two weeks since I'd come out of hospital had been, at times, purgatory. Once the euphoria produced by getting home had worn off, I was left with the stark reality of tackling life from a wheelchair or on crutches in a small cottage with steep stairs. Though I could cover the ground quickly and efficiently on crutches outside, in the house they were awkward and doing the simplest household task was frustrating in the extreme. The killer was the stairs. They were nearly vertical. Though they had taught me at the hospital how to put one crutch under my arm and haul myself up and down the stairs on the rail and with the other crutch, it was exhausting, rib-wrenching and quite frightening — especially coming down. By the time evening came I was usually so aching and sore that all I longed for was a hot bath, and then bed.

In the first few hardest days I simply wouldn't have survived without Richard. He was endlessly patient, constantly encouraging. By the evening, sometimes my arms just gave out and I couldn't haul myself one step further. Then, always treating it lightly and as a joke, he would carry me upstairs while I desperately tried to laugh too, though sometimes I cried with pure frustration.

But somehow we managed. And managed not only to achieve a semblance of domestic organisation but to pack the caravan we had borrowed to live in, to clean two sets of harness and organise a horsebox.

Herbie had done her best with Bear during my long absence, but even as I had an emotional reunion with him I couldn't help thinking that his coat was not nearly as well groomed as usual and his stable not as clean or tidy. Reading my thoughts, Herbie made an embarrassed apology saying she too hadn't been well recently; her back had been troubling her and she found riding and mucking out a bit painful. Looking at her hard for the first time I thought that she didn't look herself. She had never been sylph-like but appeared to be piling on even more weight (though it was hard to tell under her habitual baggy jumpers) and her face had a drawn, almost gaunt look. Still, we'd all had a rough couple of months.

My biggest achievement was giving Bear a haircut a couple of days before we left. Getting his mane hogged was low down on his list of tolerances and even when I was able-bodied was a task I approached with great respect. But Richard didn't know how, Herbie didn't know how and that left me. I had to abandon my crutches altogether and use Richard, arms encircled round my chest, as a human crutch. With Herbie grimly hanging on to a twitch in one hand and bridle in the other, I slowly wandered up his neck. When I came to the no-man's land between his ears there was nothing for it, I had to stand on a stool to reach. Balancing there on one leg while Richard held on for grim death, the sweat running in a cold trickle down my back, I realised how vulnerable I was; how one quick movement on Bear's part would topple us both and do God-knows-what to all Miss Robinson's efforts. He never moved.

And somehow, everything got done, everything got packed and at the appointed hour our little cavalcade set off. Richard and I (and my wheelchair) in the Land Cruiser towing the caravan and Griff, Richard's helper from the shop, and Herbie in the horse box towing the trailer.

The journey was uneventful, my delight at just lying and watching the passing countryside quite child-like. Finally we drove to the correct field in Windsor Great Park and set up camp for our attempt at the National Championships. Spirits were high and we all worked well. I was appointed Chief Harness Cleaner as that was one job I could do unaffected by my leg. Herbie was cheerful and excited, though visibly wincing when moving heavy bales and boxes. I made a mental note to get her to my osteopath as soon as we got back. Without her, I didn't know how we would manage at all.

Dressage for our class wasn't until late into the afternoon of the next day and so we had plenty of time to polish everything to perfection. All my misgivings about Herbie's health vanished when I saw Bear; he was beautiful, glowing in the late afternoon sunlight. She had done him proud. Richard drove him down to

Smith's Lawn — how apt I thought — where the presentation and dressage were to be held and I followed in the Land Cruiser, having discovered I could drive perfectly well despite my hip. Herbie got my wheelchair out at the other end and I sat patiently in it until it was time to go in.

I had had a last minute tussle with Richard the night before when he had suddenly developed grave misgivings about me going in the trap. What if there was an emergency? What if the horse bolted? How could I get out quickly? It wasn't safe. It was too risky. His objection firmly, though perhaps not happily, over-ruled, I sat feeling a bit of a twit in my large straw hat in my wheelchair. Then Griff and Herbie somehow man-handled me one-legged up beside Richard and we were off. The presentation went well. The judges said very little, but I knew it had gone well and then we went in the dressage arena.

I had rehearsed this moment many times lying in hospital and it was one of those rare occasions in life when reality turned out to be even more lovely than the dream. It was a perfect late autumn afternoon, warm, calm and faintly misty, and Bear covered the hallowed turf of the Guards' Polo Club with beauty and precision. His test was accurate and full of impulsion and sitting next to Richard as Bear trotted rhythmically and gracefully around the arena, I thought I would burst with pride and happiness. It had all been worth it just to experience this.

Richard halted Bear, saluted to the judges and left the arena. I hugged his arm.

'Oh, that was a lovely test, really lovely. I'd forgotten just how good he can be.'

'Just needs a good driver, that's all,' Richard teased.

In the collecting ring Herbie came up wreathed in smiles.

'That's the best I've seen him do yet. Clever lad,' she crooned, patting him.

We all indulged in an orgy of self-congratulation.

'Come on,' Richard said suddenly, 'I want you out of here. I'll not feel happy till you're back in that chair.'

'Richard, I'm fine,' I protested. I had no desire for my lovely drive to come to a premature end.

'No, out you come. Herbie, come round and help her down.'

Herbie left her customary position at Bear's head and came round to me. It had been tricky enough getting in but suddenly I discovered I just couldn't manoeuvre myself into a position where I could get down on one leg, even with help from Herbie. Richard grew more concerned. He got down from the trap and came round to the back to help Herbie lift me down.

It registered mechanically in my brain that Bear was standing there quietly all on his own, that no one was holding him. That there was a golden rule somewhere about that. But he seemed quite happy. Then I was concentrating on getting into my wheelchair and enjoying letting Herbie and Richard fuss over me. Enjoying it too much to notice the lorry draw up beside Bear, concentrating elsewhere than on the show jumps the men were hauling to the side of the lorry. The words were forming in my brain; the instruction ready to shout 'Herbie, for Christ's sake, grab Bear!'

But it was too late.

The large wooden multi-coloured jump reached the side of the lorry, toppled and hit the ground with a sickening clatter. Richard and Herbie simultaneously dived for the Bear.

But it was too late.

Eyeballs whirling in panic, Bear whipped round, knocking Richard off balance with the trap as he did so, and leapt forward. Feeling no pressure on the reins, no restraint, no reassurance, in two strides he was galloping. Galloping straight for the exit to the collecting ring.

My warning died, impotent, in a strangled gasp. Richard was on his feet and running after the trap but he never stood a chance of catching it. People yelled and squealed in panic, waved their arms and scrambled out of the way. This only had the effect of making Bear accelerate further. The entrance of the ring was narrow and he wasn't heading straight for it. To the side of the entrance a little car was parked. Whether in a desperate attempt to correct his course, or to shake off the rattling, uncontrolled vehicle behind him, he suddenly veered sharply to one side. One wheel of the cart hit the front of the car; it rolled up the bonnet, through the windscreen and over the roof. At this point gravity took over and the entire vehicle overturned. Amidst a tangle of broken leather and wood, the wreckage was still firmly attached to poor Bear who, absolutely terrified by the dragging, flapping mass behind him, now headed over the beautiful level turf of the Polo field at a desperate gallop, the wreckage gouging great holes and grooves in the grass as he went. A couple of cars were now in pursuit and one took a wide loop to detour and head him off.

I watched the entire scene from my wheelchair in complete silence. The noise, the confusion and the pursuing figures receded into the misty light.

I closed my eyes for a few moments and they were all gone. Nothing spoiled the quiet beauty of that English evening.

Nothing could possibly have gone wrong in such perfect surroundings. I held stubbornly on to that thought. The horrific images had been so unexpected and over so quickly, they had never really happened. Yes, that was it, it had never really happened. It was a fleeting daytime bad dream, the sort of thing I'd been afflicted with in hospital; scenes of Bear hopelessly trapped in a bottomless cesspit, his eyes pleading for help. Monstrous black horses getting bigger and bigger, filling the whole of the sky just before the sky began to fall. But it was all right now. I'd woken up. Any moment, Richard would drive up and put me in the trap to go back.

I became aware of Herbie desperately shaking my arm, clawing at my hand and sobbing, 'Oh God, no, no. Do you think I should get a doctor? She won't speak to me, she hasn't made a sound since he bolted. She's just come out of hospital herself, you know. Carol, please talk to me, say something!' Her voice was rising to hysteria.

My eyes focused and my brain cleared. Reality returned like a lead weight.

'I'm fine, Herbie. Shush, shush, I'm fine.'

She put her head on my lap in the wheelchair and cried, but gradually calmed. She raised her swollen eyes to mine,

'Why?' she demanded angrily. 'Why? Why!'

'Because we broke the rules. You were both more concerned with me than the horse. Richard was right, I had no place in that vehicle.'

On the horizon a mass began to form and to draw nearer to us. I strained my eyes and soon could distinguish separate shapes. There was a car, some people and . . . a man leading a horse! My heart began to race. Oh thank God, thank God. Whatever else there was to face, there were no broken limbs. I longed to rush up and meet them, to lessen the waiting, and I cursed the wheels that held me fast where I was. Torn between caring for me and getting to Bear, Herbie was in a dreadful state. I sent her off to meet them and she loped clumsily across the field.

'That poor girl's back must be really bad,' I thought yet again.

First to draw up was a Land Rover with a trailer behind. On the trailer lay the corpse of my good trap. Its mangled and broken body was almost beyond recognition. The shafts were broken, the seat and wings just splintered stumps and somewhere amongst the assorted pieces of wreckage lay two battered and flattened pieces of bright metal. They had been Richard's best carriage lamps. Tears scalded my eyes and rolled down my cheeks. I had been so proud of that trap. Obsessively proud. It had represented months of effort, of searching the country to find parts to make it a whole, and now it lay there like so much fire wood. It would have been very easy to give way then but I found the strength from somewhere.

'It's only wood and metal,' I told myself. 'Very special wood and metal, but it can be replaced. It's not flesh and blood; what if it had been Bear lying on that trailer?' That thought shook me so much I wrenched my eyes from the wreckage and saw Richard, Bear and another figure approach. The figure was familiar; it was George Bowman. Richard and he were holding Bear, one on each side, both soothing him. They halted beside the trailer and Bear seemed to view the wreckage with as much horror as I had. He was drenched in sweat and trembling gently now and then. From a very dry throat I managed to get far as 'How . . . ?'

'He's OK,' Richard was grim-faced, 'but he's had a hell of a fright. If George here hadn't headed him off and got him stopped when he did, God knows where he would have ended up. He's got a few cuts and bruises about the legs where the trap's been hitting him but, miraculously, there seems to be little other damage.'

Other carriages and traps on their way to presentation were driving carefully past us, asking anxious questions as to our welfare. With every vehicle that came up behind Bear, as soon as he heard the wheels, his eyes rolled and he took a great leap forward then stood there trembling.

'I'll tell you what,' George said to Richard, 'this horse has had one hell of a fright; about as much as he can take I should say. He'll be one to watch from here on, I'm afraid. You'll be lucky if you can ever trust him again. I've had it happen to me a time or two. They're never the same, never the same.'

My spirits which had raised a little at the sight of Bear intact now sank again to new depths. Never the same? Bear? Never the same? Surely not. He'd had a fright, an awful fright. But he'd survived far worse, he'd survived the slurry tank — surely he would get over this.

People were now gathering round chatting, offering advice, offering help. The evening had begun to turn chill and in my silky blouse and straw hat I began to shiver. How much of the trembling was cold and how much shock I didn't know but I felt very weak. The Land Rover set away with the wreckage to take it back to our camp and Herbie stripped Bear of the broken remains of his harness and put a rug over him against the evening chill. Oh my harness, my beautiful, beautiful harness.

Bear seemed a little quieter now. Not relaxed, just exhausted and drained of all emotion. Herbie put a head collar and lead on him, and led him quietly away.

'Come on,' said a familiar and concerned voice behind me. 'You look like death and half-frozen too. You're not driving yourself back in that state.'

Richard began wheeling my chair back towards the Land Cruiser.

'Oh Richard, I . . . '

'Shush. Not a word; what's done is done. It could have been worse.'

'But if I . . . '

'I don't want a word out of you. I just want you back in that caravan and a nice cup of tea into you. You'll feel better for that.'

'Oh yes. I'm sure I'll feel great. And what about Bear? What are we going to do with him? Give him a nice cup of tea too?'

'No' said Richard, graciously ignoring my sarcasm. 'I'm going to put the work harness on and drive him out in the other trap.'

'You're what! But you can't; he's exhausted, he's terrified.'

'Carol,' Richard said with cold firmness, 'if that horse doesn't drive tonight, he may never drive again.'

The atmosphere inside the caravan that night was awful. Between them Richard, Griff and Herbie had indeed managed to get Bear harnessed into the trap and for a drive. Well, not so much a drive, Richard had admitted grimly later, as a controlled bolt. The big question was, what to do the next day. What would be best for Bear? Just to pack up and go home and rest him quietly or to compete? There was nothing stopping us from competing. There had been no error made in the competition ring. In fact the latest ironic twist on the thumbscrew of life had placed us well in the lead of the class after his super dressage test.

We picked morosely at what would otherwise have been a celebration meal and weighed up the pros and cons. There was no physical damage to Bear. The vet had examined his few minor bumps and bruises and pronounced him perfectly fit. Physically, that was. What would be the best for him mentally? We decided to go for it. A good long drive might just exorcise the willies from him and if he did well, if he sensed our elation and rising spirits, he might respond in the same way. He usually did.

None of us slept well that night, but it passed all too quickly and suddenly there we were at the start of the marathon. I sat in the Land Cruiser watching anxiously as Richard drove Bear round and round in circles. There was no question of him standing still at the start line, there was no question of Bear standing still at all. Already his coat was breaking out in dark, damp patches and even at some distance from him I could see the tension wrinkles where his neck joined his withers. Restless and anxious, he milled round and round. The official starter called two minutes, then one minute, then called Richard to come up to the line.

'I'll start from back here,' Richard shouted back.

'Ten, nine, eight . . . ' The familiar countdown proceeded. 'Three, two, one — away!'

But Bear was already powering down the road out of sight, Griff hanging determinedly on the back of the trap.

I looked at Herbie, 'What now? It's going to be a long two hours. Do you want to watch him through the hazards?'

'Do you?'

'No, but I feel we should.'

'So do I.'

'It's not quite turned out the way we expected has it?' I said.

'Does it ever with you?'

She had my wheelchair beautifully positioned at the notorious sand quarry so I could get a perfect view. Trouble was, I didn't know if I could bear to watch.

The tannoy system announced the next competitor would be Richard Smith driving Conwy Blaze and the adrenalin began to pump. Suddenly he was there, plummeting over the edge of the sandy bank, so completely wet with sweat he appeared almost bay rather than chestnut. But he was powering on, responding to Richard at the right moments, going in the right direction. There was a flurry of applause and he was gone.

'Well, he looked fine,' Herbie said encouragingly.

'I don't know,' I replied dubiously. 'There was something not quite right, not quite Bear.'

'How do you mean?'

'Well, he was — oh, it's hard to find the right words. He never looked at that hazard, he was oblivious to it all. He was just going on mechanically. Yes that's it — mechanically; like a toy that's been wound up and it's just going to keep on running until it either hits something or runs down. His body drove that hazard but God knows where his mind was.'

'Let's get back,' said Herbie, pushing me firmly towards the car.

In the afternoon the scores were posted and Richard, smiling for the first time in two days, informed me that we were not only in the lead but with such a good lead he could afford to have four cones down the next day and still win.

'So, sweetheart, if the old boy can just keep his cool for a few minutes in that arena tomorrow, he will be National Champion, despite everything that's happened. And then he can have a good long rest and get over all this. By God, I hope he does it, I really hope he does. If ever a horse deserved it — he does.'

'You deserve it too! Look at the work you've put in with him and all you've been through this summer just to get him here. Oh Richard,' I was beaming now, 'I dreamed of this all those weeks in hospital. Well, I hadn't dreamed of it happening the way it has but it's what we need. It's what we all need — some good news for a change.'

We poured ourselves a glass of wine that we'd been saving for a special occasion and settled ourselves down in the caravan for a welcome few quiet minutes together. There had been precious few of those in the last couple of months. Precious few in our entire relationship, come to think of it.

'You know,' Richard said, putting his arm around me, 'all this will pass.' He gestured with his free hand at the wrecked trap and my wheelchair parked outside the caravan. 'Because what we've got is unique. Well, there's us for a start — we've got to be a pretty unique pair.'

The wine, after all the tension, had gone straight to my head and I giggled in my glass.

'Then that horse; I know you think he's special, but you're too besotted with him to see the truth. He is special; very, very special. He's got guts, intelligence, stamina and presence — he's got it all. Oh, I wish I had another one like him. Another one like him and I tell you we could beat the world. Do you realise that? Beat the world!'

There was a discreet knock on the caravan door. 'That'll be Herbie,' I said. 'Ask her in to join us for a drink. It's as much her moment of glory as ours.'

Richard squeezed past me and opened the door.

'Mr Smith? Richard Smith?'

'Yes.'

'Look, I'm sorry to be the muggins to have to tell you this,' the little man looked very uncomfortable, 'I've just come from the Course Stewards' Meeting. I'm afraid you've been eliminated. You missed going round a white flag on Section E. You're not the only one — it caught several people out. Damn shame when you were doing so well. Look, I can show you where it was on the course map if you want.'

'No. No, thank you. I'll take your word for it,' said Richard and quietly closed the door.

We withdrew Bear next morning and packed for home. Perhaps we shouldn't; perhaps it would have been more sporting to drive the cones and appear at the tail end of the final parade, but we just didn't have the heart.

Herbie insisted on riding Bear out just to make sure he had no stiffness in him after the marathon before his long journey home. She looked quite desperate when she got back, white and shaking. She said it was her back hurting her again but even so she insisted on lugging most of the harness boxes and bales into the horsebox. It was as if she was seeking total exhaustion as an anaesthetic against the events of the weekend. I envied her in a way, as I could only drag myself clumsily around the caravan and watch the preparations to leave. Very little was said by any of us as we pulled out in the late morning.

The long journey home was so different from the journey down. Our hopes and dreams were as bruised and battered as the trap, the harness and poor Bear. We stopped only once to eat on the motorway. Herbie would have nothing, she said she felt sick. Poor lass, of us all it seemed to have hit her the hardest; she looked dreadful.

We arrived back about seven at night and unloaded Bear into his stable. At least he seemed to have travelled all right.

'Right,' said Richard, 'we do no more this night. We can sort out the rest tomorrow. Herbie, you go on up home and I want you to have a hot bath and an early night, do you hear? And tomorrow, I don't want to see you before about ten o'clock. I'll come down and feed and water Bear.'

She nodded miserably, gave Bear a last pat and set away slowly up the hill.

By eleven o'clock the next morning she had not appeared. Richard had seen to Bear early on and then organised me for the day but he was anxious to get off to the shop and sort out whatever problems might await him there. He decided he'd better go down and find out what was going on.

When he returned some twenty minutes later he looked even more ashen and shaken than Herbie had the night before.

'Richard, whatever is the matter?'

'Are you ready for this?'

'Dear Lord, not more bad news. I don't think I can stand much more at present.'

'Her sister informed me she's in hospital. I asked if she had had an accident and she said no, she had had a baby boy. About midnight last night.'

'Oh, my God!'

All the pieces, all the clues fell into place: the sickness at events earlier in the year, the baggy clothes and big jumpers even in hot weather, the obsession with fishpaste sandwiches. The poor kid, the poor, frightened kid.

'Why on earth didn't she tell us?' I finally managed to say.

Richard sat down by the fire very wearily, 'She didn't tell anyone, not a soul. Not even her mother. She didn't really admit it to herself and then it wasn't going to happen. Just put it completely out of her mind. It's what they call a 'concealed pregnancy' apparently.'

'But the risks she has taken. Do you realise she rode for an hour just yesterday? And the stuff she carried and humped, all the mucking out she's done. She's had no ante-natal care, no dietary supplement, no preparation. Nothing! She could have seriously damaged herself and the baby.' I was horrified at the thought of all that could have gone wrong.

'Apparently,' said Richard smiling faintly, 'she had a rapid, uncomplicated delivery and has a healthy, bouncing baby boy. Just shows how wondrous Mother Nature is.'

'But why,' I insisted 'why didn't she tell us, or anyone, or at least her mother?'

'Well, she became pregnant in the same month that her father died. The baby's father is some unemployed yob in his late twenties. She felt she didn't dare tell the family, especially her mother who was in such a bad way after the death. But in the event the mother, now she's over the shock of last night, is delighted and feels that the baby has been sent in some way to replace the father. They're going to call him Clifford after the father and there's no question of Herbie being turned out on the streets or anything. In fact, with a family her size, they'll probably spoil them both rotten. She'll be OK.' He patted my hand encouragingly.

Still numb with disbelief at this latest turn in events I sat in my wheelchair by the fire cradling the cup of tea Richard had made me. After a while, concern and alarm for Herbie's well-being were replaced with more selfish thoughts.

'What's going to happen to Bear?'

'How do you mean?'

'Without Herbie. I'm useless, you're at work and Bear's penned up in a stable. We've no land, Richard; not a square foot to turn him out on. Now there's no one to exercise him during the day, no one to take him out for an hour or so's grazing, no one to muck out. What's going to happen to him?'

Richard's carefully composed cheerfulness had slipped.

'I don't know, sweetheart, I just don't know. I do have friends with fields but not in this part of the world. We may have to send him away for a while, that's all. But not today; I can't handle that one today. Look,' he got up slowly, 'I don't want to leave you; I can see you're upset but I've got to get in and see what's been happening at work. I'll try and get back early and I'll bring Griff with me and we'll get the horsebox unloaded and I'll take Bear for a walk.'

After he'd gone I just sat there a long while and took stock. It was not encouraging; in fact the outlook was totally black. I was in the middle of a divorce, financially insecure, disabled and immobile. I had a three-year-old daughter whom I'd been parted from for most of two months. During a few brief and unpleasant communications between coming out of hospital and leaving for Windsor, it had been made abundantly clear that Ian no longer considered me fit to care for Megan full time. 'Physically and mentally incapacitated', I think was the phrase in the lawyer's letter. In short, I had the very thing I had dreaded most on my hands — an all-out custody battle. Until the date and place for that was fixed I was to have Megan for only half the time. I was 'involved' — what a dreadful word that was, 'involved' — with a man I hadn't known six months ago, who was fifteen years older than myself and who had just lost his business and all his personal possessions in a fire. My aspirations for my horse's success, my pride and joy that had sustained me through so many weeks of despair, had dwindled into a pile of wreckage and an unhappy animal without a stable or field to call his own. So much for independence, so much for a new beginning. So much for my better way.

The misery of the last few days swept over me. I gripped the arms of my wheelchair and cursed the unfairness of it all. I swore at the empty air of the little cottage until it turned blue and then subsided into helpless sobbing. I was so completely engrossed in my misery that I never heard the back door open, nor anyone enter the kitchen, till a voice behind said, 'You'll feel better for that, gettin' it off yer chest like. Aa came up to see if Aa could do owt.'

Deeply embarrassed and still snuffling, I turned the chair to find a small, wiry lady with rosy cheeks in the kitchen door. She looked vaguely familiar.

'I'm sorry, I don't seem to . . . '

'Janice, Janice Witton. We've met in the Post Office and chatted about hosses — Aa keep the ponies in the field behind the stable you rent. Aa live down the bank next door to the Herbert family. Ther's trouble on there, but Aa 'spect you know ba now. Aa know Carol Herbert well — know she looks after yer hoss, like, and she told me about yer accident an' so on. So Aa guessed you'd be stuck now wi'out her like.'

I was so taken aback by her unexpected appearance it had effectively put the finger in the dam of my outburst.

'You must forgive me. I don't usually, well, carry on like that. It's just that you're quite right — I am stuck, I don't know what the hell to do. Everything, and I mean everything, has gone wrong these last few months.'

'Oh, don't apologise. Best out, that's what Aa say.'

'Would you like a cup of tea?' I was suddenly aware of social proprieties.

'That'd be luvely,' she said beaming from one rosy cheek to the other.

In fact she stayed well into the afternoon and organised us both a bit of lunch. There seemed to be nothing or nobody in the village that she didn't know about. My first impression was that she was the most down-to-earth, practical and realistic person I had ever met. It was to prove an accurate assessment. She had a husband and three children all approaching their teens, several dogs and cats, a large house in constant need of attention, a small motor bike and two ponies in a rented field. Her budget was exceedingly tight, she was always 'strapped' for cash and would do anything to earn an honest bob or two. She could muck out and I couldn't. She could empty ashes, fill coal and do other jobs in the house that were impossible for me. For a very modest sum she would do all these things, and anything else I required, five days a week. And the extra free bonus was she was great company, and that, if the truth were known, was what I needed more than anything. By the time she left, the clouds had rolled back a little and there was on the horizon a glimmer of light.

'Yes,' I thought as I peeled the spuds for an evening meal, 'after a disastrous start, the day is turning out better than I'd dared hope.' What I didn't know was that the day was not yet over.

True to his word, Richard arrived home by early teatime. I had made an enormous effort to pull myself together, cobbled together a passable evening meal and made myself presentable. My efforts were rewarded by the smile of relief on Richard's face when he came in.

'My word, you look smashing and something smells good. I was really worried about you when I left this morning.' His own haggard, worried expression had lifted and he was positively twinkling for the first time in many weeks.

'I've got some good news,' I said.

'So have I — I think,' he replied mysteriously.

'Go on then,' I urged.

'No, you first.'

'Well, I've found a pair of helping hands.' And I quickly filled him in on the providential appearance of Janice.

'That's marvellous. Truly marvellous. That should solve all our immediate problems beautifully. My news hasn't such immediate impact — it's more of a long-term plan if you like. Are you sure you're ready for this?' He seemed to falter in his resolve momentarily.

'Try me. I think I'm about ready for anything.'

'Right. Well, on the way to the shop I kept thinking about what you said about not having any land, not a foot of our own. I popped my nose in to the shop and there was not much doing. Too little really — but I shall set about that problem when I get this off my mind. So I went to see an acquaintance of mine, an estate agent, to see what he had on his books. You know, small country manor with a thousand acres, that sort of thing. No seriously, I asked him if they had anything, anything at all that had land, even an acre or two with it at a sensible price. And guess what?'

'Don't tell me!'

'There is a smallholding up for sale by a brewery, at a place called Stanley. It's a house with a range of outbuildings and ten acres of land and it's only six miles from here.'

'But it'll cost a fortune!'

'It's up for the highest offer. The brewery just wants rid. It's been rented to two old brothers who farmed it for years. I've been to have a look and, I'll be honest with you, it's in a hell of a state. In fact nobody in their right mind would buy it.'

'This conversation keeps occurring in my life.'

'But it's got land, real land, not a paddock. Ten acres of land. Think of how many horses you can keep on ten acres!'

'Richard, we only have one.'

'At the moment, at the moment. I haven't come to my second

bit of news yet.'

'Oh Lord.'

'After I'd been to Stanley, I realised we have a more immediate problem with Bear that can't wait till we get a place of
our own. So I went across to Lanchester to a horse dealer friend
of mine who has land over that way. It's a fair journey
away I admit, but I thought he might let us rent some grazing
over the winter. And guess what?' His face was alive with
excitement.

'You've tried me with that one already. I daren't imagine.'

'He's got a young cob. Oh Carol, what a lovely animal. Only
three, and just broken to ride but not to drive. A bonny, bright
chestnut, just like Bear with a white blaze and four white socks
too. If he had a flaxen mane and tail instead of chestnut he'd be
the spit of Bear. The very spit.'

If I hadn't been sitting down I would have had to do so as I
could never have supported myself on one leg.

'And?'

'And he's not daft money. Enough, but not daft for what he is
or what he is going to be. God, what a match and right on our
doorstep. What a pair of horses!'

'Pair of horses!' My face was registering genuine alarm now.
'Pair of horses! Richard, what on earth do we want with a pair of
horses? We can't even provide for Bear at present. Look at the
state I'm in, and we've practically no income coming in. And
smallholdings? And derelict houses? Where's the money
coming from?'

'From you.'

At least he looked me straight in the eye when he said it.

'Me?' I could barely gasp.

'You said the other day that your financial affairs are practically sorted now. What do you intend doing with that little sum
of money after the divorce when you get it?'

'Well, I, er, well, I've the future to think of. The future for
Megan and I, a home to provide and God . . . well I hadn't really
thought about it yet.'

'Don't I figure in that future? Or Bear? Have you considered
how you're going to support your talented, marvellous horse in
the style to which he is accustomed?'

'Not really,' I answered lamely.

'Well, it's time you did, and it's time we did.'

'I don't want to hear about the future; the present is difficult
enough.'

'But don't you see, sweetheart, if we don't look to the future we'll be stuck in this present for ever? In a rented cottage that isn't yours and isn't mine and is costing a lot of money weekly but isn't an investment. It won't get us anywhere. And you've nowhere for your horse.'

'Richard. I'm afraid, that's all, afraid of making commitments at present, of making new bonds that I might have to painfully undo again. How can I think of my future, of starting a new life, when I don't even know how I'm going to cope when I get out of this thing?' I slapped the arms of my wheelchair angrily.

'I'm willing to take the risk if you are. I know I'm not the world's greatest catch. I've got no capital of my own but if you put your capital into this venture I shall contribute our income and the manpower to rebuild the place providing the materials as and when we can afford them. If personal commitments frighten you, don't think of it as a personal commitment — think of it as a business venture. Partners in a business venture.'

'What sort of venture?' I was still suspicious.

'Well, the place is called, of all things Mount Pleasant Farm, so how about "Mount Pleasant Carriage Driving Centre"? And it'll become the centre of excellence for Competition Carriage Driving for the whole of the north of England!'

'Richard, you've flipped.' But I couldn't help giggling. 'You've really, finally flipped!'

He leant across and held my hand tightly. 'We can do it, sweetheart. I promise you we can do it. After all we've been through separately and together we've got to fight back, got to get what we want out of life. You want a home and security for you and your daughter; we'll get it. You want honour and glory for that horse of yours; we'll get it — and a whole lot more. I promise you.'

He meant it, I could see he really meant it.

The rollercoaster of my life was ploughing on again, away from all my carefully considered plans, all the carefully constructed paths I'd thought to travel. So why not? What the hell? None of those plans had come to any sort of fruition and caution wasn't going to change the present situation. I took a deep breath: 'I'll go and have a look at the place in the morning.'

'And the young horse?' His eyes were glowing with hope.

'In the afternoon.'

He would have made a good estate agent, would Richard. He had the right, sneaky, tactical approach. It was a lovely, late autumn morn; just enough mist around to give a hazy edge to not very pretty sites. Then of course he approached the place from its 'best side' — from the back where the land was, not from the street at the front where the house was. Helping me down out of the Land Cruiser, he handed me my crutches and helped me hop across the verge. He put his jacket on the grass and we sat down and gazed across a couple of badly drained, badly fenced, badly over-grown fields.

'You see,' he enthused, 'the place hasn't been managed properly for years; that's why it's so cheap! Just look at the space though. Where else are we going to get a chance to buy this amount of land at a price we can afford? Don't look at it as it is now — look ahead, think of the future. Just imagine this field populated by a herd of chestnut Welsh cobs!'

It was a lovely morning, still and warm. The upset and worry of the last week gave way for the first time to the pleasure of being out in the fresh air together with time on our hands. Little did I know how exceptional the climatic conditions at Stanley were that day. It was as if the place was showing itself to its best advantage in a desperate attempt to gain my attention and approval.

I'm sure Richard waited for the exact moment when he sensed I had drunk in sufficient of the pleasant, calming scene to lower my defences a little. Then he drove round to the front of the property.

I wasn't so far gone as not to get a terrific jolt. There was a relentless row of red brick, grey-roofed terraced houses. They opened directly on to the road that ran between them without a windowbox or blade of grass, let alone a garden. It was tarmac wall-to-wall and punctuated right down the street with disproportionately large telegraph poles festooned with electrical conductors and wiring and large orange street lights. That's all there was, that one long grey and black street, and it was quite the ugliest, the most desperate-looking place I had ever set my eyes on. It had been briefly a flourishing Durham pit village but the pit and that prosperity had long since gone. Nothing appeared to have moved in to take its place. At the far end of the street the road widened to allow the buses to turn round and to accommodate what must surely have been the uncontested winner of the most vandalised, graffiti-covered bus shelter in the country.

Behind this stood a long, narrow, very neglected terraced house. Well, it had been a terraced house but the houses to one side had all been pulled down and an alley separated it from its neighbour to the other side, a rather desperate-looking pub.

From the ruinous byre Richard built a stable

. . . and together, from dereliction, we've made a home

The start of our dream. In the back streets of Stanley Crook, Bear and Blizzard are put together for the first time as a pair

. . . and now look at them

Our wedding

Pride at Brighton — second place in the Horse Driving Trials

Disaster at Kelso — the Boys career past the castle at a flat-out gallop having deposited both Richard and the referee on the ground

Ken Ettridge

Behind the house could just be seen the collapsing wood and tin shapes of some outbuildings.

'Don't tell me, that's Mount Pleasant Farm?'

'In a word, yes.'

'I think we'd better go back.'

'But you haven't even looked yet!'

'Richard, there is no way, no way at all that I could live in this . . . this place. I'm sorry.'

'You can't say that, not without looking!'

'Oh, yes, I can.'

'You're bigger than that.'

He was, as I say, very sneaky.

I allowed myself to be propelled down the alley between the house and the pub. Richard produced the key he'd procured the day before and unlocked a peeling, rotting back door. It was not actually one house, it was two. Or to be perfectly accurate a house and a cottage, joined at ground floor but not first floor level. The house was a typical two-up, two-down terraced house, characterless and damp, dismal and unbelievably depressing. The roof had been leaking long enough for the two upstairs bedrooms to have been abandoned long since in a rubble of crumbling plaster. But the house was structurally sound and I had had sufficient dealings with properties described as 'in need of renovation' to know how relatively easily it could be transformed.

Richard seemed far more reluctant to take me into what had once been the cottage at the back. It was old, truly old, probably pre-dating the house by a hundred or so years. And it had been abandoned for the last seventy. There were only two rooms, one up, one down, connected by a ladder rather than a staircase. The red pantile roof had mostly fallen into the upstairs room, the floor of which was so bad you could stand downstairs and see the sky. At the furthest end of the stone-flagged room the sandstone lintels of a fire place stood surrounding a place where presumably there had once been an iron range, long since pulled out. But here was the remains of the heart of the little cottage. The stone lintels were flanked on either side by little wooden cupboards, recessed in the wall, the pine weathered and silvered with age. The hearthstones were still just visible in the rubble. Three small windows opening into the alley allowed a diffused light into the room. Half closing my eyes, I could imagine the range burning there, the kettle on the hearthstone and there would have been a wooden chair in that corner by the fire. Yes, someone had sat for many an hour in just that spot, in the comfort of the fire. It was very old and very peaceful. Richard came crunching over the rubble and stood behind me.

'Perhaps you're right, perhaps I got carried away. It's in a hell of a state, far too much for us to take on, particularly with you as you are. I'm sorry, I shouldn't have even brought you. Of course you can't live in a place like this.' He turned and walked away slowly.

'But I like it! Well, not the place, it's awful and the house is pretty depressing. But this part, this cottage; can't you feel how peaceful it is? I always judge a house by its vibes. Yes, I could be happy in here.'

'If I live to be a hundred,' muttered Richard, 'I will never, never understand women.'

I was given a quick tour of the outbuildings before we left. I use the term loosely. A more miserable collection of collapsing timbers and tin sheets I had rarely seen. None of them was usable though the most promising was a long ten-stall cow byre. The wooden superstructure was collapsing but the floor, partitions and half walls were of brick and quite sound despite being under eighteen inches of accumulated cow muck.

Fortified by a pub lunch on the way, at which I foiled Richard's attempt to get me slightly tiddly, we arrived at the horse-dealer's establishment.

'I shall not be rushed into anything,' I decided firmly. 'I've been very lucky once with a horse bought on impulse. This time I've got to be critical and unemotional.'

Mr Plummer led the way along the front of some loose boxes and, despite my every attempt to appear blasé, my wretched adrenalin let me down as always. Before we even got to the box a large friendly chestnut head with a mop of a mane was stuck out of the door. The mane was chestnut and the blaze down his nose a good deal wider but somewhere I'd seen that expression, that hopeful, outgoing youthful expression before. Oh dear.

'Steady, get control of yourself!' an internal voice warned.

Naïve though I still was in the company of hardened horse-dealers, I had enough sense not quite to believe all the marvellous qualities Mr Plummer was attributing to his merchandise.

'Aa tell ye. He's the best young hoss, the best hoss Aa've ever had thru me hands. Aa'm loathe ter part with 'im, e's a champion.'

Close at my elbow in case my crutches slipped in the straw, Richard whispered, 'He says that about every horse he ever sells. Mind you, I've bought a few from him and I'll say this much: he's never sold me a wrong 'un.'

Mr Plummer led the creature out on to the yard.

'Can we see him more, Bill? Can you put him on the lunge?'

'Ee, Aa dowt he's dun anything like that, he's only a bairn, only a bairn. Barely backed to ride really.'

'Well, find me a length of rope and a whip and I'll have a go.'

Mr Plummer grunted and waddled off in search of a rope. The young horse watched the proceedings with great interest, never fidgeting on the end of the halter rope Richard held. I took a step towards him and he lowered his muzzle hopefully.

I scratched his nose and he responded ecstatically, nudging me for more, nearly knocking me off balance.

'Well, he's friendly enough,' I conceded.

'He's a pet,' said Richard.

Mr Plummer returned and the lunging began. Well, it wasn't exactly lunging; lunging is supposed to take place in a smooth circular motion around the person holding the rope. This movement was more octagonal than circular. Thinking he was free the horse would trot a few yards in a straight line, then feel the tug of the tope and twist round before setting off again at a slightly different angle. On several occasions he got his legs so tangled up he nearly over-balanced. Where had I seen that before? The lack of co-ordination, the look of mild surprise as previously unknown muscles were put to work? Seven years ago, a summer evening. A young horse doing his very best to progress in a straight line. I felt a familiar pang. Oh dear, oh dear.

'Steady!' I said to myself, I must be objective. Of course the animal wasn't moving fluently so it was difficult to tell. He was similar to Bear and yet different somehow. For a start he was much more powerfully built; Bear had certainly never had stocky hindquarters or a neck like that when he was just rising four. And his stride, it was shorter, the action different — flatter, choppier. But he was a baby, he'd had no schooling; time and experience could change all that.

'How's he bred?' I enquired of Mr Plummer. My knowledge of Welsh cob breed lines was about as extensive as the language but it sounded the sort of thing I should be asking as a prospective buyer.

'Aa haven't a clue,' he answered, 'he's there as he stands. He's either right for yer or he's not.'

'But he is a Welsh cob?'

'Does he look like a Welsh cob?'

'Well, yes,' I stammered, 'he does, that is I think he does. What about his papers?'

'What papers?'

'Registration papers?' I gritted my teeth hopefully.

'Oh, I've nowt like that. Would they make him a different horse, like? A better animal?'

'No . . . but!' My God! I was buying a mongrel!

'Well, there you are then, there you are,' Mr Plummer grunted, his case fully proven. Richard was leading the horse back to the gate. The young horse looked exhilarated by the exercise, his bright, friendly eyes gleaming.

'Well?' asked Richard hopefully, 'What do you think?'

'I think he's very nice,' I answered truthfully, 'but,' I tried to whisper through clenched teeth, 'he's got no papers!'

'Oh, I know that!' answered Richard cheerfully.

'You do?'

'Look. If you want a horse for driving in a pair you trust your eyes and your heart. Does he match well enough, does he move right, does he have the right temperament, does he feel right? Bits of paper only put the price up but don't do anything for the horse.'

Mr Plummer smugly folded his hands as if to say 'I told you so'.

'Do we buy him or not? It's up to you, it's your money, it's your horse.'

I knew the asking price and felt quite alarmed at laying out such an amount of money for a young, unknown animal. A pious voice was telling me I had much more important priorities to think of, like a roof and food. I knew there was no haggling to be done, Richard had already done it. The price was down to £800 for cash. My mind reeled. Good driving horses, I was lectured repeatedly, were like gold, and a sound investment.

'I do like him and I'll certainly consider it carefully. When do you need to know?' Gosh, that sounded very 'woman-of-the-worldish'.

'Now.'

'Now!' Hang on, I'd heard this conversation before. How had it gone?

'I've got him and three others ready to take away to the sales tomorrow,' said Mr Plummer. 'It's no skin off my nose. If you don't want him, there's plenty others that will.'

Richard said nothing to persuade me, nothing to push me. He just stood there quietly holding the horse who was breathing gently down his ear and sucking the collar of his coat. But Richard's eyes were pleading, 'Trust me, trust me. He's right, I know he's right and I need him. I need something to replace all that's gone, all that's been lost. Something to work towards again.'

'If you want pound notes, Mr Plummer, we'd better go before the bank closes.' A pious voice inside me hissed, 'Idiot, now what have you done? Another mouth to feed, four more feet to shoe and where are you going to put him?'

'Oh shut up.'

10

'I'm a vet, not a psychiatrist'

SO NOW I have two horses I kept telling myself, somewhat stunned. Mr Plummer had said he would graze the young cob, and Bear too, over the winter if we wished. For a price, of course, and he was a fair distance away from the cottage so it wouldn't be simple to check on the horses every day. It wasn't an ideal solution but the best we had to date.

But I had a far more pressing concern that evening. I couldn't just keep referring to our new purchase as 'the young horse' or 'the new cob', he needed a name. Given, God willing, that he would be appearing in public some day in a pair, the name had to be chosen carefully. People tend to pair their horses' names as well as their appearances. The names had to be similiar enough to go together but different enough so the horses could tell them apart. I thumbed relentlessly through the dictionary. Bear, of course, always competed under his registered name of Conwy Blaze, so it had to go with Blaze. BL, BL, BL, my finger ran down the lines of words, and stopped abruptly when it came to Blizzard. 'Blaze and Blizzard'. Oh yes, that was most definitely it.

Late into the night, Richard and I discussed plans and dreamed dreams.

'What are our priorities for the next few months?' he asked.

'Where do you want me to start? Trying to buy Mount Pleasant Farm; trying to get off these crutches; then there are little things like our respective divorces and the custody battle for Megan and you've got to sort out the insurance from the fire and get yourself back into business properly again.'

'All that's going to happen anyway. That's just the background against which we live our lives at present. No, I mean priorities with the horses.'

'Of course, silly me,' I said, half-joking, though in the months and years to come I was to learn that there was only one priority

166

in life so far as Richard was concerned.

'We haven't got this new horse just to look at.'

'Blizzard,' I corrected him.

'Am I right in assuming that what we both want to do more than anything is to succeed in competition driving? You wanted me to drive Bear because you wanted him to achieve the highest honour, the best he could and — with respect — I've had a lot more experience than you. But my heart isn't in single driving, it's in the pairs class. And I want us to come out with a pair next year that'll set that class alight. Now I'll say this once, then it's off my chest. They're your horses, both of them. Once I start driving them together as a pair, where does that leave you? You wanted so desperately to drive F.E.I. and I can't see us ever affording to put a pair and a single on the circuit.'

I was amazed how easily and how honestly my answer came.

'You're right about how much I wanted to drive. But I've learnt a lot recently, and I know that it takes a lot more than the person at the reins to make a winner. You need the best you've got at the reins, that's true, and there's no question in my mind that that is you and always will be you. But you also need back-up, dedicated, well-organised back-up, to keep on top of all the training and work at home and to plan and pack for the events. And that, it would appear, is what *I* am best at. Right now, I can't say whether I'll ever ride or drive, but God willing I hope to do both again. I wouldn't like to think I would never be able to compete again. I'm still determined to do a full F.E.I. one day with Bear. But for the rest, no, let's combine our resources; your driving, my organising and exercising, Bear's talent and the new,' — I stopped myself, and gave him his name — '*Blizzard*'s promise, and let's see just how far we get together.'

It was a rosy picture.

'Very well,' said Richard, 'if that's what you really want, then we have to start right now.'

'But this season's only just finished,' I protested.

'Yes. But have you any idea how much work there will be to do if we want to put a pair together for next season? Have you any idea how quickly it would be upon us? Be brutally frank. What have we got? An unbroken, unknown youngster and an old hand who's had a very nasty experience and a hell of a shock. And we've lost our groom.'

'But we've found Janice,' I reminded him.

'Janice is a married woman with three kids. How much time is she going to be able to give? Now, if we want to start work with these horses we can't do it from a field over in Lanchester, and

Bear only has a single stable.'

'It had crossed my mind,' I said glumly.

'Well,' he said cautiously, 'I have a solution. Not an ideal one, but it's the best I can come up with at present.'

I looked up hopefully.

'At the back of my shop premises there are still the stables where I used to keep my horses. I say stables, but don't let your imagination run riot over pretty boxes and so on. It is a tin-roof-covered area with three sorts of corrals divided by metal railings and then there's a sort of lockable room where I used to keep harness and so on. It's pretty awful and very depressing. Very little light ever gets in as it's tucked away down a back alley. Actually, it used to be a slaughterhouse. You can see all the channels in the floor. That's why I was able to keep my horses there in the middle of town, even though the Council didn't like it; it had always housed animals. But as long as they get out every day for exercise it's not so bad and it's free and it's all we've got. Till we get Mount Pleasant, that is,' he finished encouragingly.

'Well, I suppose in some ways it's no worse than Bear being in a stable all day here on his own. At least he'll have company with the new horse.'

'Blizzard,' Richard chided.

'Sorry. The main problem is going to be travelling though, surely?'

'Well, it's not so far away. You would have to come over in the mornings with Janice and see to the mucking-out and grooming. I'd already be there at work and I'd have to work the young horse in the middle of the day with Janice. Then you can both get away in time for you to pick up Megan from the nursery school. I'll have to check round and feed before I leave work.'

'Well, it sounds as if it should work. When do you want to start?'

'Anything wrong with tomorrow?'

Actually it took a few days to accomplish the move. The rosy picture glazed over slightly when I first laid eyes on the damp, dripping, dingy area that was about to become my horses' home. It had been disused for many months and smelled and looked it. Janice, however, seemed undaunted by anything and set about with brush, shovel and barrow cleaning stalls and knocking down cobwebs. I cursed my crutches for the umpteenth time as they monopolised what *I* needed to use —

my hands. But I did manage to balance on one crutch and free a hand to clean the one smeary window in the building and to allow just a little more light in.

The next day we returned and sorted out the little room that was to become our harness, feed and tea-making room. Megan thought it was tremendous fun, and stomped around in her wellies. Richard arrived with a trailer-load of shavings and hay and feed and other bits and bobs. Once we got a bag of lovely clean aromatic shavings down in the two stalls, the place at least smelled a lot better and looked a lot cleaner.

Ever practical, Janice enquired, 'What do we do about muck? We can't have a midden in the back street, surely?'

'I'm not sure. Richard? What do we do with the muck?'

'Bag it.'

'Pardon?'

'Bag it into polythene sacks, then tie the neck with string, and once a week I take it away on the trailer. It's a hell of a nuisance but it's . . .'

'I know, it's the best we can do.'

We got the place if not pleasant at least ship-shape that day, and next morning Richard took the trailer over for Blizzard. He travelled very well for a baby, barely sweated up on the journey and having explored the confines of his 'corral' rolled ecstatically in the clean shavings.

'One down, one to go,' said Richard and went off for Bear with Janice.

I couldn't believe my eyes an hour later when the ramp went down. This wasn't Bear? Surely not my Bear who had so nonchalantly travelled hundreds of miles without ever making a fuss. He was dripping with sweat as he backed down the ramp, trembling in little ripples all over, his eyes rolling with fear. We put him quietly in his stall, threw a sweat sheet over him and he stood shaking and dejected in the corner. He didn't even look at his rack which we'd filled with good hay.

'Whatever is wrong?' I asked, genuinely alarmed.

'I don't know,' admitted Richard, 'he wasn't too keen on going in the trailer but did in the end. But every time we hit a rut in the road and the trailer rattled and bounced, you could hear him throwing himself around. I didn't dare stop; I thought I'd better just keep going and get him here. He'll probably settle soon. Just needs a bit of peace and quiet.'

Blizzard, who'd been attacking his hay with all the relish of youth ever since he arrived, suddenly seemed to become aware of the silent stranger in the stall beside him. He walked across and made small, friendly, encouraging noises but Bear totally ignored him.

'How about a cup of tea, then?' said Janice cheerfully, trying to ease the strain of the situation, 'I've got a brew on in the tack room.'

We were sitting sipping gratefully at our mugs when all hell broke loose. Richard flew out and started shouting, Janice followed and I brought up the rear. Bear had finally moved across to the rail that divided the stalls. No doubt Blizzard had continued to make friendly overtures, and Bear had responded by lunging and biting and squealing at him. Not in the way most horses do when they first meet — a short squeal of protest. This was for real. Like a snarling, snapping mongrel, he was lunging at poor Blizzard, ears flat, eyes blazing and teeth bared. Blizzard was yelping like a hurt puppy and then he backed off and retreated, baffled, to the far side of his stall where Bear could not reach him.

This was to be our pair? These were the horses that had to work together in total, united harmony of body and mind?

'They'll get used to each other,' said Richard optimistically.

They didn't get used to each other. It got worse. In the end Richard had to erect a solid partition between the stalls in order to give Blizzard some peace. Every time the poor creature moved towards the front of his stall Bear attacked him, and there was worse to follow.

Bear would not eat. He would pick half-heartedly at his hay rack for a few minutes occasionally but other than that, nothing. In a few days the effect was already showing. Within a week he began to look dreadful. Perhaps worst of all, he was completely unrideable. Janice tried several times to take him out and each time returned with a sweating, jittering horse.

'He jumps at every mortal thing,' she declared. 'Cars, people, dogs, trees, and when he runs out he jumps at nothing at all; I've ridden a few horses in my time but, Lord, it feels like sitting on a keg of dynamite with a slow fuse. I don't know about *his* nerves, but it ain't doing mine any good.'

Finally the day came when she returned home on foot, towing a lathered, dancing animal behind her. For a horrible moment I thought she'd been thrown but she shook her head sadly; all that was thrown in was the towel. She admitted defeat.

'I hate to tell you this, Carol, but he's dangerous. Really dangerous.'

And all I could do was to groom him and talk to him and stroke him, none of which he liked me doing any more. In fact he seemed positively to resent me. Instead of coming to greet me when I approached, he would turn his head miserably into the furthest corner of his stall. Instead of revelling in the sensation of the brush massaging his skin, he tensed with each stroke as if it was sending an alarm throughout his nervous system.

This went on for weeks. It so clouded my view of the world that I was oblivious to all the progress being made with Blizzard. He was behaving beautifully for Janice, going out completely fearlessly when she rode him in the busy town traffic and long-reining in harness with Richard every day. Another week or so, and he'd be ready to go in the cart Richard told me, in an effort to cheer me up.

With each morning a growing dread developed. Impossible though it seemed, Bear seemed to be growing visibly more emaciated. He was taken out by Richard for enforced exercise every day, walked down to a piece of common land nearby and allowed to stretch his legs and graze. But he wouldn't graze; it was as if his nervous system forbade him to relax and he had to rove relentlessly at the end of the rope.

One day in early December, Richard sent me ahead to the common with some harness and a tyre on a long rope.

'Perhaps,' he theorised, 'if we take Bear back to basics, back to square one like Blizzard, it might help him.'

Nothing could have been further from the truth. As soon as he felt the weight of the tyre behind him dragging on the ground, Bear completely panicked and tried to bolt. With enormous difficulty, Richard held on grimly and finally brought the trembling animal to a halt, his legs entwined in the ropes.

I sat in the car, horrified, watching the whole procedure, slow hot tears running down my cheeks. My horse, my wonderful, gifted, brave and fearless horse . . . This emaciated, trembling wreck . . . This couldn't go on, something had to be done.

Richard's vet of many years, Mr Peacock, was summoned. He examined Bear carefully and said he could find no physical cause. He did blood tests that only proved what superior haemoglobin Bear had. He gave him vitamin injections and, as a last resort, steroids. I plied Bear every day with tempting meals that surpassed those we got ourselves — full of Guinness and black treacle and raw eggs. Each evening Blizzard would guzzle the lot with relish.

Winter bit with a vengeance and it seemed all thing conspired

to bring me low. My pre-Christmas check-up with Miss
Robinson showed the hip joint still to be inflamed. She was
adamant that I spend at least another six weeks on crutches.

'You'll thank me for it in the long run,' she pronounced,
seeing my face sag at the news.

The custody hearing was to be in January. More than anything
I need to be off those damn crutches, otherwise who would
believe I was a competent mother? Blizzard was now driving out
daily with Richard. So what? What earthly use was that — what
use was anything when I had to suffer the anguish of daily
watching Bear fade before my eyes? And fading away in total
rejection of everyone and everything he had once loved.

Our offer was accepted on Mount Pleasant, my divorce
settlement money was through. It was nearly ours.

These things Richard constantly begged me to hold on to. But
it was no good. What use was a farm and land without Bear?
Where was the dream of fields dotted with Welsh cobs, if Bear
wasn't amongst them? What good was a family home, if I no
longer had a family? I became obsessed with the thought that
my long run of ill-fortune was going to go on for ever. I was
going to lose Bear, I was going to lose Megan. Maybe I was
going to lose my sanity.

Our first Christmas together came and went and needless to
say was not one I care to remember. In the New Year the snow
came, and huddled in his dark corner, with many rugs on to try
and warm his bony body, Bear stared blankly at the world. Mr
Peacock came yet again and I trembled all morning, dreading
hearing the words 'nothing else I can do . . . can't let him go on
like this . . . best put him out of his misery.'

In the event he shook his head and said, 'Well, he's got me
beat. There is nothing physically wrong with this animal. I'm
sorry, I'm a vet, not a psychiatrist.'

When he'd gone, I huddled into Bear's hairy neck and he
stood there, barely enduring my touch. What were we doing
wrong? Why wasn't he improving? He reminded me, he
reminded me . . . of course! The similarity hit me like a clear
beam of light — he reminded me of myself. I remembered
feeling the way he looked now — despairing and depressed,
rejecting all that was familiar and comforting, including food,
just wanting a dark hole to hide in. Feeling only fear, feeling
only hopelessness for the future. And what had wrought the
miracle for me? What had brought me back from the edge of that
bottomless pit? Two things; a change of surroundings, and a
good friend wise enough to give me a kick in the backside and

make me fight for survival again.

'Oh Bear, oh Bear,' I said out loud, 'I think I understand now and I think I know what to do.' I gave him a quick hug on the neck and hopped off to find Richard in the shop.

'Richard!' I said breathlessly.

'My goodness, that's the first time I've seen you smile in weeks. It's a welcome change, you look almost human.'

'Richard, listen, please. I know what's wrong with Bear!'

'Well, everyone else seems baffled.'

'He's had a nervous breakdown!'

'Oh, of all the ...'

'No, Richard, listen,' I pleaded, 'I'm not joking.' And I patiently explained, adding, 'And something else, this stable he's living in. He hates it. It frightens him. Didn't you say it had been a slaughterhouse?' Richard nodded. 'Well, don't you see, he knows that. I get vibes about old buildings, why shouldn't he? I think he thinks he's here waiting to die.'

'Carol, even if these theories of yours are correct, what do you propose doing about it?'

'It's so simple, so stupidly simple. Turn him out!'

'What! In this snow when he's been in since September? He's not hardened off. It'll kill him!'

'He's going to die, anyway, at the rate he's going. Don't you see! He'll either have to start and fight back or give in completely — and I don't think he'll do that. If he had a change of surroundings, fields to walk round, exercise to give him an appetite, some peace away from other horses, I'm sure he'd fight back. Bringing him here with Blizzard was the worst thing we could have possibly done. On top of the dreadful shock he's had, he's had to contend with an upstart youngster. He's not mad, he's mentally ill and my God there's a difference, a world of difference. I know — I've been there. Mental illness is like any other illness; given time and the correct conditions, a wound to the mind will heal like any other wound.'

My psychological theories were obviously too much for Richard who, ever practical, came back with, 'And where exactly do you intend putting him?'

'On our land. On Mount Pleasant Farm. Oh I know it's not strictly ours yet. But the offer's accepted, the deposit is paid and there's nothing else on it. Oh, Richard, say yes, please, it's his only chance.'

He thought quietly for a while. 'All right. But . . .' he warned, 'this is your decision, he is your horse. If we find him frozen solid in the snow then there's to be no recrimination. As you say, we've got to try something radical, and soon. Poor old lad, he's pitiful the way he is.'

So next day Richard led Bear out of his dark corner for the last time and set away up the long hill to Stanley. We had decided that to try and box him for a journey of only two miles would not be worth the distress it would cause him.

'I only hope he's got the strength to make it up that hill,' Janice muttered.

We followed in the Land Cruiser, taking a couple of bales of hay and a New Zealand rug. We got to the farm long before Richard and I was just beginning to panic that he hadn't made it when a very weary creature almost stumbled round the corner. Three months, three months, that's all it had taken to reduce a magnificent animal to this shambling wreck. Janice had stowed the bales of hay in a dry corner of the semi-derelict byre, but first she'd filled a hay net and attached it near to the gate into the field. Together we put his New Zealand rug on and Richard opened wide the gate. A large lump formed in my throat and I was suddenly seized with doubts. Was I doing the right thing? How could I turn him out into that white wilderness?

'Well, it's kill or cure, old son.' I patted him in a pathetic attempt to make light of the situation. But those two words rattled round my brain for hours. 'Kill or cure, kill or cure, kill or cure.'

11

'I'm just as scared as you are, Bear'

As IMPERCEPTIBLY AS the turn of the year and the slow lengthening of the days, I came gradually to realise we were making progress. Janice and I called in every day to see Bear and for the first few days I thought I'd done the wrong thing. Not a wisp, not a blade of hay disappeared from his net and there was no question of getting near Bear. He roamed restlessly and relentlessly around his large field, occasionally putting his head down to snuzzle in the snow but then, not trusting himself to be off his guard, he would take a quick nervous bite and be off. Sometimes he would canter round and round and round the field. Where he got the energy from in his weakened state, and on so little food, I was at a loss to know. I was convinced he would collapse with sheer exhaustion.

Two things stayed set fair, thank God; there was no more snow and his New Zealand rug stayed put — there would have been no question of catching him to adjust it. I tortured myself over what I had done, but at least he was moving and in the fresh air; anything was better that his utterly miserable immobility in that dark stable.

'Let him be,' said a voice inside me, 'let him be.'

And one day the hay net seemed flatter and the next day if definitely needed filling. From then on it was filled twice a day, once in the morning by Janice and once in the evening by Richard. Bear would not come up to the fence when we were there, but would stand a long distance down the field. He was a stranger to me, this aloof and indifferent creature, but at least, I consoled myself, he had ceased his downward slide. He was fighting back, he was alive. Let him be, let him be.

There were other hopeful signs. Because of legal complications the custody hearing over Megan had been postponed into the following month. It gave me a breathing space, a chance to get off my crutches.

I was very, very weary of those crutches by this time. I thought I would have become more accustomed to them with

175

the passage of the weeks. The reverse was true; I resented them more and more.

Two things kept me sane: being able to drive a car, which meant I could get away and visit friends or just take myself off when it got too much for me, and being able to swim — it was only in the water that I could go where I wanted without the aid of metal or wheels.

But still I was often restless, despairing that I would ever again be able to do all the things I had once taken for granted, like walk down the street, pick Megan up and carry her, ride my horse, drive my horse. Richard often got the brunt of these storms of frustration and he bore them remarkably patiently. One day, however, I complained just a little too bitterly.

'Well, then, don't just moan and rant on about it, do something positive.'

'Such as?'

'You drive a car perfectly well, don't you?'

'Yes.'

'Well, what's stopping you driving your horse?'

'That's below the belt, Richard, that is: that's downright cruel. I can't even get near my horse and as for driving, we don't know if he'll ever do that again.'

'I mean your other horse,' Richard said quietly.

'Blizzard?' I said after a stunned pause.

'That's the one. I'm glad you remember him, you've been so bound up in Bear's troubles and your troubles. Blizzard doesn't have any troubles. He's a super little animal, as honest as the day is long. In case you hadn't noticed, I've been driving him out every day for weeks now, and I can honestly say he has never put a foot wrong.'

'But I don't really even know him,' I squeaked.

'Well, then, don't you think it's high time you did? What could be better than you driving him out with Janice every morning instead of me? I've got more pressing things to do with my time.'

My mouth was dry with a mixture of excitement and apprehension. 'Do you think I could do it? Honestly?'

'I wouldn't be suggesting it otherwise and I certainly wouldn't want to take any silly risks with your neck or any other part of you. You would be at a disadvantage because you couldn't get out of that trap in a hurry and back on your crutches. But with Janice on the back step she can be at the horse's head in a flash and Blizzard's bomb-proof in traffic. And I'm talking about very steady walking-trot exercise on decent roads. No cross-country or clever stuff. It's time you got off your backside and did something, rather than laze around in that wheelchair all day!'

A couple of days later I swapped my hand-powered wheels for horse-driven wheels. We devised a system for getting me quickly and safely in the trap, with an extra sponge seat to cushion my hip against bumps, and stowed my crutches. Janice stood on the back step with the rope leading to the horse's head, so she had instant contact with the horse in case of emergency. Richard stood at Blizzard's head till we were all sorted out, then quietly took a step to one side.

'Off you go then!' he chided gently.

Trembling, I took a firmer contact on the reins — how strange they felt in my hand after all this time — moistened my lips and said as clearly as I could, 'Walk on.'

The oh-so-familiar yet definitely different chestnut creature in front of me pricked his ears and obediently set off at a gentle walk. We ambled down the back lane, my hands reacting automatically as the rest of me was still certainly stunned. Once we were clear of the main streets I gave the command to trot and we were off. And oh the feel of it, the glorious, glorious feel of air sliding past my face, of being able to go faster or slower as I dictated, of choosing pace and direction, of having to think with and for the horse at the end of the reins. It was freedom, it was glorious freedom from beds and pulleys and crutches and chairs — I was free. My spirits soared. My God, what an ungrateful fool I was, how little I valued how lucky I was, how much worse my accident could have been. If I could drive that vehicle, pain-free and completely independently, suppose I did have to use crutches, was that really the end of the world?

A hand gripped one of my shoulders and a tissue appeared over the other. How had Janice known I was crying?

'You okay?'

'Oh yes, yes I'm fine. I'm just so happy, that's all; I can't believe this is really happening.'

'I understand.' And I think, gruff and Yorkshire-practical as she was, that she did.

After the initial surprise and delight of simply being in the driving seat again, I was able to focus my attention on Blizzard. I was strongly aware it was Blizzard — or rather that it wasn't Bear — I was driving. This animal had a feather-light mouth that easily over-responded, he had a short, choppy gait which made our progress at the trot both bouncier and slower than with Bear. He was relaxed and responsive, but relied heavily on

me all the time for instruction and direction. He had no
experience on which to base what he was doing. Bear had come
to driving a mature and widely experienced horse. Blizzard had
all the innocence, all the lack of co-ordination of youth.

By the time I proudly drew up in the back yard of the stable,
Blizzard was no longer simply a horse that I owned. Though I
had almost ignored him from the day he arrived, on that first
drive together he had unlocked my heart and trotted straight in.

From then on I drove Blizzard every day that I could. Little
actual snow fell that February but the temperatures were very
low. Some days when Janice and I got back it took long and
painful minutes to restore the circulation to our fingers and toes,
even though I had had the extra comfort of a hot-water bottle
strapped round my middle under my driving rug. Only on days
of treacherous freezing fog did we not venture out. In those
weeks Blizzard was my salvation both mentally and physically;
he gave me his legs when I had none of my own, he gave me a
challenge when I most badly needed one, and he gave me
purpose when the rest of my life hung by frighteningly thin
threads.

Having dragged so slowly from the previous summer, time
suddenly began to accelerate alarmingly. There was so much
about to happen, so many important days on which so much of
the future rested.

The first of those days found me striding up the corridor of
Shotley Bridge Out-Patients from an appointment with Miss
Robinson. After being X-rayed, I had sat trying, not entirely
successfully, to be patient until she called for me.

She smiled when I went in but didn't waste her time on social
pleasantries. She put two sets of X-rays on her screen and
compared them long, hard and in infuriating silence, then
switched off the screen.

'How do you feel about coming off those crutches?'

Could I believe my ears? Did she mean it? I had longed and
prayed for this moment. How did I feel? My God, I felt . . . I felt
. . . Without those crutches I would have to put my foot to the
ground. Without those crutches my hip would have to support
the weight of my body for the first time in over six months. I
would have to walk. Could I walk? What I felt was frightened.

'I very much want to,' I answered truthfully.

'Fine. Just leave them in the corner there.'

'Now?' I experienced pure panic.

'I thought you wanted to get off them?' she enquired mildly.

'Oh I do, I do, but . . . well . . . I thought it would be gradual.'

'How can it be gradual? You either come off them or stay on them.'

'Well, don't I need a walking stick or something, to help me, to begin with?' I was truly frightened.

'If you need support, stay on your crutches.' Then she added more gently, 'If you feel you need to be on them longer that's fine, really it is.'

'I don't need them and I certainly don't want them,' I exploded, more angrily than I meant.

'OK then, walk over there and put them in the corner.'

'Miss Robinson, that's just it, I don't know if I *can* walk any more.' I said it in a rush.

'I think it goes something like one foot on the ground, the other one in front, and so on,' she answered brightly.

Well, if I did over-balance, if the hip or pelvis did give way, better do it here in her office at the hospital than back at home. Walking? No problem. But first I had to stand up.

With both feet on the ground I gripped the arms of the chair and pushed myself up. I had to over-ride an instinct that made me bend my right knee and keep the foot off the ground. With clammy palms and dry mouth I straightened up. And I stood. I picked up the crutches that were leaning on the chair and, taking a deep breath, which I held, lifted my right leg up and forward and put it down again. This was the point of no return. With the sort of courage born of desperation I used to experience when learning to jump on Bear, I forced my body weight forward on to my right leg then quickly brought the left leg up to join it. I had done it — I had walked!

'A small step for man but . . . ' I trailed off lamely as I saw Miss Robinson was not much impressed with my effort.

Remembering to start breathing again, I took another tentative step and another and one more. I was standing in the corner. I put the crutches down gently, turned round and a little more confidently returned to my chair.

'See, nothing to it,' she teased, then added more seriously, 'well done. Did you experience any great discomfort? Any sharp pain?'

I shook my head. 'No, nothing. Honestly, it was fine. It just felt, well, strange, unreal — as if the leg didn't belong to me.'

'You'll know it belongs to you tomorrow,' she chuckled.

'You'll have aches and creaks and groans like stink but don't overdo it, that's all I ask, don't overdo it. When it gets really tired and sore, listen to it and take a rest. Now, off you go, and be sensible.'

I reached into my handbag. 'I have something for you.'

She opened the buff envelope and took out the framed enlargement of Bear at Windsor with Richard and me in the trap, all in our finery, all ready for presentation. It had been taken only minutes before the dreadful runaway. She looked at the picture very carefully and then placed it on her desk.

'Thank you,' she said. And away I strode.

Miss Robinson was a lady of her word. By the next day I was so stiff and sore that I limped round home all day. But my delight and joy at having my mobility and the use of my hands back outshone any discomfort. It was a good omen and a much-needed confidence restorer.

The date of the custody hearing was set for the following week. And practising my walking kept my mind off that dreaded day of judgement. In the weeks leading up to the hearing I'd been so deeply wounded that I had begun myself to doubt the wisdom of what I was doing.

It had begun when I received a letter from John who, as my solicitor as well as my best friend's husband, had a more than difficult role to play. In his covering letter he warned me that I might find the enclosed contents upsetting, but I wasn't to get upset, such tactics were normal practice in a custody battle played at the pitch mine had now reached and we would simply have to retaliate even more strongly. The 'enclosed contents' were copies of sworn affidavits submitted by the other side. Solemn sworn statements from various people all saying, one way or another, the same thing: that I was an unfit person to have control of my daughter. That mentally, physically and certainly socially, now that I was living with such an ill-educated and socially unacceptable person as Richard, my daughter would be happier and more secure in the care of her father. And all of them, every one of them from people I had once considered good friends or good neighbours or good professional advisors. That Louise would take this action I had expected. She was now living with Ian and so that was obviously where her loyalties lay. I thought of how tirelessly we had battled together for Bear's life after his accident. How unfathomable life's pattern was sometimes. But that two of

Megan's godparents should do this! And the Harrisons of Bell's House Farm! Each word I read wounded and tore into me deeper than anything I had ever known. Tactics they might have been, but the world suddenly became a darker and uglier place for them.

I wept long and bitterly over those statements but eventually shock turned to anger, the wounds to determination and by the appointed date I had gathered together my retaliation — from Megan's other two godparents, from doctors and psychiatrists, from social workers and from my new neighbours. And their message was that yes, I'd had some appalling and dark times, yes, I'd been completely incapacitated at certain points. But I hadn't gone under and I hadn't given in. And now, still in the midst of many and very serious problems, I was not only coping, but I was coping remarkably well.

I won the psychological battle when I walked unaided, without a trace of a limp, into the courtroom. I won my personal battle when I replied coolly, calmly and, most importantly, truthfully to everything the opposition barrister fired at me. I won the war when I walked out with complete care and control of my daughter, Megan.

Though spring never comes early to so high and exposed a spot as Stanley Crook, by early March there were hopeful signs. Longer days, less biting winds, new vegetation appearing. It was a symbolic spring in many ways as my life too turned in new and hopeful directions.

I was walking further and better each week, only rough ground really causing me to ache any more. The legal transactions to buy Mount Pleasant were complete and Richard and I were now officially partners. Janice and I continued to drive out Blizzard daily and his stamina and co-ordination improved all the time.

There were clouds and worrying developments, such as our livelihood. The insurance wrangle over Richard's shop was concluded and the final settlement was far short of what he needed to re-build the business he had once had. I had been so bound up in my own problems for so long I'd paid little attention to the real problems Richard was having. In the end he decided to sell his own shop property in Crook and move into rented shop accommodation in Bishop Auckland. The days of antiques and shipping abroad were over. There was no other title for the premises he was moving into other than a second-hand furniture warehouse. And to be honest, that was being kind to it. The place was appalling, stuck up a dark and littered alley with one little window opening on to the outside world. It was smelly and dirty and utterly depressing, and was known locally as 'Ted's Shed'. Worst of all, it was the coldest, most bone-chilling place I had ever been in in my life; an hour in there and it was a toss-up between hypothermia and manic depression. But it had an established and regular trade selling an astonishing quantity of indescribably awful second-hand furniture and re-conditioned electrical applicances. It was a painful decision for Richard to make and I think his biggest fear was what my reaction would be — would I really want to be associated with, let alone live with, someone who made his living in such a way?

I thought of all the unfailing, constant support he had given me over the last months and realised that now, probably more than at any other time in our lives, was when he needed me. I didn't understand the workings of his business — or any business come to that — nor the legacy of problems he had from his past life. But I assured him that I had every confidence in whatever decision he made and that I would help him in any way that I was able. I teased him that he now had five mouths and fourteen legs to feed and, that at the end of the day, that was all that really mattered!

Of course, with the sale of his shop we also lost the stables. I was not sorry; I had hated them from the first time I had laid eyes on them and couldn't help but blame those premises for Bear's decline. But they had given us a base for Blizzard and all our equipment and now, with Easter approaching, we had a deadline to be out. There was no panic as we had somewhere to go. The trouble was that, though we had fields, we owned not a single usable building and Blizzard, clipped out and in regular work, needed a stable. The solution, Richard pointed out, was very simple; we must *make* a building usable.

So, taking a week off work, he and the two lads who worked at the shop demolished the wooden superstructure of the cow byre, hauled in van-loads of second-hand timbers, breeze blocks, tin sheets, sand and cement and set to. In seven days, from the stumps of the cattle stalls, an edifice arose without a true ninety degree angle in it. Richard and the lads worked so hard from first light till pitch dark that I simply didn't have the heart to voice any objections or misgivings. Certainly, if I'd been having dreams of stylish loose boxes opening on to an immaculate and elegant yard I would have to think again. Like God, on the seventh day, I stood back to admire the handiwork. I suspect

God was better pleased with his efforts.

Richard noticed my expression, grasped me by the shoulders and said, 'Look, it might not look much at present but it is a building and it's weather-proof, and there'll be a yard here, you'll see. Never a grand one, or a fancy one, but a good sound workable yard with feed room, hay shed and harness room and a workshop for me and a place for the carriages. And from that yard do you know what we're going to do?'

'No, tell me.'

'We're going to drive those two horses to the top. To the very top. Now, do you believe in that dream or don't you? Because if you don't, I won't have the heart or strength to go on. I'm not a builder or a joiner by trade, and what you see here isn't much, I know that, but it's a start. It's a start.'

Feeling deeply ashamed I buried my head into his cold, damp coat.

'Why are there five stalls when we've only got two horses?'

'At the moment, at the moment. Who knows, we might have a team one day!'

Next day I drove Blizzard up to his new home. For the rest of the morning Richard and Janice shuttled backward and forward with the van bringing up feed, bedding and all the rest of our tack and equipment. I settled Blizzard in his new stall, which took little doing; as long as there was a hay net and a bucket of water Blizzard was perfectly happy. But I wasn't — I was agonising over what I should do about re-introducing him to Bear. It was all very well Richard talking about pairs of horses when Bear seemed to loathe every hair of his new partner's body. Poor Bear; I hadn't given him much thought in the past few weeks since he was turned out. He seemed more settled and was certainly regaining his weight. I checked he had hay and water every day and at least he would now come up to the gate when I arrived — not to see me, I soon realised, simply to get his hay. He would tolerate me adjusting his New Zealand rug while he munched, but although I could have caught him and made a fuss of him he disliked any attempt to get hold of his headcollar so I didn't bother him. Yes, tolerate, that was the word. He now tolerated us, but didn't want us around him any more than was necessary.

Richard must have read my thoughts.

'When are we going to do the deed?'

I knew exactly what he meant. 'I don't know, I'm dreading it

— look what happened the last time they were introduced.'

'Well, that could have been due to a number of things; Bear was very down then, they were introduced indoors and there was only a rail separating them and there was nowhere for Blizzard to go to get out of the way. Now they've got ten acres to avoid each other in, and Bear does seem slightly more amicable these days.'

I looked very doubtful.

'Carol, it's March. The season starts at the end of April; I want to be driving these two as a pair by May or June by the very latest. Otherwise, what on earth is the point of all this?' He made a sweeping gesture at the building.

'What if there's a kicking match?' I winced at the thought. I didn't want either of them getting hurt.

'Then one of them will win and the bruises will heal. Actually, what they need to do is establish who is boss. Horses are a bit like hens, you know, they need a pecking order. Look, it's quite a decent afternoon and this little horse hasn't had a good romp in a field for weeks now. He's had plenty of work and exercise but no fun, and all youngsters need fun. I'm going to turn him out.'

Richard had spoken and I was beginning to learn that there were times when it was best not to argue further. However, my knees were knocking slightly as he walked Blizzard to the gate and turned him loose. Bear was at the other end, about as far away as it was possible to be. Delirious with joy to be free and unencumbered with rugs or anyone on his back, Blizzard gave squeals of delight and, sticking both his tail and nose in the air, began to trot in an exaggerated fashion up and down the side of the fence. The noise must have caught Bear's attention and suddenly he raised his head with a jerk. That movement caught Blizzard's eye and he came to an abrupt halt, frozen immobile, nostrils flaring. For a full minute they simply stared at each other from opposite ends of the field then, never taking their eyes off each other, they both advanced. Like a scene from a spaghetti Western, they slowly and relentlessly closed the gap between them until they were only a few feet apart. There was a tense moment as they tried to decide who should move next but, in the end, they both moved simultaneously. Their noses met and there was the ritual exchange of breath.

'This is it,' I thought, gripping the gate with white knuckles, 'any second now.'

Their shrill indignant screams ripped through the air, both horses half-reared and lunged at each other with their front feet, then dropped, wheeled round and lifted their backs to lash out. But even through my half-closed eyes I could see that the lift wasn't sufficient, the kicks not strong enough, the distance between them too great. They were bluffing. The nostril contact and the squealing procedure were repeated a couple of times and then they began slowly to circle around each other. Suddenly, at an unseen signal, they both took off at a flat-out gallop and a chase ensued round and round the field, interspersed with skidding, juddering halts in corners where a quick boxing match would take place before they careered on again. I could not have told from watching who had the upper hand in this delicate psychological balance but one thing was sure, Blizzard certainly wasn't standing for any nonsense from Bear. He was giving as good as he got. Finally, the game having been played to some ancient and intricate conclusion, they stopped as suddenly as they had begun and started grazing a little way from each other.

'Don't you dare smirk!' I said to Richard before he had time to get a word in. 'Just you concentrate on how we're going to persuade Blizzard to come back in again.'

'No problem, he's got no rugs on and it's getting colder now. More importantly, it's nearly his teatime.'

He was smirking, he definitely was.

Sure enough, an hour or so later, one rattle of a feed bucket was all it took for Blizzard to come trotting hopefully up to the gate. And — dear Lord, could it be true? — just behind him, an equally hopeful expression on his face, came Bear.

'Well, I'll be . . .' began Richard, then swiftly said in a low voice to me, 'don't touch him! Just leave him, let's just see what happens.'

He opened the gate and took hold of Blizzard's headcollar.

'Come on, son, let's have you. Nice new bed for you tonight and fields for you to run in now. Clever lad, that's it.'

He led Blizzard towards the stable, leaving the gate wide open. He completely ignored Bear who, after a moment's hesitation, slowly followed behind till he was standing with his head in the stable door. I quietly walked up beside him and put my hand on his neck. Beneath my touch the muscles relaxed and he swung his head towards me and gave me a gentle nudge, his expression warm and alert, filled with intelligence and life.

It was a timeless moment, an unforgettable moment.

From what seemed to be a great distance away I heard Richard say, 'All that animal wants is a nice warm bed and some supper;

are you going to leave him standing in the doorway all night?'

He'd forgotten his hanky as usual, and was wiping his eyes on the corner of Blizzard's blanket. I used the sleeve of my coat for my own tears.

For the first time I began to think seriously about what I had taken on by agreeing to make this bleak and exposed place my future home. A day's routine was that, after turning Bear out in the field, we would muck out, then harness Blizzard up and take him for a drive. By now he was fit enough to manage an hour and a half of hard work every day. One thing was sure, this was going to be a hell of a place to get horses fit from. There was quite simply no place to go out for a drive without going down a hill. The only choice was steep, very steep or vertical. Every drive ended with a hard pull uphill. We would then allow Blizzard out for a romp in the field with Bear while we finished the stable work. After lunch we would bring both horses in, put all the harness in the car and drive home. I then had about an hour and a half in which to do a few trivial things like shopping, cleaning, cooking and washing before I had to collect Megan from school at three-thirty. In the evening either Richard or I had to return to give the horses water and hay. In a day I could travel up to fifty miles, all silly tiring little journeys and all using a lot of fuel. A few months earlier I had not known how to get through the long tedious hours of the day. Now there simply were not hours enough. I seemed to go around in an exhausted blur. Richard was also finding the days more tiring, now that he was travelling further to and from work. Every month there was rent to pay on the cottage as well as a mortgage on the farm. Most of our time, energy and money went on our commuting to the farm, and the cottage was rapidly becoming just a place to eat and sleep. But the house at the farm was uninhabitable, derelict, so what choice did we have? In yet another of Richard's memorable manoeuvres, I was soon to find out.

Having come home very late the previous evening, he announced nonchalantly, 'I'm not going in to work in the morning till later, so I think I'll come up to the farm with you.'

I was immediately suspicious. Richard, I had discovered, developed a sort of twinkle whenever he was up to something. The next day my suspicions were proved correct.

'Well, what do you think of it?' he asked breathlessly. 'It' was about forty foot long, battered, sludgy green, and parked behind and parallel with the stable. I didn't dare trust my tongue for an answer so I just stood there, speechless.

Luckily, Richard took my astonished silence to mean that I was overcome with wonder. 'It was a bargain, a real bargain,' he crowed with glee. 'Come on, I'll show you inside.' Shaking slightly, which Richard also took to be part of my overawed condition, I allowed myself to be propelled through the door. The caravan, or to be more correct, mobile home, had, judging from the outside, seen better days. The inside, however, came as a considerable relief. It consisted of three rooms: a bedroom with built-in wardrobe and chest of drawers, a kitchen with a miniature enamel sink and draining board and a small gas cooker and a table that folded down, and an almost spacious living-room with a gas fire, and a large picture window at one end.

'We are going to live in here?' I tried to make the question blasé. I thought of my cosy little cottage, with its lemon bathroom suite and Laura Ashley wallpaper. My spacious kitchen with pine dresser and table. My fridge-freezer and washing machine. The dishwasher. The log fire. And I tried very hard to keep hysteria out of my voice. I had a mental picture of Megan in her neat little uniform at her new convent school. 'And do you know your address, Megan?' 'Oh, I don't have an address, Sister, I live in a caravan.'

Megan! Had Richard become de-railed? Had he forgotten there were three of us?

'If it's not a silly question, where are we all supposed to sleep? There's only one bedroom.'

My last thread of hope that, in his enthusiasm Richard might have overlooked this small point, thus making the whole exercise void, snapped when he gave a theatrical 'Aha!', moved to the wall at the top of the living area and pulled a handle. The wall tipped forward and down and, suddenly, there was a double bed.

'Megan gets the bedroom, she needs the privacy and quiet at night and room to put her toys and so on. We sleep in here. Cosy, isn't it?' He wiggled his eyebrows roguishly.

I sat down with a thump and gazed out of the main window. The view was quite lovely, across our own land then over other fields to wooded hills beyond. I certainly couldn't live anywhere nearer the horses, they were about a yard away, just the other side of the stable wall.

'I wanted to give you a surprise.' Richard sat down beside me.

'Oh, I think you can say you've achieved that.'

'Think of all the advantages. We'll save a lot of money on rent and on petrol. It'll be far less tiring for you — no more traipsing backwards and forwards. And before you say it, there's no problem with Janice; I've discussed it with her and she's happy to come on her moped each morning. More importantly, it means I can get started on the house. That's what it's all about, isn't it? Making the house habitable. Getting moved into our own house?'

I had to agree with everything he had said so far. It all made sound economic and time-saving sense.

'What about all my furniture?'

'Sweetheart, that's the least of our worries: I've got all the space in the world to store it upstairs at the shop.'

'And how long do you think we could be living in here?'

'I like to think we'll be in the house by the end of the year.'

Yes, it all made sense, very good sense and the idea was beginning to grow on me. Summer evenings. The horses sauntering past our windows as we ate breakfast. Opening the door on to a daisy-speckled field in the morning. How exciting! Megan was going to be thrilled.

'How soon do we move in?'

'What's your tenancy on the cottage?'

'I've got it on a weekly rental.'

'It looks like next week, then.'

It was amazing just how much stuff you could get into a large green tin can if you packed methodically. Megan was thrilled with the whole idea, and with her bedroom. I stuck up a couple of rolls of Laura Ashley wallpaper left over from the cottage bathroom and cut up and re-made the bathroom curtains to fit her small windows and it did look lovely. The kitchen I had to be ruthless and practical about, and pack away for storage things like dinner services and deep fat fryers and all the assorted paraphernalia of an ex-cookery teacher. Richard laid on, by one ingenious means or another, an electricity supply and water. The living area, which now boasted a colour TV, a stereo record player and a dimplex radiator for added warmth, looked really quite luxurious. I took only what clothes I thought I would need in the coming months — basically trousers, shirts and jumpers — and the rest I packed into suitcases and took to my mother's for safe, dry storage. She, poor soul, if she did have misgivings about the latest unconventional twist to her daughter's life, kept it to herself. Few people could have been as blessed with such a long-suffering and patient mother as I. At least Richard and I didn't have to quarrel over space for our respective possessions. His were still pitifully few after the disastrous fire.

With Megan exhausted with excitement and safely snuggled under her covers, Richard produced a bottle of cheap fizzy plonk and, unable to find any glasses, I picked up two earthenware mugs. We climbed cautiously into our new bed, which look suspiciously like a large wooden orange box on legs, and which creaked in protest at our combined weight.

I was overcome with giggles.

'Do you think it's safe?'

'I don't know about safe, but it's certainly not very big.'

Richard filled our mugs and we clanked them together.

'To our first night on our own land.'

'Amen.'

The first week in our tin can was a memorable one. There were things that were good — like not having to spend half the day commuting, being able to check the horses frequently — and things that were not so good — like a chemical toilet, no bath tub and having to be ruthlessly methodical and tidy all the time.

But all this was pushed aside by the most memorable, the most wonderful thing of all. Janice had gone home after work as usual, and I was enjoying the first pleasant day I had known in my new hill-top home. The air was relatively still for once and, though not exactly warm, the bitter edge had gone from it. A bright sun shone from an almost cloudless sky and down the field a lark was hovering and trilling her glorious song. I didn't have to collect Megan for about three hours and I had, for the first time in weeks, some time on my hands. The horses were grazing down the field and, feeling I couldn't let such a lovely day go to waste, I pulled on my boots and set off for a walk.

Though I had viewed the fields from all angles and walked over bits of them, I'd never actually explored our land at leisure and it seemed a good day to do it. The clear fresh air was very exhilarating and I realised for the first time just how far you can see from our hilltop. Miles and miles and miles. What a strange place. Ugly and depressed and cramped at the front, open and free and beautiful at the back.

I became aware as I drank in the view of a presence behind me. It was Bear. I knew it was Bear without turning to look.

'Hello, bonny lad, do you like it up here then?'

In answer he moved closed till I could feel the breath from his muzzle on my neck. I turned and hugged him. He'd filled out so much in the last few weeks that he was unrecognisable as the emaciated skeleton who had come here in January.

'Oh, it's so good to see you looking well and like your old self!'

A few short months ago he'd been a hopeless case and I'd felt pretty hopeless myself, stuck on my crutches. How far away the whole of last summer seemed. Already I was taking my legs for granted, the wonder of simply being able to walk fading away. And Bear? He too looked no different than he ever had. Had his wounds healed too? His mental, wounds, his deep fear?

There was, I realised, only one way to find out and it would be a test not only of his courage but of mine. I took a deep breath and drank in the smell of fresh and hopeful growing things. If the weather was an omen, then there would never be a better day than this.

'Come on,' I said quietly, getting hold of his headcollar. He followed me up to the stable.

All tacked up, I led him back out into the sun, then paused, realising that I was frightened — but of what? If you are frightened of a horse, be sure that he will be the first to know. You can never lie about your emotions to a horse. Everything you feel goes straight down your reins and straight through your legs. But I wasn't frightened of Bear. Was I? I examined this thought carefully. No, I wasn't: I was frightened of myself maybe, but that was all. Frightened of what would happen when I tried to swing up on to his back. Could I indeed do it? Would it hurt? Would the nuts and bolts in my pelvis allow me to settle comfortably back into my beloved saddle?

I decided to come clean. I put my hands under Bear's chin, leant my forehead on his nose and said quietly, 'I'm very scared, Bear; very, very scared and I guess you know that. I'm not scared of you, or I wouldn't be doing this. It's just, well, I don't know if I can do it any more and it's so important to me, so terribly important. I expect you're scared too and you want it to be like it was, just as much as I do. I just want you to know there isn't another horse in the whole world I would try to get on. Please believe me, I'm just as scared as you are Bear, just as scared as you are.'

This was it. Should I find something to use as a mounting block? No, that would be cheating; I had to know if I could swing up into the saddle. I took the reins in my left hand — at least with his unhogged lavatory brush of a mane there was plenty to grab hold of. I checked that his girths really were tight as the last thing I wanted to happen was to end up with his saddle under his belly. I placed my left leg in the stirrup. Thank God it was my right hip I had damaged as I don't think I could have taken all the swing up on the other leg. He was standing perfectly still as if he was holding his breath. He who hesitates is dead. I bounced lightly on my right foot, pulled hard on his mane and I was up! He pranced gently around, snorting a little, more with surprise than alarm I hoped. I patted his neck and made encouraging noises. My heart thumped so fast it was painful. But there was no other pain, nothing shooting up and down my leg as I had imagined, no feeling of my pelvis being pulled apart. In fact my bottom moulded itself to the contours of my saddle with comfortable familiarity. I shortened my reins and squeezed gently with my legs.

'Walk on,' I said firmly.

Without a moment's hesitation he set away at a long eager stride. We reached the field gate and I leant forward to open it. The manouevre at the gate did not upset him, but it livened him up a little. I felt the familiar pressure building up against his bit. Bear bounded gently down the field. I relaxed a little, deciding it wasn't that he was upset, rather that he was enjoying himself. His ears were forward and there were no ugly damp patches of sweat appearing on his neck as had happened whenever Janice had even put his tack on a few months ago.

Another horrible thought struck. Blizzard! Supposing Blizzard gallops up and scares Bear? I confined Bear to the upper edge of the field. Blizzard, I discovered, was at the other end and downhill and therefore out of view. I asked for a trot and got it at once.

To my amazement and relief I found I could still ride effortlessly and painlessly in the saddle. He trotted quickly, but not out of control, a few times in a large circle and, more importantly, came straight back to a walk when I asked him. There was a small surge of that feeling of unity that only occurs when a horse and rider through long association move and think almost as one. We trotted a little more and with the spring sun and air on my face I was totally, utterly and unbearably happy. Oblivious to anything but the feel and emotion of my horse beneath me. How I'd longed for this, how I had despaired of this! And now it was happening, really happening and I didn't want it ever to end.

'I think that's enough for the first time for both of you,' said a voice and I snapped back to reality.

'Richard! Where have you . . . ? I didn't see . . .'

'I came home early to make a start on the house. I just walked in through the gate but you were obviously too far gone to notice me. And what on earth do you think you're doing, you silly little fool? No one here, no hat on?'

'I just . . . well, it just felt right that's all. I had to try it some time and today felt like the day. Oh, Richard, please don't spoil it for me, please don't. Look, I can ride him! I can sit here and it doesn't hurt and I got on on my own. And he's fine, Richard, he's all well again, really he is. Oh, please don't be angry!'

'Angry? Do you think I'm angry? I've been standing here this last five minutes at the gate watching you and I've never been so happy or so proud in my life — of both of you, yes of both of you.'

'To tell you the truth, I'm pretty proud too — of both of us.'

'Well, wipe that silly grin off your face and get the kettle on. A fellow could die of thirst round here. No tea ready; I don't know. You want to get your priorities right, young lady.'

He held the gate wide open for us to pass through.

'Yes, Richard,' I beamed happily.

Just as I was drifting off to sleep that night in the cramped confines of our box bed a voice said, 'You realise you've got a busy day on tomorrow, don't you?'

'Mmm?'

'After what happened today there'll be a lot to do in a short time.'

'Sorry?' I mumbled sleepily. What on earth was he rabbiting on about?

'You'll have to get him clipped tomorrow.'

I sat bolt upright. 'Clipped! What on earth for?'

'Well, it's Beamish in just over three weeks and we've got Blizzard entered. Or had you forgotten? Well, I might just be able to slip an entry in for Bear if I whisper sweetly in the right ear.'

'Beamish! You cannot be serious — he hasn't done a thing since Windsor, we don't even know if he'll drive yet!'

'That's what I mean, you've got a busy day tomorrow. Goodnight, pet.'

And he gave a very final roll over and left me, mind reeling, stomach whirling and still sitting bolt upright.

It was indeed a race against time, but one we won just by a nose. There was of course no question of getting Bear fully competition-fit in three weeks, nor did Richard want him to be. All he wanted was Bear fit enough to get round the course steadily and safely and he made the decision that he would drive Bear and not me.

'But,' I argued, 'Blizzard's a baby, a total novice; he's never even seen a dressage arena or a proper hazard.'

'No.'

'But I know Bear better than anyone; I understand him, I know how he thinks.'

'No.'

'But . . . '

'No!'

Richard drove Bear and I drove Blizzard. How incredible, how unimaginable, that four years after I had stood looking longingly from the sidelines, stop-watch in hand, I should be back at Beamish not just with the one horse I had dreamed of competing with, but as the driver of another horse and the owner of two entrants.

We borrowed an extra cross-country vehicle and we shared the good trap and harness by getting one horse scheduled early in the dressage class and the other at the end. We were not after records or rosettes but set out to get our respective horses safely and quietly round the course: Blizzard the baby and Bear the shell-shocked old war horse.

Bear had gone back into the breaking sledge the day after I had first ridden him again. He hadn't enjoyed it at first and wouldn't relax, but at least he was listening to us and obeying orders. The following day Richard put him into the cart and with Janice and me both on safety lines he negotiated the field a couple of times without undue fuss. The following week Bear was back out in traffic and we were back in business.

We also needed A.N. Other groom to go on the back with me, as Richard was taking Janice with him. Who, though? The answer was obvious — Carol Herbert. Although we had only seen a little of Herbie since the birth of her baby, she was thrilled at the chance of working with Bear once more.

When Herbie, Blizzard and I passed the 'Finish' sign on the marathon I was immensely relieved. Blizzard had tried his little heart out in his first marathon and was a very tired young cob. But my mind hadn't been totally on the course or on what this

super, willing animal was doing; it was on Richard and what
Bear was doing. Quickly unharnessing Blizzard, I left him in
Herbie's competent hands to cool down and dashed back to the
finishing line to watch for Richard coming in. He shouldn't have
been far behind me, only a couple of horses separated our
starting times. Two horses came; four horses came in. No sign
of Bear. I was beginning to imagine the worst and build up a
disaster scenario when a familiar form came into view, head
down, trotting up the track. Since those first early hunting days
I'd never seen him look so tired.

'He's buggered,' said Richard as he pulled up and handed his
green card to the time-keeper.

'I can see that.'

'But that was to be expected after all the weight and muscle
tone he's lost over the winter. And this cart weighs a ton, far
heavier than the one he's used to. So I've just let him do it at his
speed. I pulled him out of the competition on Section E and let
the others overtake. If he'd wanted to stop altogether I would
have let him, but he was happy to go on at his pace, and that's
the important thing; he was happy to go on.'

Bear's breathing wasn't distressed but it was still quite rapid
and he was drenched in sweat and covered in mud. He stood,
head slightly down, trying to rub the irritating sweat off on my
anorak and devouring Polo mints as quickly as I could
adminster them. Strained heart? Damaged lungs? Nerve gone?

'Bear, you're a hero.' I rubbed his damp, sweaty blaze
lovingly.

'And little horse?' Richard enquired, his voice now suddenly
anxious.

'Absolutely super; didn't get the times in but what do you
expect? We took all the long easy routes in the hazards. But he's
willing and a trier and nothing puts the wind up him, just took it
all in his stride. Just think,' I brightened at the thought, 'we've
just got two horses safely round. For the first time we've got two
separate entries at an event!'

'Well, make the most of it,' said Richard as he unbuckled the
traces, 'because the first time is going to be the last.'

'What do you mean? They've both done well really, all things
considered. They'll do much better next time out!'

'Of course they will, of course they will. Because next time
they compete it'll be as a pair.'

12

'Nice cobs, Richard, nice cobs'

IT MADE SENSE — in theory. Both horses were now driving single perfectly well. Richard had a pairs' work harness and a cross-country vehicle he'd built himself. He had the experience and know-how to put a pair of horses together, and that was what we'd purchased Blizzard for. That was what it was all about — Richard doing what he was best at, driving a pair of horses again. The dream could begin at that point. But to do it, to actually do it — that was something else.

'Do you not think we're rushing things?' I struggled with a spaghetti-like tangle of pair harness that had been packed away none too carefully, for many months. I hadn't a clue what was what or how to put it on. Outside in the back street on a perfectly flat piece of road, oiled and ominously black, Richard's battle wagon stood waiting.

'I need to know if I can get them going together by the end of this week.'

'Why the hurry?'

'The entries for Scone Palace close this week.'

'Scone Palace? That's right up near Perth, isn't it!'

'Correct. And before you ask, the event is at the end of May. And before you say it, yes, Bear will be perfectly fit by then.'

'Surely you're not going to bring them straight out at a full F.E.I. event, are you?'

'Well, I don't see why we shouldn't. We're not going for instant victories or anything stupid. All I want is for them to get the taste of a full event together. Let's face it, with only my work cart and this harness, we can't expect to get far anyway. But there's a perfect little one-day event before Scone Palace, up in Northumberland: Shortflat Towers. It's run by a friend of mine, Ray Brown.'

That sounded suspicious.

'How soon is it?'

'Two weeks.'

'Two weeks!' I gave off a high-pitched squeak. 'But that's . . .

195

well that's impossible. Be realistic, Richard, you'll never have
them driving together as a pair by then.'

Richard gave an exasperated sigh. 'I'll never have them going
as a pair at all if you don't get that harness sorted out. Look,' he
paused for a deep breath, 'this morning they are two fit, single
driving horses with a fair amount of experience. That experience
is still going to hold good when they are going side by side.
There comes a point when you just have to put them together
and go. If by this afternoon, or next week at this rate, they're
driving that vehicle together, then they are driving as a pair. But
I don't expect them to BE a pair; to be able to manoeuvre and
turn and share the work and think together. That will only come
with time and experience, and if they are compatible.'

'I see,' I said, vaguely comprehending.

Richard raised his eyebrows. 'Do you? I'm not very good with
words but I'll try and explain. Look, I've seen lots of horses that
look alike, side by side, pulling a vehicle. Technically, they're a
pair. But that's only the first step. Beyond that you can go into a
whole different dimension; to where the driver and horses all
think and act as one. Does that sound stupid?'

'No, no, not at all. I've known that feeling with Bear often. I
just didn't imagine it was possible when driving. I thought that
the vehicle would come between you somehow.'

'Well, I admit it's a feeling that doesn't happen that often, but
when it does it's special, very special.'

'I can imagine.'

We drove Bear and Blizzard out every day and every day, after
we'd all learned how to handle the cart, they went further and
happier together. It was a very special time in all our lives. The
first, and probably hardest, step on our new path had been
taken. It was spring, I was walking, we were on our own land
and building our own house. We had a pair of horses entered
for their first competition. Our world was full of hope.

Arriving at my first event with two horses was also memorable.
It was, as Richard had said, only a one-day event with cross-
country, some hazards and then a cone course. No dressage and
no presentation. Perfect for a début. On one thing I was
adamant: I was going round on the back of the vehicle. But my
hip? Miss Robinson? I over-rode all objections. Who else could
cope better with the horses in an emergency? And the ride

wasn't as bone-shattering on the back of the four-wheeler as on a single cart. And anyway I could always stand on one leg over the bumps. And I was going, and that was that.

We kept a low profile, concentrating on what we were doing and took it gently. But the competiton carriage driving world is a small one and a new pair of horses, particularly in the hands of an experienced driver, never goes unnoticed. As Richard ticked over the finishing line in the cones and then walked slowly back to the box, Ray Brown's eyes never left the horses. As the organiser of the event, an old friend of Richard's and an experienced driver himself, his verdict was vital to Richard; on it Richard would base where and what he should do next. The verdict, when it came, was one of those glorious under-statements that still managed to say it all.

Pushing his tweed hat back, Ray looked him straight in the eye. 'Nice cobs, Richard. Nice cobs.'

On the six-hour journey to Scone Palace in Scotland, I got to know a member of my new family I'd hitherto had little acquaintance with: Plod. Up to now I'd simply thought of it as a vehicle, albeit a very large one that belonged to Richard. It was in fact a converted nine-ton furniture van of venerable age, a beloved old friend of Richard's and a vital part of our plan as quite simply it was a case of no Plod, no events. As many hours seemed to have been put in by Richard servicing and checking Plod for the season ahead as he'd spent with the horses. With Plod and the trailer, a lengthy, featureless, oblong box on wheels which Richard had made to carry our vehicles, we could go anywhere — so long as we weren't in a hurry.

With typical Smith ingenuity, Richard had been one of the first to make the adaptations that, on arrival at an event, converted his horsebox into a temporary stable and living area. Bear had been indulged in a hired loose box at most events he'd previously attended, but to do this for two horses for four or five nights was a very expensive business. So Plod carried on her sides two large, wooden 'wings' which, when supported by poles all the way round, could be slid up and out to form an effective roof on either side of the wagon. By lacing tarpaulins and more poles into position, the space beneath could be enclosed against the weather and used on one side as stalls for the horses and on the other as housing for the carriages.

The trailer became a storage place for the horses' feed and bedding. Once the horses were installed, the space they'd travelled in inside the wagon could be brushed and sluiced out and used as an area for living and working and cleaning and hanging the harness. At the front there were the Calor gas cooker and sink unit, and we also a few hard stacking chairs and a table. The grooms slept in Plod, and Richard, Megan and I slept in a tent borrowed from Janice. It was very spartan but we had the necessities for survival.

We knew of course that we couldn't make a silk purse out of a sow's ear when it came to our presentation in this competition. We only had our work harness and work cart. The rules stipulated only that harness and vehicle had to fit, be clean and safe, but there was no doubt that an elegant and showy turn-out helped the cause. Nevertheless we polished and rubbed to make the best of what we had and at least the horses were immaculate, both neatly hogged and their tails banged to exactly the same level, their lovely copper coats gleaming with the effort of love and pride. Richard wore a dark suit and black bowler hat and I accompanied him as groom dressed in black jacket, boots and hat. It was the first time Blizzard had been in a proper marked dressage arena and his first-ever dressage test. He hadn't a clue what he was supposed to be doing, but was quite happy to allow himself to be towed in the right direction by Bear. His little choppy step looked ridiculous next to Bear's high stride but he held his head proudly and when they finally came to an extremely ragged halt I wanted to leap out and hug him for trying so hard.

The following day was the marathon, their first real marathon as a pair, and my first since my accident. Quite a day! They did better than we had dared hope on the first four sections, incurring few penalties, and I was grateful that the going was not rough or bumpy enough to give my hip any bother. By the end of the marathon they'd proved themselves to have the courage and stamina that was required of a pair. To our astonishment we found that night they were lying in fourth place, a position they retained the next day despite both being a bit of a handful in the cone arena and both fetching down a cone or two. Blizzard kept coming off the bit and Bear adopted his stiff-necked, won't steer, won't listen attitude; it was amazing Richard didn't knock all the cones down.

So despite one young inexperienced horse and another battle-scarred one, a battered cross-country vehicle and work harness, to our immense delight we finished in the ribbons. It was lunacy really that a piece of green ribbon and cardboard for coming fourth could make living for four days in a damp, cold tent worthwhile. Could make those hundreds of uncomfortable miles travelling in an aged horsebox more bearable. Could make returning to an old caravan in a patch of mud behind a tin shack of a cowbyre feel like a triumphant return home. But it did. In some unfathomable way, it did.

The next event on the 1983 schedule was Holker Hall in Cumbria in June. There was a problem, though. Now we'd proved that the cobs could compete successfully as a pair, we had to decide whether to attempt the sport seriously or just to play around the edges. Whereas it was possible with a single horse or tandem to get away with one vehicle for all three sections, it was nearly impossible to do this with a pair or team. The design of the vehicle used for the marathon was so much more robust and untraditional that it was hard to make it look presentable and elegant for dressage and presentation. No, if we wanted to go forward we needed a carriage. A new one was out of the question as it would cost thousands of pounds, and even a second-hand one was going to put a large hole in funds set aside for the house. But it was a question of priorities — a presentation vehicle or bricks and mortar; so it had to be a carriage, didn't it?

Richard set off for a carriage sale, clutching our cheque book and a catalogue. Late into the night I heard the sound of the Land Cruiser and trailer bumping cautiously over the field to the caravan. He wouldn't be driving that carefully with an empty trailer. I struggled into an anorak and wellies and, opening the door, slipped out into the clear night air.

'Hello, sweetheart, what are you doing out of bed?'

'Well, I wasn't exactly asleep, sort of half-listening for you.' The suspense was killing me. 'Well?'

'Well, what?'

'What's under that tarpaulin, that's what.'

'That, sweetheart, is the loveliest thing on four wheels. A genuine turn-of-the-century German wedding phaeton. The prettiest carriage I've seen in many a long day and a perfect size for the boys.'

'How much?'

He gave me a look which said 'Oh don't ask sordid things — that'll spoil it,' and then came clean. I took a sharp intake of breath. I'd heard of putting the cart before the horse but this cart had cost more than both horses put together!

'Think of it as an investment,' Richard soothed me. 'It's an antique, it's genuine, it can only appreciate in value.'

'Or drop to pieces,' I murmured.

But in the daylight next morning, I could see that it was indeed a thing of graceful lines and lovely craftsmanship. The upholstery had seen better days and the paintwork wasn't in top class condition but it still looked pretty.

And when Richard, Bear and Blizzard drove it for the first time in the dressage arena at Holker a few weeks later, I began to think of it as money well spent.

The setting at Holker was breathtakingly beautiful — parkland surrounded by woods and the lakeland hills climbing out of the background. Herds of deer roamed loose in the park and in the early morning mist they would venture timidly right into the horsebox encampment. The weather was glorious, so living in a tent was no hardship and slowly I was beginning to learn names and make friends. Janice wasn't with us on this trip as she had family commitments so instead we brought two local fifteen-year-old girls who'd been helping out with the horses from time to time. Oh, how I missed Janice and her down-to-earth, hard-working approach! These girls had to be pushed, and their work checked all the time. Once they realised the weekend wasn't going to be the picnic in the country they'd imagined, that it was going to mean work, they became even harder to push. That lack of dedication, of attention to detail, was to prove our undoing.

Thrilled that the dressage results had once again put us close to the leaders, I was up very early to give the horses a small hard feed then I went back to bed for an hour or so. It was vital that they had virtually empty bellies for the rigours of the marathon that lay ahead. They mightn't be very happy at the time but would be thankful for empty, comfortable bellies when the going got tough. With a full belly it would be like trying to run the London Marathon after a large helping of fish and chips. As I fed them it registered through my sleepy haze that they were tied up in their stalls, not loose to roam round, and with the sides of the tarpaulin laced firmly to the ground to keep them in. We'd given the girls their instructions the night before: small hay net, let them off their ropes and make sure they were properly laced in. Richard and I wanted an early night and had left them to it. It was while I was frying bacon for breakfast in Plod a couple of hours later that the awful truth was revealed.

'Richard Smith, ain't it?' A broad Lancashire accent accompanied by a cheerful face popped round the door. Everyone knew Richard, nobody was quite sure who I was yet.

'Yes, yes — he's just out walking the course a last time. Can I help you?'

'No, Aa'm checkin' yer 'orses were right after Aa put them back like. Ba, they 'ad a grand time in't park.'

A cold finger got me in the solar plexus.

'In the park?' I gasped.

'Aye. Aa were up reet early, barely light. One o' my mares was kickin' up a fuss and Aa went ter see what's what like. Well, there's these two chestnuts, strollin' round, bold as brass, eatin' their 'eads off. Aa thought they were Richard's and saw the tarpaulin down on 't side o' wagon, so Aa thought Aa'd better put 'em back, like. Mind you, they surrendered like lambs when Aa went up to 'em, but ba they 'ad some bellies on 'em. Been eatin' for hours I'd say. Anyway, thought Aa'd just check like, just in case you were puzzled why they're tied up. I reckon the tarpaulin weren't up reet.'

'Oh, thank you, thank you so much. They could have wandered off anywhere, they could have been killed on the road!'

In the ensuing inquisition, the girls only became more sullen, defensive and uninterested. In our hearts Richard and I knew it was not their fault, it was ours. Ours for not checking, ours for not making sure. That the ultimate responsibility was ours was a lesson we never forgot from that day onwards. It was a nightmare.

On the marathon later that morning the horses were lethargic before we even started and on the steep, hard hillside section the after-effects of their binge began to bite. After heavy rain the previous week the forest track was a soft bog, churned up by many horses and vehicles before us, and in this the cobs gasped and struggled as the vehicle bedded down axle-deep. All we wanted to do now was just get the horses safely home. Both the referee, (who accompanies the competitor on the course to make sure that all sections are completed accurately, and keeps time checks as well as the groom) and I got down from the vehicle on one section, and put our shoulders to the back wheels, pushing with all the strength we had simply to prevent the vehicle pulling the horses backwards. We were miles from anywhere, there was no help at hand. It would have been dangerous to let the carriage slide backwards and drag the horses off their legs. We simply had to go on. Angry tears streaming down his face, Richard urged, shouted and swore at them. But he never once took his whip to them. It would have been no use; they were not being disobedient or lazy, they were doing their best. In the

end, breaking his most sacred rule of all, Richard too got off the
vehicle and, turning the spokes of the front wheel with his
hand, shouting encouragement to the cobs, we broke free and
crawled painfully to the top of the hill. The horses were
trembling and sweating and so were we.

As soon as the track widened sufficiently we pulled off to one
side as, in the distance, clanks and rumbles heralded the
approach of the next competitor. Even his two large long-legged
Cleveland horses struggled and gasped with the severity of the
incline and the mud and they were barely trotting as they drew
level.

'Are you all right?' A vaguely familiar voice rang out.

'We're okay,' Richard shouted back, 'but the horses are
buggered. Tell them at the next post we're withdrawing. I'm
just going to walk them back. One's just a baby — second time
out.'

'Righto — I'll tell 'em. Tek care.'

Having got a little of their breath back, his beautiful
Clevelands stretched their legs out a bit more and they trotted
off into the distance leaving us alone again.

'Who's that man?'

Richard climbed wearily back on the vehicle. 'That's Fred
Pendlebury. Why do you ask?'

'He's the man that caught the horses and put them back this
morning, that's all. I hadn't realised he was a pairs driver.'

'Oh, we're not all short, round, bald-headed and middle-
aged,' quipped Richard with a sad little smile on his face.

He was, I knew, as bitterly disappointed as I was. We gently
walked and trotted the cobs back to camp. We did not want to
over-tax Blizzard in this, his critical first few events. At the age
of four he was in fact just old enough to be permitted to compete
in F.E.I. competitions, and we only intended to give him a
limited number of events in his first season. The only other
event definitely planned for the pair, and that had a marvellous
and majestic ring to it, was Sandringham.

But if Holker Hall was to be the first disappointment of the
season, it was not to be the last.

It was the first time there'd been a three-day driving event at
Sandringham and Her Majesty had graciously given permission
for the event to be held, and for the competitors to camp, almost
within sight of Sandringham House itself. The horseboxes were
in fact parked in a field right behind the Royal Gundog Kennels.

At feeding times and exercise times, the excited babble of canine voices rose from the buildings which housed the famous 'Sandringham Sidney' line of labradors. Labradors or not, the noise obviously sounded much like the babble of foxhounds to Bear who would shoot to the front of his stall, ears pricked, nostrils flared. He'd never forgotten his hunting days, the memories all obviously joyous and exciting, and any sound even vaguely reminiscent of hounds or hunting horn would set his pulse racing.

The event was quite the best organised I'd yet attended. Down on the main showfield there was a beautifully laid out dressage arena with tiered grandstands around it and pretty striped marquees for the VIP guests. Everywhere were flags and bunting and tubs of flowers. The setting was like a latter-day Camelot. There were trade stands and displays and a fairground which had Megan squealing with delight. Janice's eyes were round with the wonder of it all.

'Aa don't care if I cannot get a bath or if Aa have to eat cold beans out of a tin, Aa wouldn've missed this for the world!' she announced firmly.

Despite being awash with nerves as Richard entered that arena, I soon began to realise two things; first, the horses felt as though they were going straighter and more together and in unison that I'd previously experienced, and secondly that sitting bolt upright behind Richard in the carriage was the last place on earth to be able to judge the horses' performance. All I could see was the back of Richard's neck. But my sensory perception must have served me well as we found, to our astonishment, that we were lying third after presentation and dressage. The horses had had a month to recover and then get back on peak form after Holker and the marathon course itself, because of the flat Norfolk terrain, was not the endurance test that Holker or even Perth had been. The hazards were tight and well built and would, as Richard classically understated, 'take some driving'. But we must be in with a chance. Not of winning, we had no thoughts of that, but of coming in the ribbons at this, the horses' first really prestigious event.

Because the terrain was not arduous, both Janice and I would ride on the back as grooms and as the marathon progressed so did our excitement. The going was perfect for cobs; light, sandy, springy soil. On the fast section which took place right through acres of lavender fields it was as if they suddenly took wings. The blue sky, the fragrant green and purple bushes as far as the eye could see, all rushed past at an incredible speed as stride for stride two gloriously fit horses ploughed on. It was a glimpse of what could be achieved, of the 'coming together' as Richard had called it of vehicle, driver and horses.

On the walk section they incurred no penalties, which left us with the breath-robbing realisation that if they could only get safely and quickly round the hazards we were in with a chance. What a monumental word 'if' is.

The first few hazards posed no problems — maybe this encouraged Richard to speed up further, perhaps to oversteer. Perhaps he lost his concentration momentarily, perhaps the horses did. But at the next hazard there was suddenly a sickening crunch and we all tossed forward on the vehicle as its momentum was suddenly stopped. We'd hit a large upright post with the front of the pole as the horses had tried to come round a hazard. Richard backed them off, realigned them and got them going again. Then I realised something wasn't quite right, Bear didn't seem to be pulling back.

'Bear's snapped some harness!' I yelled.

'I know!' (The inference was 'Silly woman'.)

'Shall I get down and try and mend it?'

'No! Stay where you are: I've still got enough contact to get round if I go steady. Both of you stay where you are until we are out of the penalty zone.'

Every hazard has a twenty-metre zone marked around it, usually in sawdust. Within that zone the stop-watch of the hazard judge would be running. A driver could drive at any pace he wanted but any groom dismounting from a vehicle would incur heavy penalties. Once outside a penalty zone a groom could dismount to effect emergency repairs without incurring penalties. A few strides over the sawdust circle Janice and I leapt off the back while Richard was still bringing the horses to a halt. Janice held their heads while I extracted a penknife and stout cord that I carried and had rehearsed using for this very occasion. Only then my hand hadn't shaken so much, my fingers hadn't felt so numb and useless.

'Come on, come on!' Richard fumed.

'I'm doing the best I can,' I hissed back.

The impact of the collision had snapped the junction between Bear's breast collar and the trace on the inside where it was hard to reach. I tied what looked suspiciously like a granny knot and yelled, 'Right!'

I just managed to leap on the back of the vehicle as it surged past me.

The next hazard was the one Richard had been having

collywobbles about; the one he had walked over and over again the previous day. It was a collection of mature trees in which large metal round cattle feeders had been placed. It didn't sound difficult but the gaps were extremely tight and the angles cunningly deceptive.

'This is where the trouble will be,' Richard had said measuring up a gap with his eye. 'If we don't come round there exactly right and at the right speed that wheel could go into that tree.'

And with prophetic accuracy that was exactly what happened. Another sickening crunch and then a dead halt. But this time, when Richard tried to back the horses off, nothing happened. If you went forward the front wheel ran up against the tree and wedged. If you went backwards the back wheel went into the cattle feeder and wedged. After several fruitless attempts, by which time the horses were getting hot and bothered, he put us down. Better to incur penalties than disqualification. After five minutes in a hazard it was all over. Heaving and tugging at the horses' bits Janice and I tried to lead them forward. They came willingly a step or two then, crunch, and they could go no further. Quite a crowd had gathered round the hazard to watch the goings-on by now and I felt colour rising in my cheeks as I flushed with anger, disappointment and embarrassment. It wasn't fair, they'd been going so well. After a little while Blizzard just refused to move at all, and stood there, bemused by it all. Once he gave up, Bear seemed to find the exercise pretty fruitless too. The adrenalin was surging round me by now. I knew the seconds were ticking by and we couldn't, we just couldn't be stopped by something as stupid as a tree. In one desperate last attempt I slapped Blizzard on the nose and pulled his bit.

'Come on, you stupid animal, for God's sake at least try to move.'

'Don't you dare hit that horse, he's doing the best he can!' Janice rounded on me.

'He's not even trying! He's not moving a muscle!'

'Don't you dare lay a finger on him!' Janice bristled in his defence.

That did it. Something snapped; some primitive emotional safety valve gave way and I lashed out.

'If you didn't have him so spoilt rotten he wouldn't be so namby-pamby and useless!'

Cheeks flaring red with passion and anger, Janice tried to push me out of my position at the horses' heads and grimly I pushed back.

From far, far away a voice said, 'Carol, for Christ's sake!'

Oh dear Lord, what was I doing? I was virtually brawling with another woman in front of a highly amused crowd. I was making a complete and utter spectacle of myself. Shame washed over me. From the edge of the hazard a whistle blew. It was all over.

'Do you think you two could manage to get these horses out without coming to blows?' Richard said coldly.

Without exchanging a word, heads bowed, Janice and I held our respective horses' heads while Richard unhitched them and we led them the long bitter way back to the horsebox.

I felt so terrible. So guilty and ashamed. What on earth had come over me? I had never, ever in all my life experienced such reckless, stubborn feelings as I had in that hazard. I had thrown all common sense and common restraint to the wind. Tears rolled down my cheeks as I trudged back to the box with Bear.

It was not long before Richard, with a willing band of helpers, puffed in pulling the vehicle.

'Look at this,' he called us. 'Just leave the horses tied up where they are and look at this. When we hit that first hazard we must have bent the pole by about eighteen inches to one side. There was no way, no way at all that the horses could get a straight pull at it. When they got stuck, it was bound to keep coming over to one side and hitting that tree. So it wasn't their fault and it wasn't your fault; it was just one of those things.'

'Oh, Richard, I feel so ashamed.'

'Good. What are you going to do about it? Have you sorted it out with Janice?'

'Not yet. I don't know what to say.'

'Well, you're a big girl now, I'm sure you'll manage.'

And I did somehow. After a terse exchange and then a few tears and a round of 'it was my fault — no it was mine — no honestly, I started it off,' and so on, the dust was truly laid.

I never did fully understand the violence of my reaction that day; it was something that has happened to me only that once, and I wouldn't want it to recur. Losing control of one's emotions is a slippery path. But it taught me how deep-rooted my feelings were for what we were doing. If I had kidded myself I was just playing at this game, after that day I realised I was involved for real. I'd always denounced having a competitive streak, at being ambitious in any way. The illusion that I wasn't, was shattered at Sandringham. And if we were going to succeed it would be by hard, consistent work and cool, careful organisation. We all needed to become more professional. We'd dropped out of one event through mis-management and now a second by the grooms losing their cool. We couldn't afford to let it happen again.

Back home at Stanley, there wasn't the purposeful optimistic atmosphere there'd been after Perth. It was nearly August. The summer was slipping by and as far as the pair were concerned their first season was over. Three events — one success and two disasters. Should I have expected more in their first few outings? I wasn't sure. A few short months ago simply to put the whole thing together, compete the pair at an event, was an impossible goal. So surely we'd achieved something?

Richard was adamant that Blizzard did no more. Not at his age. Young horses could be so easily soured and never regain their full zest. No; he'd been working hard all year, time for a rest. But I was dissatisfied, unhappy, restless. Partly over the horses, or to be precise, Bear. It seemed such a miracle to have him back in full health, driving again. It seemed such a waste to stop now in mid-season: he was eleven years old and fully mature, be didn't need a short season, he needed his full potential stretching again.

However, the greatest source of my dissatisfaction was the caravan. It sounded idyllic — parked in a field, horses at your door, small spaces to keep clean, a minimum of housework. The outdoor life, the fun, the novelty. The problem was the novelty soon wore off with the lack of space, lack of privacy, lack of proper sanitation.

But salvation was at hand. My source of information was Edie from the corner shop. She knew everyone and everything that related to the village. Including the fact that there was a little terrace house empty and to rent at the other end of the street. It was very modest but had two bedrooms and, oh joy, a bathroom. It took me three days to scrub it out and two more to organise my furniture. We were moved in within the week. The caravan became our new harness and tea room. Of course we moved back a step because it meant paying out rent again, but we were still within five minutes' walk of the horses and we were warm, clean and sane. Megan, quite aptly, christened our new accommodation, 'The Inbetween House'.

I was just recovering from the exertion of the move and mentally disciplining myself to stop thinking about horses and driving for the rest of the year and start thinking about bricks and mortar when Richard stuck another unexpected spanner in the works. He'd entered Bear for Castle Howard Driving Trials. Single.

'You've *what*?'

'Now, you're the one who was moaning that it was criminal for him to be wasted for the rest of the season when he's so well again!'

'Well, I admit that. But for a start we don't have a single presentation vehicle any more, or had you forgotten?'

'We've got your cross-country vehicle.'

'Have you seen the state of it recently?'

Richard murmured in his infuriatingly reassuring way, 'I'll soon slap a coat of paint on it.'

And of course he did and of course we went. It was to be an almost fairytale event. In the shadow of the great house of Castle Howard, awakened every morning by the shrill note of the peacocks, it was like taking part in *Brideshead Revisited*. And when, despite our shabby vehicle and a nerve-biting finish in the cones, Richard drove Bear to his first F.E.I. victory, the fairytale was complete. Knowing how much it meant to me, he allowed me to take the reins in the final parade and to accept the cup and rosettes from Simon Howard. Driving Bear around that arena on his very first lap of honour awoke a deeply suppressed longing in me.

When we returned home I began to work on fulfilling that longing. Or to be more precise, to work on Richard.

It was nearly the end of the season. So there were no more events to worry about afterwards . . . if anything should go wrong . . . which it wouldn't . . . I would probably never get another chance . . . Next year he would be driving the pair all season . . . I know I'd done a couple of Beamishs but it wasn't quite the same thing.

As I drove into the arena at Osberton on dressage day of my first full F.E.I. event, I began to wish I hadn't been so persuasive. I had practised that test until I was literally doing it in my sleep. I had paced the movements out on the carpet, I had even done them in the local swimming baths. But as I entered that arena to be faced by judges on three sides it was to little avail. I knew I had the best single dressage horse in the country on the other end of my reins but that was to little avail either. Crooked and ragged we swerved erratically up the centre line and managed a pathetic salute. When I tried to form the words of command to move off, nothing issued but a rattle from my bone-dry throat. On rigid wrists my hands were like lead weights that refused to do what my brain was frantically instructing them. My heart raced and my whip drooped. All this transferred itself in its telegraphic way down the reins to Bear who wobbled along, cutting corners and flattening circles, obviously totally confused by the instructions he was receiving. It was one of the longest ten minutes of my life and my smile at the final salute was of pure relief. But although the execution of the tests was poor, the content was correct. I'd made no errors and out of twenty-two entries in the class I found myself twelfth after presentation and dressage.

Richard nearly wept into his beer that night. Oh, the humiliation of it all. Bear twelfth in a dressage test. I was just thankful and astonished not to be eliminated.

The marathon the next day was frightening at times but in an exhilarating rather than tense way. Of course I drove those big hazards much slower than Richard would, but again I got all my sections and even moved up a couple of places overall. In the cones on the final day I knocked only the final cone down and was within the time allowed, and so kept my tenth place.

In the same arena where three years earlier Brian had won third prize at the National Championships I accepted my 'also ran' rosette with great contentment. I had finally achieved what had been my burning, driving ambition for so long and discovered, almost to my amusement, that I wasn't really very good at it. I got a far greater kick out of watching Richard driving the cobs. It interfered with my aesthetic appreciation of their turn-out and dressage movements when I had to try and remember the test. Most of all, I really did prefer Bear to be up among the winners where he belonged. I had driven my first F.E.I event; it would also be my last.

13

'This year the Nationals, next year the World'

WE VIEWED THE year ahead, 1984, with optimism and enthusiasm. This was the brink. We had moved into our new house in time for Christmas. It was far from finished, and far from perfect but it was our — Richard's, Megan's and my — home. We also had our horses, our vehicles and, having invested the very last of our money into show harness, everything we needed to compete the following season. Filled with zeal we entered the horses for the first main event on the calendar at the end of April: Brighton Horse Driving Trials. Plod had never before undertaken such a long journey. At the end of thirteen ear-splitting, juddering hours we crawled rather than climbed out on to *terra firma*. The horses came down the ramp as fresh as when they'd left home.

The setting in Stanmer Park, Brighton, was delightful, especially with early spring positively oozing out of the parkland around us. We were so determined to do well. However, we had had problems with exercise; the cobs were used to a really long run just before dressage to settle them down mentally, but we'd been told that for reasons of safety we could exercise only in the park itself, not go out on to the busy main road nearby. So we did the best we could, lunging them and ambling round the park on them. I realised as we drove up for our presentation that they were on fire, Bear especially. They had had precious few opportunities to drive the phaeton the previous year and had not been out in it at all as a pair since then. That was the first and most obvious mistake: Richard should have been driving them at home in it a few times. The second glaring mistake was with their new harness. Oh, it looked beautiful and it fitted perfectly. Richard and I had tried it all on and adjusted it to fit when we got it. But that was all we'd done; once again we'd omitted to give it a trial run. And now it was too late and we were heading up to be judged for presentation and the horses were far, far from happy.

'What on earth's upsetting them?' Richard asked, trying to hide his anxiety.

Trotting beside them, complete with bucket of last-minute cleaning equipment, Janice surveyed them carefully to try and find the problem.

'Don't rightly know. Summat's up though.'

Veins by now were bulging on Bear's neck. A hand with sharp nails had hold of all my internal organs.

'Shall we go back?' I ventured hopefully.

'There's no time, we'll miss our presentation. Whoa! You daft buggers! Whoa.'

'It seems to be summat wrong with their heads, at least with those new bridles,' Janice reported.

'Bear seems to be trying to shake his off, yet it fits him right enough. Why should it be upsetting him so much?' New bridles, new bridles, my mind searched frantically. New bridles; what was different with the new bridles? Of course! It was the 'drops'. The 'drops' were purely ornamental, a tear-shaped piece of patent leather which hung from the middle of the head piece below the brow band, and dangled on to the forehead. And they had never worn a bridle with one on before. As they trotted, the drops bounced slightly on their foreheads and that could be what was upsetting them. That, or not getting their usual amount of exercise. Perhaps I should have cut their feed back and made allowances for that as well. Perhaps it was all three.

'Dear Lord,' I prayed silently and swiftly, 'don't let them do anything dreadful.'

The presentation judge was extremely understanding. There was no way Richard could get them to stand still at all. I tried standing in the allotted place in front of them but twice nearly got mown flat as they shot forward.

'Good morning, sir,' Richard doffed his bowler and flashed Major Coombes his most boyish of grins. 'Spring would appear to be in the air. I seem to have my hands rather full!'

'So I see, Mr Smith, so I see. Just walk them quietly round if you can; I'm sure I can judge you on the move.'

When that part was over, both gentlemen solemnly doffed their bowlers to each other again and I made to climb up into the back of the vehicle.

'Don't get in the back! Sit here beside me,' instructed Richard. 'You'll be able to get to the horses' heads much quicker if you are in the front.'

Having been nearly flattened at my last attempt, I did not see what earthly use I could be even if I got to their heads. With slightly knocking knees I sat beside Richard.

'I'm just going to drive quietly round till it's time for dressage and see if they settle a bit. Anything could happen when they get into that arena. Anything.'

I must say that did a great deal to reassure me and so intent were we on watching the horses' every move that the minutes just slid by and the next thing we knew a car horn sounded.

'That's it! We're on!'

Clutching the underneath of my seat for dear life, Richard turned the horses for their approach. I felt as if I were on board a hijacked airplane that could explode any minute. As soon as they had charged up the centre line and halted, they stood like lambs while Richard saluted the judges. Then they set away at a brisk, but not silly pace and settled down to drive the test. My heart and respiration levels began to return to normal. My prayer had been answered; it was going to be all right. A car horn pierced the spring air.

'Funny,' I thought, 'they can't want another competitor in here yet.'

Then the senior judge left his car and began to walk slowly across to us.

'I'm sorry, Mr Smith,' he said pleasantly, 'but the rules firmly state that in a four-wheeled vehicle the groom must at all times sit behind the driver. I'm afraid I've no choice but to eliminate you.'

Just like that. All those hours and all those miles; all the work and preparation and we didn't even make the first fence.

We returned silent and shocked to the box. Even Janice was utterly speechless. I became aware of Richard minus his suit, jacket and bowler, standing behind me. I turned to say something, determined to handle it in an adult manner. I opened my mouth to speak and the next thing I knew my face was buried in his crisp, best, white shirt and I was sobbing my heart out. Richard held me and stroked my hair.

'Shush, shush, there, there.'

'It's not fair, it's not fair. We hadn't done anything wrong.'

'It's a rule and if you don't know the rules you shouldn't play the game.'

'But I . . .' more slobbery sobs were deposited on his shoulder. I was shattered.

'Shush. Shush. Look, I knew that rule as well as the next one. But I was concentrating so hard on settling the horses down that I forgot about you. Forgot you were still sitting beside me, that's all. I just heard that car horn and went.'

'But I didn't know!'

'You will another time. That's one mistake you'll never make again.'

So the marathon the next day was purely academic. The competitve pressure might have been off but that didn't make the going any easier. I had travelled harder marathons, steeper marathons, twistier marathons but never, ever a bumpier marathon. The hard flinty tracks were incredibly punishing for horses' legs and vehicles' wheels and rattled the teeth and bones of the drivers and grooms. Hanging on to the back for dear life Janice and I were shaken to jelly and I had to concentrate far more on trying to keep the weight off my bad leg than on balancing the vehicle over the course. And that was stupid, really stupid. A one-legged groom more worried about her own safety than that of the horses was a complete liability. Because, academic or not, Richard was driving that marathon for real and had a mishap occurred that would have been for real as well. But, thank God, nothing untoward happened and we finished the course shaken, but not stirred.

We competed in the cones for form's sake on the Sunday and prepared to depart for our long journey home early on the Monday morning. I'd been very stiff and sore all over on the Sunday, but then so had Janice so I was not worried. By the Monday morning the general stiffness and soreness was wearing off, except in one place: my hip. By the time we'd completed our tedious, uncomfortable journey I was having great difficulty in putting any weight on the leg at all. By the time the week was out I had to admit the full extent of my foolishness and phone Miss Robinson.

She again sat for long infuriatingly silent minutes staring at the X-rays she'd had taken. Long minutes that allowed me to sweat a bit. I'd broken the rules, I knew that, but what if I'd done some irreparable damage? Hadn't she once said the repair to the joint could become unstable anything up to two years after surgery? Something about disrupting the blood supply to the head of the bone? Oh, why had I been so arrogant, so stupid?

'Mmm.'

'I know I've been silly, but it's been fine for months, honestly. I haven't had so much as a twinge till now, and I did a few marathons last year,' I blurted out.

'Mmm?'

'Well, only one or two.'

'It's badly inflamed but there doesn't seem to be any irreparable damage. It's going to have to be well rested, given a chance to recover.'

'Oh, I'll take things very, very gently for a while,' I assured her.

'You certainly will,' Miss Robinson replied, 'because you'll be back on crutches.'

'Crutches? Oh but I . . .'

'Or would you prefer traction?'

I conceded defeat. 'I'll take the crutches. How long for?'

'Only two weeks if you behave yourself and take these anti-inflammatory tablets regularly.'

Only two weeks proved to be a minor eternity. How on earth did I manage before, all those months without my hands free? I was irritable, harassed and very humbled by the end of it.

Returning my crutches to Miss Robinson I meekly promised never to be so stupid again. I had been let off lightly.

The depressing thing was that I saw all my involvement with the horses slipping out of my hands. Apart from dressing up in the presentation and dressage and sitting in the good carriage, I would not now be taking an active part in competitions at all. To add to my misery, Richard seemed quite relieved by Miss Robinson's decision.

'She's absolutely right. The back of that cart's no place for you. I've got to be very honest, it keeps my mind off my job when I have to be worrying about you on the marathon. I don't really want to have to carry two grooms, it's all additional weight and handicap for the horses. But neither you nor Janice could manoeuvre the back of that cart on your own, it takes a great deal of strength. No disrespect to you lasses, but I'd feel much happier with a man on the back. I always used to carry a man. You can leave them to worry about the cart and you can concentrate on your horses.'

'Oh, so actually you'll be glad to get shot of me?'

'I didn't say that, sweetheart. I'm just trying to explain.'

'That I'm a liability! That I'm a hindrance rather than a help! I don't know why you don't just leave me at home altogether. Just take the horses and go.'

'I'll put you across my knee in a minute, young lady, if you talk such rubbish.'

My feathers began to unruffle, my balloon of hot air to deflate.

'Oh, I'm sorry. I didn't mean it like that. You're right, that's what hurts; you *are* right. I wanted so hard and for so long to do this sport. It was all that kept me going at one point. I lived and breathed to compete well some day. Then I find that my horse competes much better without me driving him, then he goes into a pair and I can't drive them anyway and I now find I can't even go round the marathon with him. I'm not bitter and I'm not envious, I just feel . . . redundant . . . that's all.'

'Do you want to give it up? Say the word and I'll pack it all in tomorrow. We can't really afford to do it, anyway. You could sell Blizzard at a tidy profit. Or sell them as a pair, they'd fetch a lot of money as a pair.'

I realised with horror that Richard was deadly serious.

'Sell Bear?' I croaked.

'Look, there's no point in keeping them if you don't want to compete them.'

'But I do! I do!' I protested 'Don't you see I want to be involved — that's all, involved!'

'I think you mean you need to know you're indispensable. Okay. I'll tell you a few home truths.'

Richard fixed me with one of his penetrating looks that rendered me temporarily speechless.

'You've come a long way, a very long way, from your original plan. You know, the scenario of you, your horse and your trap. You now own one of the best pairs of horses in the country. Oh, I know they haven't actually won much yet, but they're going to, believe me they are going to. And I intend to drive them to that success. That's my job — to drive them, and I do it better than you and that's a fact.'

I gave a solemn, silent nod of agreement.

'But your job is just as vital, every little bit as vital. And actually a lot harder than mine. You've got to keep on top of them at home, every day. Watch their exercise, watch their feed. You've got to organise and pack them, us and a million other things into that box and trailer for every show. I wouldn't know where to start. You're in charge of turning them out to a standard of perfection that I have come to expect, but I would be at a loss if I had to try and do it myself. And I know how difficult it is for you, believe me, coping in that cold, smelly horsebox and a damp tent. But somehow you provide hot meals and keep us all right. And that's your job and it's every bit as vital as mine. Involved? We'd never get ten yards from home if you didn't do your job right.'

'Who are you going to put in my, I mean our, place on the cart?' I finally managed to ask quietly.

'I know exactly who I want on the back of there. Newcastle Brown.'

'What? That's a beer!'

'In this case it's a nickname, for Ray Brown. You know, my friend who organised the Shortflat drive. He used to drive a pair of ponies but has nothing of his own at present. But he knows this game, oh he knows this game.'

And Ray certainly did. The results in the next couple of months spoke for themselves; third at Perth, third at Holker, third at Sandringham. Partly it was because the horses were getting more experienced every time out, partly it could have been luck. But partly it had to be Ray Brown, effortlessly swinging the back of that heavy vehicle round very tight hazards, then giving his famous broad Geordie holler 'Gan on Dick!' at which Richard would chase the horses on and take valuable seconds off the time it took to get out of the hazards. Our marathon scores improved beyond belief and I discovered a new masochistic pleasure — watching the pair in the hazards. It did everything, if not more, for my adrenalin than being on the back of the vehicle had without the bumps and with a better view. I was content.

Reading the local newspaper one day, I noticed a very small advert that read 'Experienced groom — three months to fill — anything interesting considered' and that's how we got Alison Cowley.

She was twenty-two carat. An extremely experienced head girl from a big eventing yard and waiting to go out to South Africa to take charge of a pony stud. On the phone she admitted she knew nothing whatsoever about carriage driving and didn't know if she could help us in any way. I tried to assure her she could. That the driving was really the end product of much careful ridden work. That although Blizzard was doing very well on the 'grunt and grind' part of the event, his dressage still left much to be desired. And neither Janice nor I had the required skill and experience to help his progress any further. So Alison came for a trial afternoon and stayed for two days.

I met her down in the market place in Crook and tried desperately all the way to Stanley to apologise for our ram-shackle building, our muddy yard, our lack of facilities. She was one of the few people I took an instant liking to. She was everything she appeared to be — competent, experienced and cheerful.

She took Blizzard in hand and gave him the biggest shock of his young life. It was with an astonished expression he found he could, if pushed hard enough, loosen his joints, lengthen his stride, get his hindquarters under him. She was quite the best rider I had ever seen. She made it appear totally effortless.

From then on she came two days every week. And she taught us other things — about stable routine and fitness programmes, about feeding and supplements. In a few short weeks Alison made us realise we were really rank amateurs, dedicated amateurs admittedly, but there was much, much more we should and could know. Routine was her key. A consistent, balanced routine, of work, of feeding, of play. The horses thrived.

We took them to Castle Howard where Bear had won the single class the previous year and were thrilled when they came second. It was the best result of their career so far.

Full of renewed optimism we tackled Lowther. It was renowned for its arduous marathon and its lakeland weather. For five days it rained solidly. The horses were wet, cold and miserable and so were we. The dressage wasn't too bad considering the appalling weather but our good carriage and harness got soaked. Damp and dull, the harness hung on the walls of the horsebox looking as forlorn as we felt.

On the morning of the marathon I awoke to a very unpleasant sensation, one that was very cold and went squelch. To try and accommodate my hip we now slept on a proper double mattress which we placed on a groundsheet in the tent. During the night the rainwater had accumulated, flowed down the slight slope we were camped on, crept in under the top side of the tent, flowed across the groundsheet and into the top end of the mattress. Throughout the night it had percolated slowly right down my side of the bed. At the foot of the bed was our suitcase with all our clothes — only now they were soaked.

That was only the start of a disastrous day. The course was by now water-logged. Discussions had been raging on the previous day as to whether parts of the marathon should be closed, but it was now decided it was driveable. Just. Waiting near the first of the hazards, which was actually in the middle of a river crossing, I knew when I caught my first glimpse of the cobs that something was wrong. There was no sparkle or attack in their action. They were just plugging on, heads down, for grim death. They lifted a little to Richard's voice at the edge of the river and went down the bankside at a fair pace. As they levelled out at the bottom there was a sickening cracking noise from the vehicle and I held my breath while they negotiated the elements of the hazard and came back out of the river. Then I saw the problem. The spring leaf at the back of the pole which supported it and gave it a resilient bounce had given way. Now the pole hung as a dead and heavy weight on the front of the horses' collars, and succeeded in dragging their pace down even further.

I watched in disbelief as, at the next hazard on a steep bankside, they just couldn't find the momentum to make a turn and stood there dazed and exhausted. Lowther 1984 was over as far as they were concerned. Richard nursed and coaxed them through the remainder of the course.

At the horsebox, Alison, Janice and I anxiously unharnessed them and led them into stalls into which we'd spread the last of the dry bedding. They were tucked up, miserable and completely exhausted.

'What's the matter with them?' I demanded, close to tears. 'I know it's been a hard course with lots of hills and heavy going. And I know the pole spring breaking didn't help, but surely it can't account for them being like this. The other horses aren't coming in in this condition.' The marathon had slaughtered them.

That night, having polished off a good bran mash, Bear and Blizzard looked a bit better. Huddled in the horsebox over our supper, I dreaded the thought of trying to sleep in that tent. I had dried what surplus water I could out of the mattress with towels and Richard had dug a moat round the tent to prevent another flood in the night. But it remained a damp and miserable prospect. It struck me as I put up the horses' feed in the back of the trailer that it was drier in there than it was in the tent. Morale was very low. On the Sunday we did a half-hearted cones and then loaded all our soaking clothes and equipment into the wagon and headed thankfully for home, dry clothes and hot baths.

It had not been the best of events. But then we'd had a run of good luck and it couldn't go on for ever. I couldn't get the image of those struggling, distressed horses out of my mind. They'd been so fit just a couple of weeks ago. Had we pushed them too hard? Had they done too many events? Surely not.

I questioned Alison closely on the journey home as to the possible causes.

She was as baffled as I was at first.

'We've eliminated feed and work and illness,' she said. 'That doesn't leave a lot else. And I know I asked about worming when I first came. You did say they'd been wormed?'

'Oh, yes.'

'Regularly?'

'Yes, regularly.'

She paused and thought before asking, 'How regular is regularly?'

'Oh,' I assured her, 'three time a year at least. Certainly before they go out to grass and when they come back in.'

She blanched slightly and asked, 'When were they last wormed?'

I thought back. 'Oh, about three months ago I should think.'

Looking at her face I realised what she was thinking.

'But they can't have worms!' I spluttered. 'Look at their coats, look at the condition of them, the flesh on them!'

'I'm afraid they could, very much afraid they could. They need worming religiously every six weeks all year round and the wormer has to be changed regularly so thay they don't build up a tolerance. You must make sure you've killed red worms, bots, whip worms — the lot — or you can be in serious trouble.'

Once more the gaping black hole of inexperience had nearly swallowed us. Two days later, cringing with shame, I examined their droppings with Alison. She'd wormed them thoroughly the night before. Both were full of whip worms, and Blizzard also had red worms. Untreated red worms can attack and destroy the muscles of the heart itself. I was appalled. It was yet another lesson learnt at the expense of near disaster.

Morale dropped even lower when Alison had to leave to take up her new appointment in South Africa. We'd all come to rely on her wisdom and experience so much in the previous three months.

Richard dropped a prize clanger by missing the entry dates for Osberton and that left a very large gap before the only remaining event on our calendar: the National Championships at Windsor. Through their success earlier in the season we had qualified anyway, but what should have been exciting and challenging, our first National Championships, was somehow flat. Alison made us vow solemnly to her before she left that we would compete and so great was our regard for her that we did, albeit with little enthusiasm. It had been a long and tiring season — nearly six months in all — and I did not relish the thought of roughing it yet another weekend in a tent. It was something I was almost beginning to dread.

But if we were half-hearted getting there, our performance wasn't. The long rest from Lowther seemed to have done the cobs good. All their sparkle and enthusiasm had returned. They were placed third overall. Third in their first National Championships. Four years ago that was exactly what Bear had achieved and look where we had all progressed since then. It was a good omen for the future.

'This year,' teased Richard, 'the Nationals. Next year, the World!'

14

New grooms and new brooms

THE LOUDSPEAKER CRACKLED and the announcer informed us that the train would be about forty minutes late. I cursed inwardly and trudged back to the car. I was certainly not spending forty minutes on the bleak, windswept platform of Durham Station, and the waiting room was not much more inviting. It was the first week in February 1985, grey and raw. In this unlikely setting our audacious attempt at the impossible was to begin, here, today.

Two life-altering events had occurred since we'd turned the horses out for their well-earned rest in late September. Firstly, Richard and I had been married one bitterly cold Saturday afternoon in early January. We'd both felt that finally the time was right. There were six people in the local church apart from Richard, Megan and myself. Oh, and the Rector and the Organist. We decided that although there was too few of us to sing we should have music. Megan was our bridesmaid, resplendent in pink and white and trying bravely not to shiver. The ceremony was lovely and traditional and very, very moving. We all shed our tears of remembrance and joy and hope. Afterwards we all filed into the vestry to sign the Register and then marched proudly down the aisle as the organ reverberated gloriously in the completely empty church. We did not need numbers to make our day special — all who mattered were there. The few who'd kept faith and close friendship in the past three difficult years: Bill and Charlotte from New Jersey had even flown the Atlantic in mid-winter so that Bill could give me away. He took my arm as proudly as any father and propelled me up the aisle, pausing only to assure the amused Rector, 'She'll be fine; she'd done this before, you know!'

The second momentous event took much longer in the shaping but was sparked off by an announcement towards the end of 1984 in the press that in August 1985 the first World Pairs Driving Championships was to he held, and to be held in Great Britain. There would be a team of three to represent each country

and as Great Britain was the host nation we could also enter a
further six individual drivers. All those wishing to be considered
for selection for the team or as an individual should write to the
British Horse Society at once.

One of Great Aunt Meg's favourite expressions had always
been 'Many a true word spoken in jest.' 'This year the
Nationals, next year the World!' Richard had teased. Suddenly,
the world was knocking on our door. Reading the
announcement Richard was trembling with excitement.

'I knew it would happen some day, I knew it had to come but I
never dreamt it would happen while I was still driving. And to
be in this country!'

'Where is it to be held?'

'It doesn't say yet.'

'Do you think we'll be able to close down everything at work
and go? Could we get someone to look after the horses so we
can get away and watch?'

'Of course we'll go, you silly woman, but we don't need
anyone to look after the horses; they'll be there!'

Rosy cheeks flaring, blue eyes twinkling, Richard was on fire.

'Whoa, whoa,' I said. 'Just a minute, Smith, get your feet back
on the ground. I hope you don't mean what I think you mean.'

'And that is?'

He obviously wanted the kick of hearing me say it, so I obliged
him: 'That we put your name forward for consideration for
selection for the World Championships.'

'And if I do?'

I didn't want to hurt him. I didn't want to deprive him of his
dreams, but this was for real.

'Be realistic, sweetheart.'

'But I am,' he exploded, 'I'm being very realistic. Apart from
our disasters at Brighton and Lowther last season, how were we
placed?'

'Third mostly, second at Castle Howard,' I admitted.

'And in the National Championships?'

'Third.'

'Exactly, third best in the country. And how many pairs did
they want for the team?'

'Three,' I conceded. 'But, Richard, hear me out. Surely they
won't pick a team based on one season's results?'

'No, of course not. They look over track records for
consistency, but mostly I would think it'll be based on next
season and who's doing well then. We haven't got a track
record as such because this year was the horses' first real season

together. And look what they achieved, just look what they achieved! We'll just have to show them that they can do it next season, that's all. We'll just have to go all out in every event right from the start. Blizzard is six next year, still a bit young, but he'll be better than last year. We'll just have to show them.'

Why wasn't I excited? Why wasn't I sharing Richard's enthusiasm? I felt strangely apprehensive, overawed almost, at the prospect.

'So we do a full season, every event right from the beginning of the year. How can we afford it? You know things aren't great at work — it's a struggle to keep going as we are without taking on additional commitments.' I felt like a wet blanket.

'To be truthful, I don't know and to be truthful it's a problem. But this is a once in a lifetime chance! It'll never happen for me again, Carol, never. To be held in this country and when I've got two such marvellous horses to drive? No, it'll never happen for me again, or for them. Somehow, don't ask me how, somehow we have to go for it!'

I understood then that we did, of course we did. If we failed, we failed. If we ran out of money, we ran out of money. But if we didn't try, if we didn't give both horses a chance, we would never forgive ourselves.

'Things will have to be very different from last season,' I said cautiously. 'We need a different routine, a more professional approach. If we're going to do this, then we need to be very serious about it indeed.'

'Serious? Try deadly serious.'

And I could see that he was.

So plans were drawn up, radical plans. The horses needed a regular routine of carefully structured work and care. A routine that didn't depend on my availability to ride or drive or whether my hip was niggly or not. Or whether Richard was late home from work or that I had to get Megan from school. A routine that was the responsibility of someone who knew what they were doing, a professional. Janice was marvellous in her dedication and enthusiasm, but her spare time was strictly limited and like myself she was an amateur who'd learnt the job as she'd gone along. Neither of us would have a clue how to implement a rigorous work, feed and fitness programme. Nor could either of us give Blizzard the requisite schooling and training he still needed as a young horse. We needed someone dedicated and professional. We needed an experienced, trained groom to take full charge of the horses and their training. That being so, how did we afford one?

The answer was complicated but in theory would work. One, if not both, of the part-time helpers who looked after the shop when Richard was out on calls or deliveries would have to go and that would release enough money to employ a groom. I would have to go and work at the shop in the mornings instead. It was not a prospect I relished; the place was indescribably foul and depressing but it appeared the only solution. Richard would do his calls and deliveries in the morning while I minded the shop. He would return at midday and release me to do shopping, cleaning, laundry (and perhaps the odd ride I pointed out sharply) and to collect Megan from school. And the groom would thus be in charge of the horses at home all day. Richard would drive the pair out as usual in the evenings and at weekends. In theory it would work.

Having someone 'living in' was also a big step, but the house was big enough and it was a time-honoured arrangement that worked well if you picked the right person.

So here I was praying that we had indeed picked the 'right' person. Chris Morris-Jones was one of the handful who had answered our small advert in *Horse and Hound*. We had whittled it down to Chris and A.N. Other who dropped out when she discovered she wasn't to have her own bathroom. And Chris was arriving on the afternoon train and I didn't know quite what to expect. Most grooms, in my experience, have a very practical outlook and way of dressing based on a life-style that demands early mornings and early nights, being out in all weathers and having your hair crammed under a riding hat most of the time and any attempts at nice hands a lost cause. Their make-up is often reduced to pinching some of the horse's Vaseline to relieve cracked lips. Green wellies, warm woollies and waxed jackets are par for the course. I was anxious too that I presented the right image as a 'horsy employer' so I had on sensible shoes, navy cord trousers, a navy quilted jacket and my tweed hat.

The minutes ticked slowly by and finally the loudspeaker crackled once more and the voice said, 'The next train to arrive . . .' The train snaked over the curve of the viaduct and into the station. If nothing else, I thought, Miss Morris-Jones' first view of Durham should be an impressive one with the cathedral and castle crowning their ancient rock just opposite. The train hissed and clanked to a halt and doors opened and people climbed out and clambered in, heaving luggage and folding pushchairs.

Then the sound was mostly of shutting doors and people approaching the ticket barrier.

My palms tingled with nervous perspiration: how silly of me, it was only a girl, a nineteen-year-old girl. Why should I be nervous? I vetted each person approaching the barrier, hurriedly putting them into possible or unlikely categories. Most were quite obviously not my groom and I could see nothing that remotely resembled a true possible. Oh God, what if she's missed the train? A tall girl with big glasses was striding up the platform. To say she was 'well-built' was incorrect because it is usually just a polite way of saying hefty. This girl wasn't hefty, at least the bottom half wasn't. The top half was something else though, quite something else. She had flaming auburn hair, thick, wildly curled and tumbling round her shoulders. She wore a tight jumper, tighter trousers and high-heeled open-toed shoes from which black, seamed stockings protruded. Her make-up must have taken hours to apply and was truthfully a work of art. Under one arm she had clamped a radio of ghetto-blaster proportions and her electric hair curlers. I couldn't quite make out what was under the other arm as she was carrying an enormous suitcase. She was headed, unerringly, straight for me. Six feet away I realised what was protruding under her other arm. A pair of leather riding boots and a long dressage whip.

'Mrs Smith?' she asked sweetly.

I, at least, had obviously matched up to expectations.

'Yes, yes I am,' I answered rather faintly, 'and you, you would be . . .'

'Chris Morris-Jones; I'd shake hands but I'd drop this lot.'

'Oh yes, of course, of course, how silly of me, well, let's get this lot to the car and get home.' My voice felt as if it were coming from a long, long way away.

Once in the car, we made polite conversation for a while but Chris soon broke the ice and got down to basics.

'What sort of place is it where you live? Quiet, is it?'

'Oh very, except when they chuck the pub out.'

'But you're near to somewhere bigger. Crook, is it?'

'Crook is bigger and only two miles away.'

'And does it have much?'

'Much?'

'In the way of social life; discos, clubs, that sort of thing.'

I gulped. Crook had numerous pubs and two Chinese take-aways. But discos? Nightclubs?

'No, I'm afraid not. I suppose Bishop Auckland would be the nearest place for that sort of thing. It's about eight miles away.'

But Bishop Auckland, I knew in my heart, wasn't the centre of urban sophistication and social life that Chris was obviously used to.

'It's just that, well I think it's important to get things sorted out from the start, don't you? My job is the most important thing of course; the horses. But in my time off, my free time, my social life is very important too.'

I churned inwardly. Had I made some fatal error? Had I misled this young girl on the phone as to what to expect? As to where we lived? What we were trying to do? Did she expect some busy, thriving event yard and a hectic social life? What would she say when she saw Stanley Crook? We were so proud of our new buildings, the loose boxes, the harness room, the new paint, our little yard. But she'd worked in London, in Austria. Oh dear. I felt more uncomfortable and miserable with every mile home. I confided all my fears to Richard as soon as I'd shown her to her room and left her to unpack.

'Don't jump to any conclusions,' said Richard. 'She's here to do a job of work. Let's see if she's good at that and if she fits in. You must give her a chance.'

'Yes, you're right, you're right, of course.'

And he was. Despite her fizzy chatter and her bubbly manner she was, at the end of the day, just a young girl away from home, in the unknown and trying to find her feet. Certainly next morning she appeared on the yard, jodhpured and booted, hair neatly tied up under a tweed cap. She crowed and crooned to the horses in lilting Welsh, the lovely liquid notes flowing off her tongue. Blizzard immediately became her beloved, her *cariad*, and came in for extra-special attention. Bear, native Welshman though he was, was astonished by it all. She had the strength of a man; a well-built man at that. Barrows of muck appeared from the stables with amazing rapidity and she trundled them effortlessly on to the muck heap up the ramp that had usually had me gasping and sweating. Hay she handled a bale in each hand, and when she began grooming, the horses bent under her brush. The phrase 'a strapping lass' took on a whole new dimension. She could eat more than Richard, Megan and I together.

Her parents arrived the following weekend, her mother immaculate and stunning in a plunging neckline cream Welsh wool dress and matching cloak. Apparently she had a hair and beauty salon in Caernarvon. Father followed bearing the first of a carload of cases, boxes and bedding and bottle of whisky. Both were emptied in the first hour. When together, mother and daughter exchanged endless dialogue in alternate effortless English and Welsh. They departed in an orgy of Celtic grief leaving me totally exhausted and understanding Chris a lot better.

Her room was transformed into a shrine to Sylvester Stallone, who now hovered six foot and semi-naked over her bed, and occupied by the most astonishing array of clothes, make-up, Chinese parasols and general chaos I'd ever seen, Chris now obviously felt much more at home. ,

She tried everything and everyone in an attempt to secure the bright lights and male company she so badly sought but in a few weeks had picked through and discarded most of the male population of Crook and found that spending her modest wages mostly on taxi fares left her without even the means to buy herself the odd tea bag. Happy and ruthlessly efficient in her work, she remained lost and rather miserable on her days off. I sympathised: there was little locally to interest such a vivacious young girl.

Good luck or fate stepped in when she met Sonia at the local Leisure Centre. Sonia not only lived quite locally and was good fun, but she was also keen on horses, a good rider and unemployed. Within weeks her appearances became more regular and Chris much happier. In the end I had to provide a camp bed in Chris's room for the times Sonia wanted to stay over, and suddenly we had two grooms. With short dark hair and quieter than Chris, Sonia worked well with her most of the time. Theirs was a tears and laughter relationship; fighting and huffs one minute and laughing and giggling helplessly the next. The barometer of their emotions swung radically at times, leaving me feeling quite exhausted. Perhaps I should have been firmer, more authoritarian. Perhaps I should have sent them both packing. But Chris was an only child, desperate for acceptance and finding her feet in the world. And I knew that feeling so very, very well. Sonia came from an inadequate home with an inadequate mother and very little material comfort. She was experiencing a whole new world with Chris and the horses.

And the horses were the main thing; they blossomed and thrived. Chris worshipped Blizzard, Sonia adored Bear. They were groomed till they shone and their muscles rippled and the yard was, if not immaculate, a generally happy place. Chris was fiercely loyal, taking Megan to her heart and ample bosom and putting the horses and us, her new 'family', before all else. There were eccentricities of course, but we all have those. She adored mashed-banana-and-chocolate-spread sandwiches for breakfast. She wore an astonishing wardrobe of mostly black, tight and glittering clothes in her non-working life. The image of her floating across the yard to check the horses early in the morning in green wellies and a slit-sided black negligée, a black eye-mask perched on top of her flaming Titian curls, will remain with me for the rest of my life.

By April 1985 all the preparations were complete: the horses were fighting fit and in glorious condition. Richard had built a new cross-country battle wagon, the back of which Chris had learned to handle and to swing through the hazards with contemptuous ease. Any thought on the horses' part of slacking pace at a critical moment would be met with a torrent of ear-splitting Welsh abuse. Even Plod had had a coat of paint and the girls had begun the major task of planning and packing for the season.

I had the job, the enormous pleasure, of packing the trailer.

I had made a bargain with Richard. He would have my whole-hearted support for the year to come; I would work in the cold, miserable dirty shop cleaning cold, miserable dirty cookers every morning, provided I did not have to spend one more event in the cold, miserable tent. If I had to spend upwards of ten weeks of the coming summer living, cooking and sleeping in a field, I wanted to do it in reasonable comfort. The memories of Lowther the previous summer, with streams of living water flowing right through my bed, were still too fresh for comfort.

Richard put his mind to the problem. First he considered adapting Plod; putting windows in the front end and installing a proper kitchen and separating a living area off from the horses. But it would have meant a serious loss of space for carrying equipment, and anyway where would the girls sleep? It wasn't fair to ask them to live and work in a cold, miserable tent either. We also considered, and discarded, the idea of getting a caravan — we hadn't the capital for a start and there were events, the really long hauls like Brighton, where we saved fuel by taking everything in Plod and the trailer and leaving the car at home. The solution, as it so often is, was right before our eyes. At Lowther I had complained at one point that the only dry place we had was in the trailer where we kept the horses' feed and bedding. Richard installed a window and an access door at the front of it and behold, we had a light, dry, interior for living instead.

At the front end under the window he fitted a sink unit. A

full-sized sink unit with draining board and cupboards beneath and a tap that worked by a pump and a drain to the outside world. Beside this, I had a full-sized Calor gas cooker with an oven and three rings, and a work top in the corner. Down the side he put a kitchen dresser for storing food and crockery and a wardrobe and a chest of drawers. At the far end (lashed against the wall when in transit so the carriage could get in) was a full-sized, really real double bed with mattress and legs. A pine table and benches completed the furnishings. There were times (not many) when owning a second-hand furniture shop had its advantages.

I set about in a frenzy of domestic ecstasy to make it our second home. I chose red and white for my colour scheme; it was clean but warm at the same time. Soon bright curtains fluttered, the windows gleamed to show off the better my gleaming white paintwork and poppy-red doors and the red carpet. I simply could not believe that after seasons of roughing it I was going to be able to cook pleasurably, eat in spacious comfort and sleep in a warm, dry bed. I couldn't wait to get on the road.

Within the confines of our budget, we'd gone as far as we could to make the attempt a serious one. We had two smashing and keen girl grooms and a new mean-machine for the marathons. Gone were my black riding hat, hunting jacket and rubber boots and gone were Richard's bowler hat and one and only dark suit. This year, he said, we had to dress the part. So it had to be grey topper, wing collar and black jacket for Richard and full livery for me. My coat was the darkest of greens, my breeches and stock white, and my black top hat a family antique. I owned my first-ever pair of real leather boots, complete with mahogany tops, and if I felt like a flat-chested chimney pot at least I was a very smart flat-chested chimney pot.

Packing went on frantically till late into the evening before our departure. Richard had gone to bed. We were leaving at three o'clock the following morning and he had an exhausting drive ahead of him. Nobody but himself could handle the monstrous bulk of Plod plus trailer. We were as ready as we would ever be. From Brighton we were going straight on to the Royal Windsor Horse Show which was a qualifier for those aspiring for selection for the World Championships. So we would be on the road for the best part of a fortnight. Had I honestly packed every article of clothing Richard and I would need in that time, down to the last collar stud, driving apron and leather glove? Every piece of harness, tack and clothing the horses would need? Everything they would eat and sleep on? Most of what we

would eat and all of our bedding? The lamps? The whips? The
wet weather gear? Hot-water bottles, first aid kit, matches and
toilet rolls? I had checked my lists over and over, done my
menus again and again. I had even packed the small tin bath. It
was late and I was very, very tired. My brain refused to work
any more. If I'd forgotten anything vital I would no doubt find
out in due course. It hardly seemed worthwhile going to bed,
but four hours' sleep was better than none, and after all I could
sleep for as much of the forthcoming thirteen-hour journey as I
wanted.

At three in the morning it was freezing and pitch black. The
horses, at first blinking in astonishment as the lights came on in
the stable, soon realised what was going on and happily left
their warm beds, walked up the 'ramp like lambs and started
munching their hay nets contentedly. They seemed as keen as
we were to get the season under way. Chris freely admitted to
not being a 'morning person'; she certainly wasn't a three
o'clock in the morning person and I think she dressed and
loaded the horses by touch rather than sight, so swollen were
her eyes behind her glasses. Finally, with a dull thud, the ramp
went up, the bolts were put in and the trailer was hitched on.
The lights were connected and checked out and I passed the bag
full of flasks and sandwiches into the cab. One by one, Chris,
Sonia and I hauled ourselves up and the girls snuggled themselves down on the rugs and foam cushions behind the main
seat. I sat in the front beside Richard and pulled my door firmly
shut.

'Ready?' he said.

I took a deep breath. 'Ready.'

Plod's throaty engine throbbed to life and clouds of diesel
fumes flowed down the back street. Throttling back a bit,
Richard engaged first gear and we rolled gently forward.

Four people, two horses and two carriages, a home-made
trailer and an old furniture van turned horsebox off to take on
the best of the rest of the country.

It wasn't easy to sneak a nine-ton wagon and a twenty foot
trailer down a back street at 3.30 a.m. but Richard did the best
he could.

The journey was every bit as long and awful as the year
before, but when we got there Stanmer Park was every bit as
lovely. It had been the cold and raw tail end of winter when we
left Durham. It was spring in Brighton. Though stiff and tired
when we got out of the wagon in the late afternoon, the bracing
air and the general excitement of having actually arrived soon

revitalised us and we started the ritual of setting up.

Normally this would have involved me in erecting stables, organising horses' beds, and putting up the tent. But not this year. The first of the major changes in our organisation was about to bear fruit. As soon as the trailer was unhitched, Chris and Sonia lowered the ramp and removed the carriage from the back. Then they turned their attention to getting the horses out and letting them stretch their legs after their long journey. On their return, the girls tied them to the far side of the horsebox with a hay net to amuse them; I was packed off firmly but politely to my trailer to get organised in there. I was definitely surplus to requirements, because the two fit, strong girls achieved in an hour what Janice and I would have struggled with till bedtime. The stables were up in a crack, the wagon emptied and brushed out and sorted in a jiffy. I could have begun to feel a bit sorry for myself — old, past-it, redundant — if I hadn't been having such fun in the trailer. No tents and tent pegs and mattresses on the floor this time. Instead I was putting red and white china on the dresser, crisp sheets and duvet covers on the bed and the casserole I had prepared the day before at home into the oven. I laid the table, complete with cloth and glasses for wine, and went out to savour the evening air. Contented munching noises came from the stable where the horses, fully rugged and bedded-up, were firmly laced in for the night. All the bedding was neatly stacked and covered against the night dew, as were the carriages. From inside Plod I could hear the girls moving around, sorting out their own beds and belongings. Settling in.

I'd long since learned that on arriving at an event the first thing Richard did was to go 'walk about'. After the hours of driving, the physical and mental strain, it was his way of unwinding, but also to get hold of any event literature that was ready, to see his friends and pick up any news or opinions on the course, the hazards, Fred's new carriage or Mary's new cob. To dive back thankfully into his world, the driving world. To immerse himself in the people, the feel, the atmosphere of it all. For myself I was utterly content to wander around and just absorb the sight, sound and smell of it all. If you own a beautiful picture you cannot fully appreciate it when your nose is right up to it for too long. You can get too close. To see it all, to get the right perspective, you must stand back. Or leave the room altogether and return to view it through fresh eyes. We were among the earlier arrivals and other boxes were dotted around the field, these first-comers usually parked conveniently near to a water supply. By the next day I knew all those places would be filled. A bustling community of people, horses and dogs would temporarily lay claim to this peaceful spot. But for tonight it was peaceful; only the occasional noise of a restless horse, distant conversations and the throb of a lone generator stirred the evening air.

I had wandered further than I intended and turned and re-traced my steps. In the now rapidly fading light I saw the large, dark bulk ahead. In there, Chris and Sonia would have organised what was to be their home for the next few days. The horses would be settling down for the night. Were they excited too by what lay ahead? The soft, warm glow of an oil lamp came from the trailer window. The trailer that was my home. I stopped and surveyed it all from a respectful distance. From the exact point where the perspective was right. The equipment, the horses, the people. The whole assemblage here poised at the start of a World Championship season. How had it happened? Did this honestly have anything to do with me? I had dared to dream hard enough and suddenly, here it all was.

Plod seemed hugely impressive in this light. 'SMITH' Richard had painted across the front. Just that — 'SMITH'. And I was a Smith now; yes, this was mine, all mine, just as much as Richard's. This was now my world as much as his and, I realised, I loved it and needed it with an intensity as fierce as his. Yes, the picture, the whole picture looked very beautiful from where I stood.

I was not alone in my contentment. At dinner that night, eaten in previously undreamt-of comfort in the warm trailer, we were all tired but very, very happy. We were well prepared, well organised and completely dedicated to the task of showing ourselves and our horses to perfection. Later that night as I snuggled down between crisp, clean sheets, Richard on one side and a hot water bottle on the other, a thought struck me.

'Do you realise this is the first night we've had away together since we were married? Do you think this constitutes a honeymoon?' The long, long day had already claimed Richard. I got no reply.

The next day was preparation day. Preparation of horses, harness and carriage. Richard did the carriage and the lamps as he always did. After a good ride out we set-to with the horses. I'd always prided myself on my ability to turn them out well but I hadn't ever reckoned on having a hairdresser's daughter for a groom. After the normal routine of shampooing and hosing, which Bear tolerated and Blizzard loathed, Chris came into her element. Tails weren't just washed; tails had to be conditioned.

Bottle after bottle of salon conditioner, generously donated by Mum, were massaged in. Chestnut tails had to have a henna rinse, blond tails a blue rinse. It would bring out the lights in them so much better, she explained. Then, while still damp, her creations were put into numerous long plaits — to set them in waves she explained (I was dubious, they looked more like Rastafarian dreadlocks to me). As a finishing touch, she bundled the whole lot into an old nylon stocking in lieu of a hairnet. Had she produced a hairdryer, I wouldn't have been surprised except we had no electricity. Having made so much fuss and commotion over the hair at their tail end, she then began to ruthlessly defoliate them of every single stray whisker on any other part of their bodies. For two hours all I heard was the patient snip, snip of Sonia and Chris wielding scissors.

They had already spent upwards of two days on the harness before we left home, but late into that evening they were up giving the brass a last buffing and fitting it all together before hanging it in the box pinned behind flannelette sheets to keep the damp air out as this would make the brass go off. They never stopped work. They actually freed me to indulge myself in things I'd hardly ever had time to do at events before — walk the course and inspect the hazards with Richard; meet people and explore the trade stands; relax and enjoy it to the full. I realised that, despite early misgivings, we had made a very fortunate choice in Chris. And that Sonia had been an additional bonus. The omens were looking good.

Heads turned and acquaintances stared as we headed off for presentation next morning. We were on quite early and we had all been up since very first light: the horses had been exercised and then their legs carefully re-washed and dried before they were given a final grooming and had the curlers taken out of their tails. I had never seen anything like it. Their tails were a cascade of soft, glimmering, slightly wavy hair which sparkled in the morning sun; warm rich red from Blizzard and dazzling silvery white from Bear. Against their chestnut bodies it looked fabulous. Resplendent in our top hats and frock coats, Richard and I looked very impressive in the carriage. Friendly voices rang out: 'Good luck!', 'You look the part!', 'By hell, Smithy, you look a toff!'

The judge for presentation was George Bowman. Now that had to be a good omen. He ran his eye approvingly over my jacket and white breeches and shining top boots, over the harness, the gleaming horses and the new improved Richard. Saying little he smiled faintly. We had applied for consideration

for the British Team; George was to be the Team trainer. He
certainly knew now, right from the starting gate, that our
attempt was a serious one.

Stifling horrible memories of the previous year's humiliating
elimination, I climbed into the back of the carriage well before
the dressage test. In the time-honoured fashion of grooms,
Sonia and Chris were waiting anxiously in the collecting ring,
the horses' rugs draped around their shoulders. When we came
out they were grinning from ear to ear. It had been a nice test —
not outstanding, but very nice. Day One was over and we'd
gone well — the gauntlet had been thrown.

On marathon day Sonia and I saw them off at the start and
then paced about in a state of high anxiety for nearly two hours
till they were due at the hazards. Right on time the distinctive
rattle of our battle wagon, which Richard had painted an
unmistakable pillar-box red for the season, could be heard
approaching. I always reckoned that by watching the horses
approach the first hazard I could judge just how much running
power and energy they had left to tackle the last and most
crucial part of the course. They crested the hill like golden eagles
and swooped towards the hazards. Nostrils flaring and ears
pricked forward, their front legs lifting and pounding in unison,
they looked magnificent. Chris swung the back of the seven
hundredweight vehicle to negotiate the stout timber uprights
and rails as easily as though it were a pushchair. The Sussex air
was pierced with her blood-curdling Celtic battle cries if the
horses so much as shortened their stride. Boadicea herself could
not have been more awesome.

And so it was at each of the successive hazards, Sonia and I
tearing breathlessly here and there to get the best vantage points
we could. The vehicle, the horses' legs and Chris on the back
step all survived the punishing flinty tracks to roll over the
finishing line well within their given time. Richard and Chris
had grins like Cheshire cats and the horses look pretty pleased
with themselves too. And later in the day, when we found we
were lying second after the marathon, we were all indeed pretty
pleased. It only remained the next day to hang on to that
advantage to keep our place.

Gregg Willett, with his Irish cobs, was in the lead — not by
much, but it was unlikely he would make a mistake in the cones
and lose his place. Which indeed he didn't and so, swapping
my livery for the garb of a lady passenger and with Chris
accompanying us as groom, I proudly sat beside Richard in the
award ceremony. It was the first time I'd sat beside him at an

event as Mrs Richard Smith and what better way to start off a truly special season. Our new grooms, wielding their literal and metaphorical new brooms, had done us proud.

We'd never packed up at one event and gone straight on to another without going home in the middle before. It was indeed to be a season of firsts.

To begin with, the Royal Windsor Horse Show was hardly another 'event'. For teams and pairs of horses only and strictly by invitation, the Harrods International Driving Grand Prix formed but part of the tapestry and pageantry of the largest Horse Show in the world.

It was not until we were driving into the showfield itself under the shadow of the ancient castle that it fully hit me. Somebody, somewhere, must be taking our rather audacious attempt at selection seriously or else we would not be here at an international class at the Sovereign's personal favourite equestrian event. My little horses and our home-made vehicle all the way from our Durham pit village to the splendour and pageantry of Royal Windsor. If we were seeking the limelight, we were going to be well and truly in it for the next few days. I said a swift, silent prayer that it would all go well; that we would not disgrace ourselves or the horses. Death before dishonour and all that.

It was a mind-blowing few days for which there are inadequate superlatives. Every breed, size and colour of horse doing any and every activity man in his ingenuity has devised for the species was to be found there: in hand, lead rein, riding, jumping, driving and tent-pegging classes. Thoroughbred, Clydesdale, Arab, Shetland and Hunter classes. I drooled over the Welsh cobs in hand and laughed and cried simultaneously over the Shetland Grand National. But the abiding memory of that, my first Royal Windsor, was the display of the Royal Artillery. Oh, I'd seen it done before on telly, but nothing, nothing could have prepared me for the real thing. The very ground trembled as gun carriages hurtled at break-neck speed behind snorting, galloping horses. In the darkened arena, the cannon roared and through the clouds of concealing gun smoke, the chink and jingle of approaching horses could be heard. As they charged through the smoke, their guns rattling and bumping behind, their riders urging them on, it was a truly living picture from the past. In their final charge they criss-crossed the arena to faster and faster music at speeds approaching sheer lunancy and missing each other by inches. At full gallop they swept from the arena as the last of the smoke rose heavenward towards the round tower of Windsor Castle. It was quite unforgettable.

As was the afternoon, when in that arena we lined up to receive our rosette. Only the reigning National Champion and a world-class Swiss driver had beaten us and we were justifiably proud of our third place. We waited with bated breath while Her Majesty herself presented the rosettes to the team drivers and to the first two pair drivers. But the field was very muddy, the schedule tight and we were in the next row back. Her Majesty's Equerry presented us with our rosette and we tried our very best not to be too disappointed. The ceremony finished with a grand parade right around the arena past the Royal box and on past the grandstand.

A small group of people rose and waved and cheered like mad as we approached. I stared harder and made out a group of our Yorkshire friends, among them the familiar figures of dear Joan and John Sykes from Boroughbridge. They had travelled down especially to give us their encouragement and support. It made an already marvellous event that extra bit special.

Heading back for home for a quick re-group before we left again for Scotland, we all had happy memories, a tremendous sense of achievement and the first tingling awareness that the impossible, the unbelievable, might not in fact be beyond our reach.

There were four events on virtually consecutive weekends, which was tiring and punishing for horses and drivers alike, but all four events were qualifiers for the World Championships and so we had to put in an appearance at them all. All this was giving our finances a terrible hammering. Not only was Richard going to be away from work for the best part of a month but the amount of diesel we needed to travel the length and breadth of the country was staggering. We had left the shop open and in caretaker hands, but, with the best will in the world, the lads did not know what they were really doing and business slumped drastically. Common sense said, 'Whoa, you've got your priorities wrong here. Your livelihood must come first, not the horses. Without your livelihood there can be no horses.' But gut reaction said, 'We can't stop now! Look how far they've got, look how well they're going. They'll never get another chance like this.'

There are no true professionals in carriage driving. At the top end, the amount of money that can be spent on the sport is quite literally limitless. The best carriages, harness and horses, carried in the best custom-made horseboxes and trailers and looked after by professional grooms, could run into tens, if not hundreds, of thousands of pounds. At the humbler end of the league table, the sport could be enjoyed, as I had originally set out and proved, with a single family horse and the minimum of equipment and horse-transporting facilities. The teams, of course, drew the most attention, the most publicity and cost the most to run. In 1985 several of these teams of horses were commercially sponsored — a trend that was only very slowly developing in the sport. Perhaps that was because of the fact that no matter how much money was sunk in or how well the team did you could never, ever, recoup any of your money. In a sport where running costs for a team might cost over £20,000 for a season, the winning prize money for a major event was unlikely to reach one hundred pounds. As the entry fee was around the thirty pounds mark you'd be luck to get a tank of diesel out of the prize money. So we battled on with our ancient horsebox, home-made cross-country vehicle made largely out of old bed irons, and our shoe-string budget. Every event was attempted on a wing and a prayer.

And there was no way, no matter how well we did, no matter if we won every event we attended, that we could help finance our competition costs by a streak of winning luck. Richard was adamant that this was a good thing: if prize money were to become more than a token, if really big money ever did get into the winners' arena, then the sport as we knew it would vanish forever. Gone would be the camaraderie, the sportsmanship and the friendly rivalry. It would all be in deadly earnest. Before long, it would become as ruthlessly professional as show jumping. No, it was better, much better with things the way they were. Though we had to admit, had anyone waved a large cheque under our noses, we would have taken their hands off!

Scone Palace in Perth had been the scene of our pair's first F.E.I. competition two years previously. They had come fourth on that occasion and third the following year. Given that they were now more experienced and on top form, could we dare to hope to do any better? The weather certainly didn't help our cause. It was cold, dismal and wet throughout the event. Lying snug, warm and dry in bed, Megan tucked under her Paddington Bear quilt on her camp bed, I fully appreciated our trailer home that weekend. But bad weather and heavy going did not affect

Richard's driving skill or the fitness and performance of the horses. We notched up another second, but barely had time to celebrate or ponder on our success before we were on our way to Cumbria, to Holker Hall.

Holker had long been my favourite event. The setting, the atmosphere, the early June weather were all quite special somehow. After the dismal rain at Perth, the sun in its unfathomable English way came out at Holker and shone for five glorious days.

The cobs, now fully into their red-gold summer coats, gleamed and shone under Chris and Sonia's muscular ministrations more vividly than ever before. They looked so fit and beautiful that they turned heads whenever we rode or drove them out. After the dressage they were lying a respectable third. They would have been placed higher, had Bear settled and worked smoothly instead of bending his neck and evading Richard at times. We did not mind this display of stubbornness and fitness too much though — in the gruelling Lakeland marathon to come Bear was going to need all the guts and determination he could muster.

I positioned myself so I could watch them come into the first hazard, to make my judgement as to just how much running they had left in them, whether they had enough stamina and enthusiasm to tackle the hazards. It had become a sort of ritual with me, an adrenalin-pumping, nerve-racking ritual and one I like to indulge in totally on my own. They crested the hill into the first hazard as if they had just been for a trot round the block. How, oh how, I asked myself in stunned admiration, could those two animals cover over twenty kilometres of gruelling up and down hill gradients, pulling seven hundredweight of metal and thirty-six stone of human flesh behind them and still be bursting with power and enthusiasm? Bear's eye caught the flags of the first hazard and instantly his ears came forward and he changed up half a gear, surging into his collar. I had the uncanny feeling that had Richard put the reins down at that point they would have gone straight into the hazard and driven all the gates, all in the right order, totally unaided. I also wondered whose blood, the horses' or the driver's, was the most stirred by what they were doing. Watching them it was as if this was the total and justifiable purpose for their existence — all three of them.

I raced between hazards muttering to myself a mixture of prayer and pep talk. Anyone listening would have thought me quite mad. Turning the horses so tightly they were, as a man next to me graphically exclaimed, liable to disappear up their own backsides, Richard came out of the last hazard to thunderous applause and headed for the finishing line. Breathlessly, I took a short cut across the grass to be there as he came in, to get to the horses's heads just as he pulled them up.

'That,' I said proudly, 'was fantastic — and it's going to take a lot of beating.'

Later in the afternoon, almost sick with anticipation, I sat watching an official maddeningly slowly mark up the results on the score board. It took a little time for it to sink in; in fact I had to read the row of little figures two or three times before I believed them. We had indeed won the marathon and not only won it but with points to spare. We were in the lead.

The next day the tension was almost unbearable. The obstacle course was causing all sorts of problems. Drivers were getting round cones accurately but only at the expense of time faults, or they were getting round in the time but not without a cone or two down. There were over one hundred and twenty competitors there that weekend. When Richard went in as the leader, the last to do so in his class, not one single driver had had a double clear round. Richard was to be the first of the day. The only other was to be George Bowman with his team.

I sat in the carriage with Richard and Chris for our lap of honour. And it was *our* lap of honour: we were all overflowing with pride and happiness.

'Come on ladies and gentlemen, a big round of applause for Richard Smith, the winner here today. A successful season of seconds so far, but this is his first major win. And a win which must please him in this, a selection event for the World Pairs Championship to be held in August . . . '

The music played, the applause rang out and under a bright blue sky the horses trotted out around that arena as they had never trotted before. They knew, they really truly knew, that they had won. Friends shouted and cheered and waved from the crowd and I laughed and waved back. I tried to absorb every drop of the heady joy, the sun and glory of it all. Had my life ended in those seconds, I would have died very happy.

15

Bad luck comes in threes

NOW ONLY ONE event remained before they announced the British Team: Kelso. So far we had notched up a second at Brighton, the second British score at Royal Windsor, second at Perth and won at Holker. It was tempting providence, but nevertheless tempting to presume, that unless something went horribly and drastically wrong we could not be overlooked.

Providence does not smile on presumption. The referee we balloted for the marathon was a cheerful and enormously hefty man. His weight posed no problem to the cobs, they were so fit and well they hardly noticed the difference. But when Richard came up against a post sharply in a hazard and they all lunged forward, the sheer momentum of his weight smashed the dash-board off. Without that they had nothing to brace their feet against, one more bump and Richard and the referee shot out of the front of the cart and on to the ground. Winded, Richard could only watch in horror as Chris raced from the back of the vehicle to try and grab the reins, grab the horses' heads — grab anything. She was too late. I was by preference alone on a vantage point on the sloping grass in front of the castle to view the hazards. I got a grandstand view of the horses careering past at a flat-out gallop, the empty vehicle, its wheels a blur, by some miracle staying upright as it ploughed on behind them. Officials shouted, car horns hooted and people screamed. I sank on to the grass too numbed to react.

It was Windsor all over again. The runaway, the car, the crash. Bear surviving physically and crucified mentally. A single sickening cold thought hammered in my head. This is the end. The horses and the vehicle had disappeared from view by now. God knows how far they would run, God knew if they were still even upright or a smashed and tangled heap of blood, bone and metal in a ditch. Even if, by some miracle, they were stopped intact, would either of them ever be driveable again? I sat there for what felt like an eternity before mechanically I forced my legs up the hill and back to camp. Trying at every step to brace

My Pickwickian Richard

The coveted Famous Grouse National
Championship Trophy for Pairs of Horses

A very different woman now than a decade

Richard's eye-view of the Boys   *Alf Baker*

Richard negotiating the Marathon with Chris hanging on the back

The medal winners. Switzerland (1st), Germany (2nd),
Great Britain (3rd). Richard is second on the left

Patriotic Megan and Chris at the World Pairs Driving Championships

Pure contentment at the Opening Ceremony

myself for whatever might await me there.

What in fact awaited me was a knot of people, a tearful Megan, and a very agitated Richard with a large whisky in his hand. In their stalls two familiar chestnut shapes were munching contentedly at their hay nets. Richard thrust the whisky into my hand.

'Oh, Christ, I've been worried sick about you. Where've you been? Didn't you hear the commentator on the P.A. asking you to check back here? Here, drink this, you look as white as a ghost.'

'You've been worried about *me*? What about the horses? I mean — I didn't hallucinate it all, did I? Are they all right? How did they get back here?'

I was totally bewildered, but very slowly the icy fear within me was retreating. A combination of the whisky and watching Blizzard tuck into his hay net was ensuring that.

'It was like something out of a John Wayne film,' Richard said. 'I was about three miles away when they got them stopped. Apparently Joe Moore and Archie Marshall, the course builder, set off in pursuit in their Land Rover. They finally headed them up a steep hill which slowed their mad gallop to a fast trot and then Joe drove the Land Rover right alongside the cart and Archie climbed on to the roof of the Land Rover, jumped over, managed to get the reins and pull them up. Then he simply drove them back here. I couldn't believe my eyes when I saw them stroll in. Christ, I thought they were goners, Carol. I really, really did. When I saw those two horses disappear it was like the end of the world. We will never, never be so lucky again.'

It was Richard who was now quite lily-white.

'Here,' I handed him the remains in the whisky glass. 'As long as you're all unhurt, then that's all that matters.'

'Well, Bear has a slight gash on his shoulder where the wing mirror of the Land Rover bashed him, but otherwise, nothing. The vet's been, put two stitches in and pronounced them both otherwise unharmed.'

I voiced the dreaded, the hidden fear: 'And is he, well, is he — is he himself?'

Richard knew exactly what I meant. 'As far as I can tell, he's calm, not sweated-up and not panic-stricken. He is most definitely not in the state he was after Windsor. And Blizzard is his usual cheerful self. We must have a guardian angel or something, but I think, I think, those two stitches are the only damage we have to show for today.'

He was wrong, of course. Late into the night, in the darkness of the trailer, I was awoken by what felt like a minor earthquake. I've never been in an earthquake, but I imagine that's what it must feel like. The entire trailer was shaking and vibrating; even the plates on the dresser were rattling. As I came to full consciousness, I realised to my astonishment that the source of the seismic shocks was lying beside me. Richard was trembling and shaking from head to toe.

'Richard!'

'Cold!' he gasped, his teeth clattering together, 'I'm so bloody cold!'

I shot out of bed, lit the lamp and the oven on the stove and put the kettle on. He was sitting, or rather bouncing, on the edge of the bed by now. I rummaged in drawers and produced a heavy wool sweater, some tracksuit bottoms and some socks. With an effort I got him into them. I made some tea and re-filled the hot water bottle and gave it to him. And a couple of aspirin. Gradually, the uncontrollable shaking subsided, he snuggled under the duvet and I put out the lamp.

'What on earth was that?' he mumbled.

'At a guess, I would say delayed shock,' I mumbled back.

We neither of us got much more sleep as he alternately shivered and glowed like a hot coal all night. In the morning he was comfortably cool but had a dry, hollow little cough.

'Now I know we are out of this competition, but I want those horses going in there looking as if we were in the lead. Understand?'

Chris and Sonia nodded gravely.

'Whatever happens as a result of yesterday's disaster,' Richard continued, 'whether they take it into account in reaching their decision or not, those horses have got to look as though nothing has happened whatsoever.'

Another solemn nod.

Chris and I had ridden the horses that morning, ostensibly to test their physical fitness, but more importantly to check their state of mind. We had to find out if they were in shock at all. Had the runaway dredged up any frightening and painful memories for Bear? No, both horses were totally fit, well and happy. The two stitches in Bear's shoulder caused him no dis-comfort at all and were fortunately above the level where his breast collar lay.

Glossy and immaculate, they swept into the arena. Stood immobile and arrogant while Richard saluted and then drove a double clear round in the cones. I was choked with pride and relief. No matter what decision was made on the fitness of my horses to represent their country, they had nothing left to prove to me. They were heroes, absolute heroes.

A distinguished-looking gentleman quietly approached the carriage and Richard quickly removed his top hat. It was John Stevens, the Chairman of the Selection Committee.

'Mr Smith, it's my very pleasant task to inform you that you have been selected as a member of the British Team. Many congratulations.'

He held out his hand which Richard swiftly took.

'Thank you, sir, thank you very much.'

I could see that he was incapable of saying more and my own eyes were full to the brim. In the back of the carriage, Chris was allowing her tears the luxury of splashing down the front of her black jacket unashamedly.

We had done it.

'We don't have to go.'

'We do.'

'Richard, we don't have to prove anything to anyone; there is no need whatsoever to do this event!'

'I need to prove that what happened at Kelso was a freak accident and I'm not in the habit of not completing a marathon, nor having my vehicle come apart under stress. It was put to me by one or two that, had that dashboard been stronger, the accident wouldn't have happened.'

'You're being neurotic! Everyone has bits smash off their vehicles from time to time.'

'But other people's vehicles aren't home-made!'

'Look, you're being stubborn and short-sighted. It's Monday morning, we got back from Kelso last night and you're proposing we set off for Cheshire on Wednesday?'

'I'm proposing nothing; we're going.'

'You are bloody infuriating at times, Smith. And you're not well: you keep having sweats and that dreadful cough. Where you need to be is in bed for a few days.'

'Rubbish.'

He left, of course, on the Wednesday with the horses and Chris and Sonia. I stayed behind to run the shop till the weekend and would drive down to Tatton Park on the Friday night to join them. I thought he was quite mad for going.

Rubber-gloved and choking on the caustic fumes, I vented my annoyance on the inside of a gas cooker. This was how I spent my time at least two mornings a week; cleaning second-hand cookers that were sometimes so revolting I felt like throwing up. Thick black viscous burnt-on grease, rancid, shrivelled chips, fag ash and mouse droppings — I sometimes feared to open the oven doors. I hated the shop, I loathed the sight and smell and touch of it. I tried very hard to be balanced about it all. It provided us with our only source of income; I only had to be there in the mornings, it allowed Richard the freedom to drive the horses. But somehow, as the blackened sludge dripped off my rubber gloves into the bucket, I couldn't believe that this was the career I had been seeking. I fled thankfully on the Friday night.

As soon as I arrived, I knew something was sadly wrong. Chris has one of those faces that mirror every emotion. And hers was registering pure alarm. She nearly towed me from the car.

'Oh, thank goodness you're here!'

'Chris, whatever's the matter?' I could see it wasn't the horses, they were in their stalls, happily munching hay. 'Did something go wrong during dressage this morning?'

'He should never have driven it, but it's not my place to say, is it? I offered to get a doctor but he wouldn't hear tell of it.'

'A doctor! Where is he?'

'In the trailer: at least he's finally agreed to lie down.'

In the trailer, glowing dry and red like an ember, Richard croaked at me from the bed: 'Hello, pet.'

My reaction was a mixture of anger and concern.

'Oh, Richard. I told you you weren't fit enough to drive all this way.'

I felt his forehead. He was on fire.

'Oh, it's just a chill, I guess.' He tried to make light of it and sit up to talk to me but, racked with pain and coughing, he subsided on to the pillows, gasping for breath.

'I'm going for a doctor — *now*!'

Most events supply an honorary doctor along with an honorary vet, both useful in emergencies. I left my urgent message with an event official and went back to the trailer to wait.

The skies had darkened and rain was beginning to fall. It was cold and damp and untidy in the trailer. I lit the stove and began to tidy up.

Just as the kettle had boiled to make Richard a hot drink, a bright orange Dormobile drew up in front of the trailer. A lady hopped out and came to the door.

'Is the call for the doctor here?'

'Yes, that's right.'

'Could you come and give him a few details?' She indicated the Dormobile and I trotted across.

A very short, very round gentleman with soft pink skin and no teeth was at the wheel. He reminded me of Humpty Dumpty, except that he wasn't bald: he had a head of lovely, thick silvery hair. He spoke with a softly Scottish accent.

'Now, my dear, come and tell me the problem.'

I outlined quickly what I knew.

'Mmm, and when did he have this crashing fall off the carriage?'

'Last Saturday.'

'And what age do you say he is? Mmm. I think we'll have a wee look. Hilda, come and get me out.'

With enormous difficulty his wife and I got him out of the Dormobile and up the steps of the trailer. I noticed for the first time the large disabled sticker in his window.

'Now, sir, I am Dr James McEwan, retired, but I'd still like to have a wee look at you.'

He took Richard's temperature and pulse and listened to his chest saying, 'Describe to me exactly what this pain in your chest feels like.'

When he'd finished he sent his wife back to his vehicle for pen and paper and laboriously wrote a longish note which he gave to me.

'My dear, I want you to wrap him up warmly and get him to the nearest hospital, wherever that may be. There's got to be one in this part of the world somewhere. I would like him thoroughly looked at, with perhaps an X-ray. He could have cracked something when he fell from that cart. Oh, and an ECG.'

'An ECG!' I gasped.

'Well, given he's fat and fifty, we shouldn't overlook a pain in the heart region, should we?'

They were lovely at Macclesfield Hospital, kind and thorough. They brought me endless cups of tea and allowed me to sit holding hands with Richard while he was wired up to the machines. On a Friday evening, the X-rays took quite a while to process but finally a doctor appeared at the foot of the bed.

'Well, Mr Smith, you'll be pleased to know the ECG is fine — perfectly normal.'

My own heart began to beat more normally again for the first time in hours, and I could feel the relief flood through Richard.

'But the X-rays show there's a bad patch on your lung. I

would say you have a touch of pneumonia. We're going to prescribe some strong antibiotics and also some painkillers and we'd be happier if you'd stay in over the weekend, at least for twenty-four hours, so that we can keep an eye on things.'

'Thank you, Doctor, but no, I'd rather get back.'

'But Richard . . . ' I began to protest, but he squeezed my hand very tightly and said firmly, 'I'll let my wife drive me back. I'll keep warm and dry, I promise, and I'll take all the pills.'

The doctor looked very doubtful, but could see he was fighting a losing battle.

The rain continued incessantly. It hammered on the roof of the trailer and somewhere a seam must have given way right above our bed. It was one of the worst nights I'd ever spent. I put towels and polythene sacks from the horses' bedding on the bed to try and prevent the duvet getting soaked but all night long there was a steady drip, drip, drip interspersed with Richard's dry and painful coughing.

In the cold, grey miserable morning light I was in despair. What did we do now? How did we all get home? Once again Richard was stubborn, adamant, immovable.

'Get the girls to pack up everything and we'll get away as early as we can.'

'Richard, you cannot, really cannot, drive that wagon home. Good God, you've got pneumonia. Do you want to kill yourself?'

'These pills are helping; I'll be all right, I promise. And once we get home I'll go to bed and do whatever you say. But I'm taking my wagon and horses home.'

So I made our withdrawal and set the girls to work. Anxious friends called. Several offers were made to drive the wagon for Richard: all were firmly turned down.

I thought he was being stupid and reckless but, short of tying him to the bed, I was powerless. It was a very long five and a half hours, but eventually we were crawling up the hill towards Stanley. Switching the engine off, Richard almost fell from the cab and allowed himself to be helped to bed.

He was to be there for three weeks.

We had to prove ourselves at Lowther; prove Richard's fitness, prove the vehicle's fitness, prove the horses were still on form after Richard's long lay-off. The girls had been doing a marvellous job keeping them ridden fit as they had had very little driving, what with Richard in bed and myself mostly at the shop.

Bear and Blizzard did a very nice dressage test which put us well in the running at the start of the marathon.

Having seen them off, I paced around anxiously for an hour or so before heading off to watch for them coming in at the hazards. A very distinctive shape beckoned to me from a very distinctive vehicle. It was Dr McEwan.

'And how is my patient?' he enquired as I drew level with his open window.

'Oh, fine thank you. Really recovered, though it's taken a long while.'

'It's not a thing you shake off overnight.' He consulted his schedule. 'He's due through here soon, isn't he?'

'Yes; I'm just getting myself into position for a good view. Don't know why: sometimes I can hardly bear to look!'

'Oh, that's not a problem I have. About the only advantage of not being so good on my pins is that they allow me to drive myself to get a ringside seat at the dressage arena and the hazards. I love this sport, love it. Go to all the events, even some of the Continental ones. It's a little cramped but Hilda and I have got everything we need in here. It's our hotel and grandstand all in one.'

The loudspeakers on the P.A. system gave the preliminary crackle which meant that an announcement was imminent.

'And the next competitor into the hazards will be the first of the horse pairs class. And news just come in concerning that class. Competitor number 34, Richard Smith, has withdrawn due to a vehicle problem on Section A. That's Richard Smith, horse pairs class, withdrawn.'

'But that's . . . '

'Yes,' was all I could reply. I felt quick sick. Literally and at heart. In some bizarre way the announcement came as no shock; I'd almost been expecting it.

'Bad luck comes in threes, always in threes,' Great Aunt Meg had drummed into me. Well, we'd had the runaway, then Richard's pneumonia, and now there was this.

'Oh, my dear, I'm so sorry. What on earth could have happened? Gracious, you look quite white. Now, as a doctor, I insist you come in here and sit down and have a cup of tea. Ah, here comes Hilda, she'll pop the kettle on.'

I didn't want to. I wanted to escape, to grieve over our lost hopes in peace. But my legs did feel shaky and he was very insistent.

Once I was inside and wrapped round a large mug of tea, the defences came down. I spilled it all out — what a struggle it had all been to get this far, how everything we had had been invested in the horses. How proud we were when Richard was selected for the Team. How nothing had gone right since. And above all, how any disaster, however small, could mark the end of the road. There was just no more money left. I had sold what jewellery I had, and a fair bit of furniture, to enable us to get this far. To be honest, we should have quit anyway and if an expensive repair or replacement was needed for the vehicle, I just didn't see us getting any further. Any hope of competing in the World Championships was lost.

Realising I'd rabbited too long. I thanked them both for their tea and their kindness and left, still slightly dazed, to see if Richard had got back and to find out what damage had been done. A Land Rover and trailer was just pulling up as I arrived. On the trailer was our cross-country vehicle — or rather two cross-country vehicles — it was completely snapped in two. Richard climbed wearily out of the Land Rover.

'Just not strong enough; the backbone chassis snapped clean in two. Design fault, or my fault — same thing. But it will never happen again; by hell it'll never happen again.'

He was trying to be philosophical but I could see he was deeply and bitterly disappointed. And when Chris and Sonia came in leading the horses, their red-rimmed eyes said it all.

Morale that night was very low.

'I think I should offer to stand down from the Team,' Richard said finally. 'I hope they let me compete as one of the six individuals, but I feel I must stand down from the actual Team. We've been deluding ourselves, we haven't got the back-up to do this properly. Dear Lord, you need spare vehicles, spare horses and lots of spare money if you want to do this job properly. We've tried to do it on a shoestring but I think we've run out of laces. And it's not just money. It won't cost much to repair the vehicle, just a bit more welding, but how much faith will they put in it when it's let us down twice now. And I can't afford another, out of the question. No, we've done well, very well, to get this far but I fear it's the end of the line.'

Next morning he went off to see Jim Corbett, the British Chef d'Equipe, to offer to stand down. I took Bear off on my own for an amble around the event field. There was no one else I really wanted to be with. I felt angry and empty.

A short, pink arm was waving frantically at me from an orange window. Oh Lord, I didn't want to be sociable, I wanted to be left alone with my misery. But they'd been so kind and concerned the day before. I turned Bear's head and walked slowly to the Dormobile. The doctor was holding a piece of paper in his hand.

'This is for you, my dear, and I sincerely hope it will help.'

I took it, wondering if I looked so obviously in need of a prescription. I unfolded the paper. It was a cheque for five hundred pounds.

'But, Dr McEwan, I can't accept this!'

'And why not?'

'Because, well — because — well, I don't think we could ever repay you.'

'*Repay?* It's a gift, not a loan, my dear.'

I opened my mouth again but nothing came out.

'Now listen to me,' he said sternly, 'Hilda and I have both discussed this. We can well afford it and it's what we want. If we can't do something patriotic to support our National Team at our age, it's a bad job. I think it's disgraceful, disgraceful that there's no funding for the Team, that you all have to pay your own way. This is our way of trying to put matters right. It's not for you, it's for the horses, to get them to the World Championships.'

My emptiness was suddenly filled. Somebody had faith in *us* — somebody actually believed in Richard and the horses and our whole crazy crusade. It was like the breath of life to the tiny glowing ember in me that was all that was left of our dreams. But even as that hope rekindled and tingled in me once more, I suddenly remembered Richard's decision.

'Dr McEwan, I truly cannot find words to express how I feel at this moment. The offer of the money is wonderfully kind and I would be lying if I said we didn't need it desperately. But what is more wonderful is that you should put your faith in us — nobody has ever done that before. I only hope that it's not too late. We might no longer even be members of the Team.'

'What do you mean?' he asked, startled.

'Richard's offering to stand down — oh, not just because of money. As I say, it's a question of faith.'

'I assure you that you and I aren't the only ones with that particular commodity invested in your husband.'

'I hope you're right.' I smiled weakly and, turning Bear, gently headed back. I felt like a piece of rubber, constantly trying to absorb the shock waves of life.

But Dr McEwan was right. The Chef d'Equipe would not even contemplate altering the Team. He strongly suggested we took up one of the dozen offers of the loan of different cross-country vehicles we had had. But Richard firmly opted for the 'devil he knew', assuring Jim Corbett that he would have strengthened every conceivable weak point by the next event.

That event was looming up fast. We were already into August: on the third weekend we would be travelling to Osberton and from there straight to Sandringham where they'd finally decided to hold the World Championships. It was all now alarmingly close.

We had one or two sticky moments, such as being asked to confirm we had a third horse. At international level a pair of horses actually means three, you have to have a spare.

'Oh yes, we have another one we're bringing on at home,' Richard calmly lied.

When the coast was clear I hissed, 'You know damned well we haven't got a third horse!'

'Well, I'll have to find one, won't I!'

It is a measure of the fellowship of our sport that within ten minutes we were collared by the Hancocks. Ron was the Chairman of the Horse Driving Trials Group, and for an awful moment I thought we were in hot water.

'What are you doing about a third horse?' he asked. 'You don't have one, do you?'

We were in hot water.

'Well . . . I . . . umm . . .'

'Would you like to borrow one of ours? He's been in a pair before and has his international passport and so on. He's black, not chestnut, but unless something goes diabolically wrong you wouldn't be using him anyway.'

I grinned from ear to ear with relief.

'Oh, bless you, bless you!'

We had also had a bit of unexpected limelight at home — local press, radio and television all banging on our door. Yes, it was all horribly close and we could not afford anything to go wrong, anything at all.

When Chris came bursting into the kitchen as I was making the early morning tea, my first instinct was alarm.

'What's wrong?'

'It's the boys; Blizzard's got colic and Bear's got a lump.'

'A lump?'

'On his shoulder where the stitches were done at Kelso.'

'Oh God.'

The vet was there in half an hour. Blizzard, who was trying to throw himself on the floor and roll because of the pain, was given an injection and we spent most of the rest of the day walking him endlessly round and round the block till it passed off. The vet inspected the lump on Bear's shoulder carefully. It wasn't very large and it wasn't very painful, though it did seem to be gathering to a head. He gave him an antibiotic injection to be on the safe side and said it was probably a small flare-up after the injury in June.

A day or two later Blizzard was completely recovered and Bear's lump had burst and a small amount of yellow matter came out. We applied antiseptic cream with relief, thinking that now it would just dry up and go away.

It didn't. It spread and grew and became more tender. The vet returned. It was now only a week before we left for Osberton. There must be, he decided, a small foreign body in the shoulder — a splinter from the collision or a bit of thread left in when the stitches came out. Something very, very small. Ideally he would like to open up and investigate.

Impossible! Out of the question! The wound would never heal in time. Bear would be off work for weeks.

Well then, he would have to try drugs to reduce the swelling and infection.

Impossible! Out of the question! The drug tests that were enforced at an international event could detect such substances even if they'd been in the bloodstream two weeks before.

So all we were left with was poulticing. Hot poulticing. To draw out the infection.

When the poultices came off, the area of swelling was double in size and twice as tender. I was totally frantic and so was Chris. Although not lame on the leg at all so he was keeping up with his normal ridden exercise, there was no way Bear would pass a veterinary inspection as fit. Furthermore his harness was bound to rub the area and make it more sore.

The vet said 'persevere'; the hot poulticing would eventually do the trick. It should draw the offending foreign body out. Eventually.

But we didn't have an eventually, we had something less than a week and although we didn't have to compete at Osberton it would be disastrous for our morale if we didn't as we hadn't successfully completed an event since Holker.

In desperation, I reasoned that this offending object had been happily in the shoulder since June, so couldn't it be persuaded to stay happily in the shoulder again?

I threw away the hot poultices and turned on the hose pipe. For about fifteen minutes every three or four hours we played freezing cold water on the entire area. Bear was cross and shivery at the end of the ordeal and so were we. We took it in shifts round the clock to hose him. It was no effort to get up at an unearthly hour to hose him; nobody was getting much sleep anyway. We were all staggering around like zombies. It was inconceivable that having travelled so long and so hard a road we should be stopped now by a swollen shoulder. And yet none of us could turn our minds and hearts fully to the vital job of planning and packing to go away while any doubt hung over us. I was getting paranoid: creeping down to the stable at every opportunity, unable to keep away, yet hardly daring to look when I got there. Trying to convince myself that the swelling was marginally smaller than the last time I looked.

After about thirty-six hours we all agreed it wasn't just wishful thinking, it was smaller. In a further twenty-four hours, leaving us exhausted and hysterical with relief, it had gone.

We allowed ourselves the luxury of a good night's sleep and set about the final packing with renewed vigour. Two days later we left for Osberton.

The word from the Team trainer, George Bowman, was not to take any risks, not to try and prove anything, just give the horses a gentle run round the course and use the event to whet their appetites, not flatten them.

We came in sixth place, which we would have normally considered diabolical. But no one was worried as it was clearly announced that the Team members were only there for a 'run out' not really to compete. So no one was worried — except me. I had watched Richard drive all the hazards very carefully, my primary concern being that the vehicle held together. But as I watched, a slow, sickening realisation dawned. Far from holding the cobs back, keeping their voracious appetite for hazards under control, Richard was actually having to push them at some points. Well, not both of them — just Blizzard. He was as flat and lethargic as a sea-side donkey and about as manoeuvreable in the hazards. After the marathon he picked half-heartedly at his feed.

In bed in the trailer that night I grasped the nettle: 'What's wrong with Blizzard?'

'Oh, you noticed.'

'It wasn't very hard.'

'I don't really know. There's nothing you can put your finger on. Usually he's such an honest willing little soldier but today he was just, well, not interested. Not trying. I didn't push, not really, it seemed unfair. Maybe he was just having an off day.'

'Or maybe he's gone over the top.'

You can get horses gradually fit, bringing them up to a peak of performance and enthusiasm. Then if you're careful and get all your equations right over feed, work and rest, you should be able to keep letting them down a little then bringing them back up to top form. But sometimes, even with the best régime in the world and particularly. with young horses, you reach a point where they have just had enough and all the work and all the food you can give them won't improve them. In fact, they begin to go backwards, becoming stubborn and uncooperative and losing condition. Then the only answer is to turn them away and forget about them for a long while. Blizzard was only six years old, still a baby in Welsh cob terms, and he'd had a very hard, very long, full competitive season. He'd never complained — till now. Now he was saying he'd had enough for one season.

And we were about to ask him to drive in the World Championships.

Well, if he had the courage and stamina of his breed, that unique Welsh cob quality that Richard always described as 'the fire in the belly', he was going to need it because come hell or high water we were going to have to ask him to give us his very best.

Just one more time.

16

'Flag horses in front, please'

I DECIDED I must be a masochist at heart. I tortured myself driving the car during the whole of the three-hour journey from Osberton to Sandringham, firmly convinced that if I relaxed or in any way enjoyed the journey down, something dreadful would happen. Plod would break down, the trailer would come adrift, we'd find we'd left something absolutely vital at home in Durham. Little things like that.

At last, however, and without a hitch, Plod pulled up ahead of me at a gate marked 'Competitors Only', her old engine throbbing effortlessly as if to say, 'Oh ye of little faith.'

'At first sight it looked just like any other temporary stabling area at any other show. I felt a twinge of disappointment. I hadn't actually expected brass bands and welcoming committees but I'd expected something. The man at the gate had finished chatting with Richard and Plod was trundling off slowly down the side of the field.

I rolled down the window as the gate man approached. 'I'm with him.'

'Right, miss, I've told him where to go to get to the international stabling area. Just follow him down.'

'The international stabling area?' I stared at all the horseboxes and bustle in the immediate vicinity and looked puzzled.

'Y' see, miss it's like two events at the same time and place. The normal Sandringham Trials lot are up here, but the world lot, they're down there.'

I indulged myself in a few moments of unashamed superiority as I caught Richard up.

At another gate, Richard was having the horses' passports checked. Beyond the fence I could see the canvas tops of three long rows of portable stabling. Flags waved proudly from the top of some of them. I recognised Canada, America, France and Italy, but the rest were just multi-coloured stripes to me.

'It's really happening,' I told myself, 'it's really, happening.'

'Mrs Smith?'

I jumped slightly at the interruption of my thoughts.

'We're just parking your husband up now. You'll have to take your car over there; no cars in the stable compound, I'm afraid. And here's your badge. Wear it at all times; you'll need it to get in and out of this gate.'

'Oh yes,' I gloated as I reverently handled the large green metal badge which said simply 'F.E.I. World'.

This was it. This was really it.

By the time I'd parked the car and re-entered the main gate, flashing my badge with totally unconvincing nonchalance, Richard and the girls had already swung into action. The horses were unloaded and the temporary stabling was going up on the side of the horsebox.

I discovered that all the British Team and British Individuals boxes had been parked in one area while the rest of the world were in a merry jumble in and around the temporary stabling blocks. I thought it would have been nicer and perhaps friendlier if we too had been thrown into the melting pot, but no doubt there was an official reason for the segregation. As soon as the carriage was unloaded from the trailer, I dispatched the girls to fill the heavy aluminium beer barrel we used as a water supply. Full, it weighed a ton, but excitement gave an edge to their already considerable muscle power and they plonked it effortlessly, brim full, at the front of the trailer. Richard connected up the gas and I put the kettle on for a much-needed cup of tea. Although the temptation was to explore and chat and enjoy the holiday atmosphere, there was still a lot of work to be done.

So after our tea and a quick sandwich, we all set about with a will. The girls got the horses settled in their stalls with hay nets and water and re-organised the inside of Plod to become their living quarters and harness room for the next week. Inside the trailer I packed away food and got out pans and china and got the double bed down from the wall and made up for the night. I was just adding the final home-making touch by whisking the carpet sweeper over the floor when Chris appeared at the door.

'We're all finished and the boys are quite happy,' she reported. 'We'll take them for a little ride when they've digested their feed. Do you think we can go off and have a look round for a while?'

'Of course. In fact if you'll hang on a moment I'll come with you.'

We wandered up and down the lines of stables, gasping at the

size and luxury of some of the Continental boxes parked
round the perimeter. Others, however, did not have such
palatial accommodation and there was a variety of caravans
and tents and even sun beds neatly made up in stables adjacent
to their Team's horses. It was late afternoon and preparations
were well under way for evening meals in various encamp-
ments.

We smiled and said hello to everyone and everybody smiled
back. The atmosphere was cosmopolitan, relaxed and friendly.
It was heady stuff. Many of the countries, as I'd noticed on the
way in, had their national flags flying from their stables and
some national groups were all kitted out in identical tracksuits
complete with flags.

'It's not fair you know,' Sonia grumbled, 'we've got nothing
like this, have we? We don't even have a flag to our name or
anything to show we belong to the British Team.'

Just then we came upon the American stables. Across the top
of a dozen loose boxes a beautiful blue banner with a white
scalloped edge pronounced in red letters 'United States of
America Equestrian Team'. Each stable door was framed in
scalloped bunting in the same colours with a hand-painted
wooden plaque giving each horse's name, age and parentage.
The occupant of each stable was resplendent in a blue rug
trimmed with red and white and lettered with the horse's name
beneath a small American flag. An army of red, white and blue
people bustled around, some in tracksuits, others in beautiful
purpose-made anoraks with a flag on the breast and 'U.S.A.
Driving Team' on the back.

'See what I mean?' Sonia persisted.

I thought of the thousands of miles these horses and their
drivers had come. Of the months of preparation and planning
that must have gone into that journey. Above all, of the mind-
bending amount of money that it must have cost to be here in
this field in a little Norfolk village. I thought about dear old Plod
and trying to scrape together enough money for diesel. I
thought about Richard's home-made cross-country cart and the
doubts that now hung over its reliability; of the shabby
upholstery and damaged paintwork on the phaeton and I
wondered what on earth we were doing there. For the first time
since the euphoria of arriving, my spirits sank as I realised that
we were up against the best the world could offer in terms of
talent and backing. What right did an ex-coal miner on a heap of
scrap metal with two over-grown native ponies have to take up
that challenge? What chance could he possibly have?

After our meal I pushed such dangerous thoughts out of my mind and when Richard went off for a Team briefing I defiantly unpacked a small piece of fabric my mother had given me before we left. Faded, and frayed round the edges, it was a silk Union Jack my father had taken to a Scout Jamboree in France in the early 1920s. I stuck it on to a broom handle with drawing pins and than lashed it to the trailer's side. It fluttered bravely in the breeze and I knew that my mother at least would appreciate it when she arrived the next morning. She and Megan were coming down on the train and were booked into a B & B in a nearby village.

Standing back to admire my handiwork, I heard a voice ask, 'Now are you sure you've got that the right way up? It's a treasonable offence, you know.'

I turned and saw it was Bill, one of the young Household Cavalry Team members we had met at Osberton.

'I wasn't a Queen's Guide for nothing!'

'Is that the best you can come up with?'

'I'll have you know I'm very proud of that flag.'

'Mmm. I, well, borrowed this. I'll have to have it back at the end of the week — let's just hope it's not missed.'

He handed me a large carrier bag and went off to find Chris. Which was no doubt the prime objective of his mission anyway.

'It' turned out to be a Union Jack. The biggest one I'd ever seen, about ten foot wide by six foot deep. We suspended it between the trailer and the horse box; now we had a banner worthy of our cause.

I dispatched Chris the next morning to collect my mother and Megan while Sonia, Richard and I made the final preparations for the opening ceremony that afternoon. As the host nation, the British contingent entered last; first the Team members, Paul Gregory, Fred Pendlebury and Richard and then the six individuals.

As we polished, a polite young man came up and asked in reasonable English with a strong Eastern European accent if we could possibly lend him a hammer. They had a small repair to do. His name was Imri and his sister was a driver on the Hungarian Team. We lent him the hammer, we lent him the tool box and before long he was having tea and admiring our horses. Later he came to invite us over to see their horses in the portable stables. We were introduced not only to the horses but to his mother, his father, his sister and his brother. Theirs was indeed a family affair. Apart from Imri, no one spoke a word of English. They were earnestly polite, shaking hands and bowing heads, but I thought I detected an air of dejection.

'Is there anything else we can lend you? Please ask,' I finally ventured. 'Anything you need for yourself or your horses?'

'Aah! The horses. It is you see the hay. Our hay, the hay they like, we have to leave in France. We cannot bring it here. Here they say we will be given hay, English hay. And here is English hay but our horses, they will not eat. Two days now they do not eat. Soon they will become weak.'

Beside their loose box door were four bales of hay. It was good hay. Our horses were well used to it, strong and dry and coarse and yellow; almost like straw — a product of modern farming methods and baling. I gave Richard a quick nod and a wink and he slipped back to our box. On route to Osberton we'd stopped off at a friend's farm and, anxious that we should have abundant provisions for our two weeks on the road with the horses, he'd insisted on filling every spare nook and cranny of the box with extra hay. His hay, off his own land. Soft, long, wispy meadow hay.

Richard returned with a fragrant soft green bale under each arm. The Hungarians' eyes bulged in disbelief.

'A small present. I hope it will help and when you need more, just ask.'

We grinned broadly and the father said something rapidly to Imri.

'My father is unable to say thank you enough — he says that I ask you how much, how much we,' he struggled for the words, 'money owe you?'

Richard shook his head in horror. 'Not a thing, tell your father — nothing. It's a present and a pleasure.'

But Imri had no need to translate; some gestures were universal. The brother had already broken open a bale and was throwing some over the stable door. The horses took one suspicious sniff and then set about munching frantically. The solemn, round mother had tears in her eyes and was being comforted by the daughter. The father just kept taking Richard's hand and clasping it. The brother produced a bottle and some glasses and poured out a glorious white wine. He held his glass up to ours and said something that sounded suspiciously like 'shaggy-haggy-dra'.

Imri smiled. 'My brother toasts you. Drink, please drink. It is good wine, we have in Hungary what you call a vineyard? It is family business. Shaggy-haggy-dra!'

'Shaggy-haggy-dra!'

The opening ceremony presided over by His Royal Highness The Duke of Edinburgh took place the next day. From fourteen nations, as far apart as Canada, Denmark and Australia, forty-eight pairs of horses had come to compete for the first World Pairs Championship. In alphabetical order the nations entered the arena and, as each nation entered, their flag was raised at the entrance to the arena. As host nation, Great Britain was the last to enter. In the collecting arena our Chef d'Equipe was trying to organise us in the correct order.

'Now I want the flag horses in the lead here please, and the individual drivers behind. Flag horses in the front, please! Paul, Richard and Fred, over here.'

Flag horses. The words reverberated round my brain. Horses chosen for the British Team were entitled to wear the Union Jack on their saddle clothes and rugs to show that they had represented their country. Conwy Blaze and Cornsay Blizzard: my flag horses. For the rest of their lives nothing could take that honour from my horses: they could wear their flags for as long as they continued to compete at any event. Richard had earlier been presented with his flag to wear on his jacket for the World Championships.

As the United States of America Team went into the arena to thunderous applause, we lined up ready to follow. I wasn't nervous, I wasn't overawed, I was simply totally content.

'And finally, ladies and gentlemen, the Team from Great Britain — Paul Gregory, Richard Smith and Fred Pendlebury!'

Paul led us in with his jet black Welsh cobs and the cheers rose even louder from the crowd. We lapped the arena once to a standing ovation. From the crowd, brief glances of familiar faces all smiling, all waving. The Doctor and Hilda, positioned at the front of the railings, and, oh wonderful sight, the Doctor in a supreme effort standing unaided, the tears in his eyes visible even from the carriage. A familiar voice range from the grandstand in broad Geordie.

'Howay Coonty Durham!' It was unmistakably Ray Brown who had helped us in the 1984 season. And the little girl in the pink straw hat sitting atop the shoulders of a man who'd kindly scooped her up so she could get a better view: it was Megan perched precariously and waving her plastic Union Jack for all she was worth, cheering at the top of her voice.

The carriages lined up in their appropriate slots and Chris leapt out of the back to stand at the horses' heads. Suddenly in that packed arena all the jangle of harnesses, the rattle of carriages, had ceased. It was as if all of us, drivers, horses and crowd had paused to take a breath. Then in the still afternoon air they played the National Anthem.

And nothing in the rest of the world mattered any more, nothing at all. Because everything that had any true meaning was all there, all within the confines of that green, English field. All I loved, all that had been worth fighting for through the hard times, through the painful times. My family, Richard, my horses. All my hopes and all my secret dreams. It did not really matter what happened in the next three days as long as we did our very best, gave of our utmost, for the honour was in being there at all. Yes, the honour was already ours; now we had to earn the glory.

The event was already like an organic thing, growing and gaining in identity by the hour. We could recognise many of the drivers by now, knew where all the respective nations were parked. We'd been issued with 'ration books' which entitled so many of each Team to so many meals a day in the huge marquee that had been erected. It was good just to go in for a cup of tea or coffee; just to listen to the conversations going on in six different languages around you, to soak up the atmosphere of it all. There had been an informal cocktail party given the night before and already other social events were being planned; a barbeque, a cheese and wine party given by the French Team, a grand dinner to be given on the last night by the American Team.

At the cocktail party, Prince Philip had shown his deep personal interest in the British Team and his knowledge of our strengths — and weaknesses. He had assured Richard he had an excellent welder on the Sandringham estate if he should in any way need his services. We had a 'shop' and an issuing point for rations for feed and bedding for the horses. We were living on an international equestrian camp site and it was glorious.

Suddenly it was five o'clock on the morning of presentation and dressage and we all had to report with the horses for veterinary inspection at half past six. When the alarm went I rolled out of bed instantly, my knees for the first time wobbling and the butterflies in my stomach fluttering at the reality of it all. Both Richard and I knew full well he had not been selected for the Team because of his outstanding dressage; he'd been selected because of the horses' outstanding ability and endurance on the marathon. And both Richard and I knew that Blizzard was doubtful on both these scores. Shivering, I quickly pulled a heavy jumper over the tracksuit I always wore in bed at events. It was barely light and a misty, pearly grey light at that. I moved to the front of the trailer to draw the curtains and fill the kettle for some tea. I pulled the curtain back, then froze, motionless.

In the swirling, grey void beyond the window, barely discernible, a lighter grey shape floated through the mist and then disappeared from my view to re-emerge a few moments later. Just that eerie, lighter grey patch that came and then went and then came back again. The phantom moved a little nearer the trailer on its next appearance and then a little nearer still. My apparition was a beautiful Lippizaner horse on the end of a lunge rope. Majestic and rhythmical he circled, and I watched quite entranced. Watched for long minutes until in the now rapidly spreading light I could see his groom at the other end of the long rope, and behind him another grey shape moving in circles and to the right yet another. It was the Polish Team. God knows at what time they had roused themselves from their beds to begin their exercise: not that their grooms bothered very much with unnecessary comforts like beds, I later discovered. They preferred to lie on the ground in a sleeping bag outside their horses' stable doors. Whether it was for fear of doping or simply total dedication I never quite discovered, but every morning I was treated to the same ethereal ballet in the dawn light and found it haunting and unforgettable.

Presentation was always an ordeal. This was to be a triple ordeal; three sets of judges set some fifty yards apart, one English, two Continental. We were to present ourselves to the first, then move on to the second and on again to the third.

It was a hot, still day. The heat and my tension only served to make my rigid starched collar the more uncomfortable. I stood at the front of the vehicle between the horses, trembling from head to toe. The collar stud at my throat felt like a golf ball and the sweat trickled down my back in itchy streams. I knew I was not that far away from actually passing out. What on earth was I doing anyway, togged up in fancy dress — male fancy dress at that — about to be scrutinised by six pairs of international eyes? I had a sudden desire to just walk away. I would truly rather have been anywhere than in that field just then. I raised my eyes miserably up and along the pole and they met Richard's. He looked quite calm, assured, and completely in control. He smiled very gently and encouragingly at me and said, 'I love you.'

And his love flowed through me and around me, strengthening and sustaining me as always. And I walked proud and erect at

the head of my horses from judge to judge, oblivious to the
heat, conquering all my nerves, determined to do my horses
justice.

The gap between presentation and the dressage test was far
longer than at a National event. For well over an hour we baked
and suffered in the sun. Richard did manage to find some partial
shade for the horses behind a portable building but it was mid-
afternoon, sticky and soporific.

I had loosened my collar studs so at least felt I wasn't choking
to death but my wool jacket and high leather boots were
purgatory. I was beyond nerves now; I was almost off-hand
about it all. After an hour and a half of hanging around in
harness, the horses were going to be totally undriveable any
way. Even they had given up fidgeting and were snoozing in
their collars, while the girls valiantly swatted troublesome flies
away from their ears.

Then Richard was calling me to get up on the vehicle. I moved
as if I were in a dream, my legs leaden and reluctant. The huge
arena with its flags and packed tiered grandstand and all those
eyes awaited us. We were heading straight towards the arched
entrance, there was no escape, no turning back. Sitting bolt
upright in the back of the carriage, my hands and my teeth were
clenched till they hurt. From far off I could hear applause and it
was getting nearer, we were getting nearer, we were approaching
the arch. I was terrified, the tension was unbearable. The horses
must feel it, they must react to it.

Richard turned his head very slightly and said over his
shoulder, 'It's nothing really, pet; just like sneaking on to the
Council football field for a bit of practice on a Sunday afternoon.
That's all, piece of cake.'

Gathering up his reins he addressed the horses, 'Come on,
bonny lads, trot on.'

And we turned under the arch and into the arena.

All the built-up tension, all our fears were suddenly gone. A
calm and confident aura enveloped the horses, Richard and
myself. This force flowed from Richard to the horses and from
the horses back to him. Even from the back of the carriage I
could sense its progress up and down the reins. The magical
'coming together'. The crowds, the grandstand, the pageantry
quite simply did not exist. Nothing existed for us outside the
white boards of the dressage arena. And within those boards
two horses and a man moved in total unison, worked in
harmony, and my heart sang with the joy and beauty of it.

Then there was the applause, the reluctant return to reality. It was not the best dressage test to be performed in that arena that day, but it was the best test that our horses had ever driven. Doffing his bowler to Richard as we trotted out of the arena, our Chef d'Equipe said simply, 'Who's a clever boy then?'

It turned out we needed that dressage mark. At each phase, the two best out of the three Team members' scores were accredited, the lowest score discarded. We knew we'd not been put on the Team to get a dressage mark; Fred Pendlebury and Paul Gregory were expected to do that. But Fred's leggy and spirited Clevelands took an exception to all the judges sitting in their little wooden huts around the arena, never settled and did a very poor test. So our dressage mark was accredited.

We had had what I hoped would be our last-minute crisis. Things just wouldn't have been the same without a last-minute crisis, now would they? An anguished howl had issued from the horsebox while Chris was putting the good harness away late the previous afternoon. She had knocked off her glasses and broken a lens. She was as blind as a bat without them. And of course she didn't have a spare pair. A last-minute dash to King's Lynn just caught an optician on the point of closing and miraculously he announced he could have a new lens fitted by mid-morning the next day. It was cutting things a bit close, but we weren't due to start on the marathon till the afternoon. Chris, who had seen her chances of a trip round a World Championship marathon literally slip through her fingers, changed her lament of grief into sobs of relief and yet one more hurdle was behind us.

So now marathon day had dawned and before it was over we would have asked a great deal of our little horses; Blizzard the cheeky, baby-faced youngster and Bear the battle-scarred old war horse. Seven years separated them in age and seven years in experience. And on this, undeniably the most important day of his life to date, Blizzard was still off form, flat and uninterested in food or work. Pushing him hard while he was in this frame of mind was already having undesirable results — the weight was dropping off him. Each rib could be clearly seen just beneath the skin on the barrel of his chest and his stifles seemed to sink further inward daily. Whilst perhaps acceptable on a race horse or a whippet, it was far from desirable in a Welsh cob. Not that he was in any way unfit; after the rigorous inspection by a panel of international vets at first light there was no question of that. It was just that he was not, well, himself.

I felt weighed down with the tension and worry of it all. I wandered aimlessly over to the horsebox to watch the girls strapping and grooming the horses. There was no need for it, they were absolutely gleaming, but no doubt it was good therapy and helped keep their nerves under control. Richard was in the trailer poring over his diagram of the hazards yet one more time, making last-minute decisions over route and approach. I felt as though I'd been on the marathon already; the way Richard tossed and moaned and flung around all night he'd obviously been driving it in his sleep.

I really would have to get breakfast started. The very thought of it made me feel ill but the others might be hungry and at least it would give my butterflies something to chew on. I had just reached the trailer door when two figures rounded the corner.

It was Imri and his father, Imri as charming and smiling as his father was solemn and silent.

'My father, he has something for you. A small thank you — to bring you luck on this important day,' Imri announced mysteriously.

I called Richard to join us. His father reached into one side of his jacket and produced what looked like four green pottery egg cups. How charming I thought, and how useful they would be for the trailer. Very ethnic.

'Oh thank you, they're lovely,' I muttered graciously taking them from him and turning to take them inside.

'No wait, see!' Imri exclaimed grabbing my arm, 'that is not what is for luck!'

From the other side of his jacket his father produced a dark green unlabelled bottle. From it he poured into each egg cup a colourless liquid. Solemnly raising his receptacle towards us, he said 'Shaggy-haggy-dra' and downed the contents in one gulp.

Smiling encouragingly, Imri repeated the toast and then looked expectantly at us. In unison Richard and I raised the egg cups, uttered 'shaggy-haggy-dra' and tipped the colourless liquid down our throats.

Breathing was out of the question; not that I was much aware of my lungs only the liquid fire that had hit my totally empty stomach, ricocheted up to my brain and back to my stomach again. Then somehow I was gasping air in and my eyes were resuming their ability to focus. A warm tingle was spreading throughout my body.

Both father and son were grinning from ear to ear. Richard just stood there with a slightly dazed expression and watery eyes.

'Imri! What on earth was that?'

'Slivovitch; or how you know it as plum brandy. Only this

very special — it is very old, we triple distil at our own vineyard. You don't like it?' He looked suddenly anxious.

'Oh, it's quite amazing stuff. It's just that plum brandy before breakfast is something my system is not accustomed to.'

'Aah. In Hungary we drink it in morning; it help you wake up good!'

I still only have two words of Hungarian: 'shaggy-haggy-dra' and 'slivovitch'. But perhaps they would have been wiser to use their luck-bringing potion within the family: later that day, having driven brilliantly all marathon, Imri's sister Erica overturned in the last hazard when she was well on course for an individual medal.

Chris had readjusted her newly-mended specs and checked her three stop-watches a dozen times. Sonia stood at the horses' heads uttering encouraging nonsense to them.

'You can show them — you can do it — you're as good as any other horse here, for all their posh rugs and fancy horseboxes!'

Richard was desperately trying to make polite small talk to his Danish referee who was now in her place on the vehicle beside him. But I knew his heart wasn't in it; his ears were straining for the starting official, his hands fidgeting with his whip, his whole body and mind anxious now simply to get on with it. I felt rather useless and killed the time endlessly checking the harness over, every keeper, every buckle: how ludicrous to get this far only to have something come undone.

'Two minutes!'

I paused beside Richard's foot and looked up. There was nothing to say really, nothing that wouldn't sound trite and superfluous — good luck! take care! — when he knew I was with him heart and soul every inch of the way.

'One minute!'

Sonia stepped back as I approached the horses. She knew I liked this moment with them in complete privacy. It was stupid really, superstitious almost, but I liked to give each of them 'their word' just before they set off.

What could I say to Blizzard other than words of general encouragement, to ask him to draw on whatever reserves he may possess.

'God bless, old soldier,' I said quietly into Bear's neck, knowing he would try till he dropped rather than give in. 'Look after them for me. Richard and little lad, they both need you today, need everything you've got.' Every ounce of courage and stamina and all his intelligence and experience.

'Fifteen seconds!'

Richard gave me a slight slow nod of dismissal and I stepped aside from the horses' heads.

'Ten, nine, eight . . . '

Able to count every bit as well as the official, Bear took up the slack in his collar and shuffled his feet restlessly.

'. . . three, two, one: away! Good luck!'

And they were gone, leaving Sonia and me to our nerves and our imaginations for the best part of the next two hours.

The hazards were everything World Championship hazards should be: big, tight and demanding. When they came into the first one, which was on a hillside and composed of massive timbers set around a realistic road works scenario, including a JCB with its bucket in the air, I was on the video cameraman's lookout on top of a large van. From there I could command a view of most of the first group of hazards. I'd been offered this bird's eye view on the strict condition I didn't get over-excited and bounce up and down and joggle the camera. In fact I didn't move at all, and never made a sound as they negotiated that first hazard. Heart pounding almost audibly and mouth bone dry, I watched them, forcing myself to breathe slowly and deeply, pushing air into lungs that were almost paralysed with tension. Each hazard was like coming through a severe contraction at the latter end of labour.

In that first hazard they were not inspirational; at the first tight turn on the hillside they were just not going fast enough, not coming round quickly enough and of course they stuck. While Bear struggled to get the vehicle free, Blizzard wasn't really trying at all, merely wooden and uninterested. My God, this wasn't going to be a repeat of their first Sandringham, was it? But then, with precious seconds lost, they were free and coming down the hill towards the next hazard. The down-hill incline seemed to revive Blizzard a little and they drove round the tight stand of trees and timbers in true style and were off again to a flurry of applause. Hard and painful, my heart somehow managed to keep on thumping. In fact at the next three hazards I began cautiously to dare to hope my fears about Blizzard were groundless as they had all their usual attack and speed. Then they disappeared for another kilometre or so across country and out of sight of the video cameraman's eyrie.

Thanking my host hurriedly, I set off across the parkland at a trot, my legs thankful for something to do. I got to the next hazard just as they were due in. It was a water hazard built around and across a natural stream. Full-sized sail boards with multi-coloured sails cracking and flapping in the strongish breeze were placed in and around the hazards. God help any horse that was worried by polythene bags in the wind! But the cobs had no such fears. This was as near as I'd been to them since they left on the marathon and I scrutinised them closely as they came in. Bear was on fire: ears pricked, nostrils flaring and four legs flying, he attacked the hazard. Beside him, Blizzard was valiantly trying his best and allowing himself to be towed round the hazard unprotesting. But his ears were slightly back, his expression glazed and he would try whenever possible to drop out of draft. Richard was having to tap him far more often and insistently with his whip than he normally did. This had the effect of irritating Blizzard which momentarily, if nothing else, made him go forward. They splashed through the last element of the water hazard, Chris shouting almost hysterically, 'Blizzard! Get on!'

And that was the last I would see of them before they reached the finishing line. They had two more hazards to do before that but there was no way I could see them through and get back to the finish in time. And the finishing line, above anywhere else, was where I most wanted to be.

Richard had foreseen it would be a problem. Normally the finishing line of a marathon is within a few hundred yards of the last hazard. So you can push really hard and fast, get the last supreme effort out of your horses and then get over the finishing line on the impetus you have generated. At the World Championships, after the last hazard, there was another hard, slogging two kilometres to cover before the end.

I already knew Richard would be fighting desperately to keep going, having been stuck badly in the last hazard. That much I'd heard over the P.A. system. I had stood quietly under a tree, praying as hard as I knew how, feeling the seconds tick by. But long before the five minutes that meant elimination had passed the speakers rang out with, 'And Richard Smith has now freed himself from the last hazard. That's Richard Smith, for the Great Britain Team, through the last and on his run in.'

He must have incurred heavy time faults by now; any thought of doing anything world-beating on the marathon was now gone. But that didn't matter, did it?

'Of course not; all that matters is that they complete the course correctly, don't get eliminated.'

'But the horses were selected for their marathon. We've let the Team down.'

'Rubbish: look at the dressage score they got yesterday. That's what counts, finishing the marathon safely. If they're eliminated then their dressage score yesterday would be worthless.'

'Oh God, I hadn't thought of that!'

'Calm down: they've got round all the hazards. However slowly and however tired they are they can always trot another mile. Good God, you don't think they'd give up for the sake of one more mile?'

'No, no I suppose not.'

'Bear will bring them in, you'll see. Do you think he survived all he has for no reason? The spirits and guts that horse must have to have got this far? He will bring them in safely!'

I became aware of Sonia, quite ashen with worry, standing beside me with her bucket and sponges.

'Sorry, Sonia, I was far away there. It's a habit I have — arguing with myself.'

'This has been the longest two hours I have ever known. I feel I've aged ten years,' she said.

'Well, we shouldn't have much longer to wait now.'

We were standing just behind the sign which said 'End of Section E' and could see perhaps a quarter of a mile up the track. Suddenly two blobs appeared and then were moving towards us. From a few hundred yards away I could see why they were such an unfamiliar colour; they were totally soaked in sweat, Blizzard looking more bay than chestnut. Whatever reserves he had had were long gone. He was running on pure guts. Neck and head down and out of draft he was actually only keeping up with the vehicle, not pulling it at all. All the traction was being provided by Bear who, although also dark with sweat, was still alert and full of determination. It was a very moving sight; the old horse ploughing on doing all the work, the young horse valiantly trying to keep up with him and Richard doing his best to nurse them both safely in. My heart ached with love and pride and concern for them all.

Then they were across the line and Richard was hauling in the reins to halt them. I flew straight round to his side of the vehicle; he looked totally and completely exhausted.

'All right?'

He knew exactly what I meant.

'Aye, we got round and no mistakes, don't worry on that score.'

My face must have registered relief.

'But we'll be slow, damned slow: we're sixteen seconds late in this Section and I didn't get the first Section in by a mile. And then we were tied up good and proper in that last hazard.'

'It doesn't matter! Nothing matters except you've driven it and driven it right. It's no more than we expected, really. Come on, let's get them back and get them washed down and fed. There's still tomorrow, you know. You always say an event's not over till you've driven through that last cone!'

Richard began to climb wearily and stiffly off the vehicle.

'I'm sorry, Mr Smith,' came a voice, 'would you just stay at the reins and drive your horses over to that stable?'

My insides went on to fast freeze.

'What's the problem?' It came out as a reedy squeak.

'Oh, no problem. Don't worry, we're the vets — we have to do random dope tests and we want to do one on this nearside horse. It will only take a few minutes. Please don't let your grooms give them anything whatsoever to eat or drink and I'm afraid I have to accompany you over there on the vehicle. Rules and all that.'

Random dope test? On the nearside horse? Which just happened to be Bear! Of all the horses in the world why, oh why, had they descended on Bear? Was it the amazing contrast in the picture they'd presented at the finish? Blizzard so exhausted and Bear still full of running. Did they think he must be hyped-up on something?

All the relief I'd just begun to feel evaporated. We had been meticulous about feeding: cutting out all those brands of horse cubes and coarse mix that indicated they contained caffeine, one of the 'prohibited substances' under F.E.I. rules. But what if we'd slipped up? Or someone had slipped the horses something to eat? I remembered reading about a racehorse failing a dope test once because someone had given him a Mars bar. I began to see the sense in the Polish grooms' twenty-four hour vigil outside their horses' boxes.

'The test will comprise a urine test and a blood test,' the vet informed me as I unharnessed Bear with shaking hands and led him towards a little wooden building.

'Oh, he's going to love this,' I thought, 'just love this. He's wild about needles. And how on earth are we going to get him to pee to order?'

But the experienced hands who took Bear from me were obviously well-versed in these matters. The stable was over two foot deep in dry rustly straw; rattling the straw and making whistling noises, the handler looked smug as Bear spread wide his back legs in preparation. A good long pee is often one of the first things a horse treats himself to after strenuous exercise and all that dry straw was irresistible. Bear looked mildly astonished when a second handler quickly approached with what looked like a small plastic bucket on the end of a long pole. This was whipped into its strategic position and Bear, looking slightly embarrassed about the whole thing, had little option but to fill it.

The second of the tests, two samples of blood from a vein in his neck, was accomplished just as professionally and quickly: Bear, for once, standing like a perfect gentleman when the needles were inserted. Perhaps it was the shock of it all. I mean, finishing a marathon usually signifies treats and a warm bath and a nice bran mash — not having to pee into a bucket and be attacked by vampires.

'Thank you, that's all. You can take him back now.' So we walked slowly back to our own box, Bear still slightly mystified by it all but happy to unwind and dry out the last of his damp patches in the late afternoon sun. I felt relief that it was all safely over, but undermining that relief was a new niggle. What if? It was impossible, absurd, but oh how I wished they had picked on someone else for that dope test.

By the evening the calculations had all been done and the scores were posted. Our marathon was, as we'd expected, heavily penalised with time faults but the other two Team members, Paul and Fred, had done really well. Putting their scores together with the previous day's dressage scores from Paul and Richard put Great Britain into fourth place behind the Dutch. So close behind that only a single fault in the obstacle driving the next day separated us from third place and a bronze medal. Germany lay in second place and Switzerland in the lead. Paul Gregory's score was such that a clear round would gain him the individual Bronze medal. One cone down and he would lose it.

It was very, very tight.

I decided I must have produced more adrenalin over the past couple of days than in the whole of the rest of my life. What else could possibly be keeping me going? I was absolutely shattered. Too excited to sleep and too apprehensive to eat. At least we were on at a reasonably early hour in the morning and we could get it over with. I don't think I could have handled hanging around till the afternoon. I think my stomach lining would have worn through.

Very early we had a second veterinary inspection and for all my nightmares about Blizzard, after a good night's rest and a good feed, he trotted, though a bit tucked up for my liking,

quite brightly up and down for the panel. All signs of
exhaustion of the previous day had gone and he was as sound
as a bell. His youthfulness may have been a drawback when
it came to stamina, but it also gave him a very good recovery
rate.

Since the veterinary inspection, Chris and Sonia had given
them both 'the works' and now gleaming, groomed to perfection, they looked every bit as eye-catching as they had done for
presentation two days previously. Richard was in the trailer
fumbling with his wing collar and grey silk tie.

'Come here. I'll do that for you.'

'Thanks. My hands are shaking so much I can't manage.'

'I can't promise mine'll be much better.'

'Well, this is it, I suppose.' He was trying very hard to say it
lightly.

'You do understand why I'm not coming in with you? It's just
that I'm so uptight I'm sure the boys will sense it and that won't
help you at all. Far better to let Chris go in with you.'

'Of course I understand.'

'In fact, I don't want to appear a coward or disloyal or
anything but I thought I might just go down to that pretty little
village and shop this morning. Oh God, that sounds so trivial.' I
struggled with words to explain how I felt. 'But whatever
happens today is fine by me; I'm not really worried about
winning or losing. Had we been lying in tenth place now I
would be thrilled and there'd be no suspense. It's just that being
so close to that third place makes it so unbearable. The fact is
that what the boys do today could tip the scales somehow — I
honestly think my heart would just give out if I had to watch
that.'

'Well, actually, I was going to ask you to do me a favour this
morning anyway . . .'

'Which is?'

'Please get lost — in the nicest possible way, of course. I'll be a
lot steadier not having to worry about you worrying about me.
Well, not where I can see you doing it anyway!'

We understood each other perfectly.

So I helped harness up the horses, giving each one his private
word as I did so. Then I watched Richard climb up into his seat
and take up his whip and reins. Chris, for once quiet and
solemn in her black jacket and bowler, climbed up behind him
and as the whole glittering, powerful picture moved off I quietly
slid away.

To my surprise I found myself a short while later in a pretty little Norfolk church, just on the outskirts of the Sandringham estate. I hadn't set off with the intention of going there, but the gate was open, the door inviting and somehow I found myself inside. Morning service was over and the church completely empty. It was very old and very beautiful and very, very peaceful.

I sat quietly in a pew gulping in the serenity of the place as a drowning man gasps for air. Slowly it calmed me and my heart ceased to race.

Was it so important then what happened on that patch of grass today? Yes, it was. Why? It wouldn't matter in the long run, would it? Nothing mattered in the long run, certainly not a lump of metal with a pretty ribbon on it.

Yes, it mattered. Not for myself, but for the horses, for Richard: I knew they were world calibre but it needed a medal to make everyone else realise it. And for myself? Not for myself at all? Truly?

Then the internal walls all came tumbling down. Yes, it mattered for me. Fiercely and passionately and covetously, it mattered to me. It would be the vindication that I had been sub-consciously seeking these past few years. The proof that I wasn't a failure, that I wasn't a weak, pathetic creature. I could put my faith and my heart into something and see it through. See it right through to the end. Through all the setbacks, all the problems and all the heartaches.

To those who'd shaken their heads when I left the comfort and security of a five-bedroomed farmhouse and the County Life I want to say, 'This is why.'

To those who'd shaken their heads at my determination to ride again, to drive again, to have anything whatsoever to do with horses again after my accident, I wanted to say, 'This is why.'

To those who could not grasp why I would live in a depressing derelict pit village on a wind-blasted hill and spend my days shovelling horse muck or cleaning filthy gas cookers I wanted to shout, 'This is why!'

Having at last been honest with myself, I sat quite calm and tranquil in the little church. Partly listening to the idle buzz of a fly on the stained glass, partly looking at the lovely flowers, but mostly thinking of the arena and of the course and of the battle that would be in progress there.

'A right pig of a course!' Richard had called it — not a straight line anywhere and in a very tight time limit. Individually,

Richard was lying about fifteenth so his appearance would be in the top third of the competition as they always began with the lowest score.

I was so engrossed in thought, so far away, that the minutes had just kept on ticking by unnoticed. Only the hardness of the pew which eventually penetrated even my well-padded rump finally brought me back to my senses and to my watch.

It was time to go back, time to find out. I felt I could face it all now.

In the arena the competition was still in progress. The flags and bunting rattled and cracked in a wind that was getting a bit too strong for comfort. The competitors and officials ringside enclosure was packed, as was the brightly striped marquee containing the bar behind it. On jelly legs I walked slowly in looking for a familiar face, any familiar face. The first one I saw was that of Charles Cheston, one of the American Team drivers. I stopped directly in front of him and he doffed his hat like the New England gentleman he was.

'Well, hello there. Say, are you all right? You don't look too well at all.'

'Could you . . . please tell me,' I said, forcing my tongue to push out each word carefully, 'how Richard did in the cone driving?'

'What? You mean you don't know? Well it's my pleasure to tell you that he did a clear round with only a half a second's time fault.'

'He did?'

'Sure he did — in fine style. Say, are you sure you're all right? Can I get you a drink or something?'

'Oh no, no thank you.' My smiles and my tears were all getting mixed up somehow and pulling my face into ridiculous contortions. 'No, thank you again. I don't need anything, anything at all!'

Tears streaming down my face, I pushed my way through knots and clumps of astonished people until I found what I was looking for. Relieved of his top hat, silk tie and black jacket, Richard was leaning over the arena railing in just his shirt sleeves.

I ran up to him and he held his arms open wide. I flung myself into them and covered him with somewhat damp kisses.

'You did it! You did it! Oh, Richard, you did it!'

Slightly embarrassed by the amused stares of surrounding

people he gently detached my limpet-like grip.

'Not bad, eh, for an ex-Durham miner and two over-grown pit ponies! But the battle's not over yet. I've done my bit and Fred Pendlebury's got a clear round. One of the Dutch drivers has had cones down so there's two more Dutch drivers and then Paul Gregory to go. If Paul gets a double clear then he's won the individual bronze and his score will count for the British Team as I got a half a time fault. And if the Dutch drivers don't both get clear rounds we've done it! But you know I always say a competition's never over till the last cone's been driven.'

Barely able to breathe, I stood beside him at the ringside to watch the final act played out.

The second Dutch driver in had a clear round, but when the little orange ball fell off the top of the cone half-way through the third Dutch driver's round I just kept staring at it. A groan went up from the crowd. A little orange ball — surely there was no way that one little orange ball could make any difference in the vast international game that was being played out? But a tiny excited voice was saying, 'It can! It can! We've done it!' Strictly though, 'we' hadn't done it. Paul Gregory was due in next lying in his overall third position and if he got a double clear he would get not only the individual Bronze medal but his score would be credited for the cones.

I was filled with strange and mixed emotions. I wanted Paul to do well, of course, and to win his individual medal: we had our dressage score for the Team, but after our poor marathon, if we didn't get a cone driving score, that would be all we had and we would have contributed but a small part to the total British Team score.

Paul's black cobs drove into the arena to wild applause. They negotiated all the difficult and large elements with almost contemptuous ease and then coming towards us through a pair of perfectly ordinary straight cones, there was the gentlest of bumping noises and an orange ball rolled gently on to the grass. A huge gasp went up from the crowd and I could see and experience myself the bitter disappointment in Paul's face. I bowed my head, fully realising how I would have felt had Richard been in the same situation, knowing how easily the roles could have been reversed. His wife was crying on the back of the carriage. One little orange ball: it had lost him his medal and his Team score.

Next in second place came the third Swiss driver, driving for Team Gold and individual Silver. He had a double clear to an explosion of red and white waving flags and a cacophany of cow bells. It meant that the German driver, driving for individual Gold and Team Silver, had to get a double clear or tumble to second place. He had no leeway, not a single time fault.

A hush fell in the arena and the crowded grandstand. The wind was now whipping up so fiercely that paper was blowing everywhere and people were losing their hats.

Erchacht Meineker saluted the judges, the bell sounded and he set off at a controlled pace. He was a superb driver, sheer poetry to watch. His horses, large and leggier than our cobs, were arrogant and elegant. With two-thirds of the course completed and in the most tortuous section, a terrific gust of wind suddenly dislodged a ball from its cone when he was only yards from the obstacle. With lightning reactions he hauled his horses in and put on his brake. The bell rang and the clock stopped. An official raced out on to the arena and replaced the ball. Then the bell sounded once more. The rules did not allow him to circle or prepare himself in any way — he had to go from where he stood. He had lost his impetus and his concentration; but he had not lost his courage. Setting his horses away again with icy control, he negotiated that pair of cones and the next and the next. Coming over the wooden bridge, the last of the obstacles, he set his horses into full gallop and covered the finish line with barely two seconds to spare. It was truly a display that was worthy of a World Champion, and that was what he had just become. The whole arena and everyone, of every nationality, cheered and clapped and whistled in appreciation of the brilliance of the man and of his horses.

When the tumult died down, there was a rush to the bar while the military band played soothing interlude music. Although we had all done calculations in our heads nothing seemed real until the officials had done theirs and the announcement had been made. Richard fought his way through to the bar and returned with two large brandies and Coke. I downed mine with totally indecent haste. The band music faded politely away and the speakers crackled into life.

'Your Royal Highness, Ladies and Gentlemen. I am pleased to announce the results of the first World Pairs Driving Championship. The individual medals first: the Gold Medal goes to Erchacht Meineker of Germany, the Silver Medal to Heine Merke of Switzerland and the Bronze Medal to Arc de Leuf of Holland.'

Waves of applause rocked the arena.

'And now the Team medals. The Gold Medal has been won by Switzerland, the Silver Medal by Germany and the Bronze

Medal goes to Great Britain!'
  It was for real.

That afternoon they held the medal presentation and closing
ceremony. As each nation entered the arena its flag, which had
flown over the entrance for the last four days, was slowly
lowered. We had entered that arena then filled with pride,
anticipation and hope. We now had returned for the glory. With
grooms at the horses' heads the carriages were lined up as
before and speeches made as before. Then the medallists were
called to come forward. Richard turned and pecked me on the
cheek and placed the reins in my hand.
  'Here are your horses, sweetheart.'
  I looked at him in astonishment. He had never, ever, let me sit
alone in control of both horses before. It was purely symbolic of
course; they weren't going anywhere and Chris was at their
heads, but as a symbol it was perfect.
  In front of the Royal box a podium in true Olympic fashion
with the graduated steps had been erected. As the three
individual medallists climbed down from receiving their medals
from Prince Philip, the announcer was summoning the Teams:
'And for Great Britain, Ladies and Gentlemen, the World
Bronze Medal. The Great Britain Team: Paul Gregory, Fred
Pendlebury and Richard Smith.'
  It was not a little dumpy man who climbed on to that podium,
it was a man six feet tall. I sat in the carriage holding the reins,
full of emotion but for once, outwardly I revealed very little. I
watched him remove his hat and bend his head to receive the
medal, his cheeks flushed rosy with pride and pleasure, saw
Prince Philip say a few words to him. Once again the National
Anthem played and I reflected that it was probably the first and
last time in my life I would hear it played purely on account of
something I had been involved with.
  When he returned, still six feet tall, and resumed control of
the horses, Chris climbed in and all forty-eight pairs of horses
paraded around the arena that one last time.
  It was over.
  'What did Prince Philip say to you when he gave you your
medal?' I enquired.
  'Actually he said, "I see your vehicle held together then!" '
  Of course it didn't end quite as abruptly as that. That evening
the Carriage Association of America hosted an amazing dinner
party for the medallists. We were in a tent (albeit a pink- and

white-lined marquee) in a field. But from the service, the food, the drink, the flowers and the dress, we could have been at the Waldorf Hotel. It was pure fantasy and I revelled in every second of it, refusing to drink anything but one glass of champagne, lest the alcohol dull my senses and appreciation of it all in any way.

Well into the early hours parties great and small, formal and informal, went on up and down the stable lines. Music and dance, food and wine of every conceivable national flavour spilled out into the night air. But eventually, even the most energetic of revellers sought their horsebox or caravan or tent and the only sound was that of the odd, restless horse.

The silence did not last very long. In the very earliest of dawn light, a new sound could be heard; of hammers banging and engines revving, of ramps going down and carriages being loaded.

It was time to pack up and leave.

We all worked very hard all morning, but in a wooden, methodical way. We had only been on that field for five days but it had become a very special place with a unique and heady atmosphere which we were now having to reluctantly destroy.

By mid-afternoon a huge convoy of inter-continental horse-boxes was assembled in the field. These were the wagons that were to take the foreign competitors to their airports and ferries. Addresses had been swapped, tears of farewell shed. Imri and his family had pressed yet another half dozen bottles of wine on us and the Canadians had given everyone little maple leaf badges. The front wagon blew three long deep notes on his air horn and doors slammed and people scattered. Engines revved, gears were engaged and the convoy moved slowly forward. From every cab people waved and shouted and blew kisses, and on the ground we waved and shouted back till we were hoarse. But all noise was drowned by the orchestrated bedlam of the air horns, one after another, blowing and blowing their deep, defiant notes in a glorious and ear-splitting farewell.

With a swirl of dust the tail-board of the last wagon disappeared out of the gate and on to the road. In a few minutes what had been hectic and colourful and alive was quiet and barren and dead. A strange, empty silence fell over the field. Lone wisps of hay blew past in the breeze; the odd empty stable door banged forlornly. Only in the British encampment was there any sign of life at all and the feeling was one of terrible sadness.

Suddenly it was no effort to hasten our efforts with the packing, load the horses and go home because the worst imaginable thing in our minds at the time was to be the last, the very last wagon, to pull out of that field.

17

'Owners, please join your horses'

RICHARD LEANT OVER the field gate watching the cobs graze and stretch and relax in the warm September sun.

'Penny for them?' I asked as I approached.

'Oh, I'm just thinking how much they're enjoying their rest. They do deserve it, by God they do.'

'But you're not enjoying yours?' I probed gently.

Ever since our return the previous week he'd been very low and distant, lost in the evenings without horses to drive or parts to weld or the horsebox to work on. I felt very much the same myself but at least had the house and all the normal humdrum routine of domestic life to keep my mind from dwelling on it too much.

'It's just that there's such a vacuum, such a hole. For a year we've worked towards it, driven ourselves demented at times over it and now it's over and done with. I feel lost.'

I put my arm gently through his and leant on the gate with him. Still in their summer coats, Bear and Blizzard gleamed in the sunlight. I never ceased to be stunned by how beautiful they were.

'I do understand, honestly. I feel it too, you know. It's called anti-climax, and the bigger the climax the harder the fall. But it's no use looking back; we've got to look forward. Just think; it's only twenty-three months to the next World Championships in Germany! Think about that; it's not as long as it sounds, you know.'

He gave a mirthless chuckle.

'Sweetheart, don't you know we can't look ahead six months with these horses, let alone two years? I don't even know where I'm going to find the money for hay this winter yet. This season has bottomed us, you know that.'

I nodded. I knew it only too well.

'Not only the cost of attending all those events, but the hammering that the business took while we were away. We've both got to knuckle down now, put all thoughts of horses out of our minds and work as hard as we can. Work just to survive.'

I knew the bleak economic facts only too well.

Chris had gone home to Wales the previous week. Not only was there nothing for her to do now the horses were letting down for the winter, but there was no way we could afford to keep on paying even her modest wage. All the experience, all the ability we now undoubtedly had — all to go to waste. It was enough to make us weep: and it did. Richard and I had talked briefly and painfully about next year, about whether we could afford to get the pair to any events at all, whether it was worth it if we couldn't do the whole season, whether we should just play with one of them single again.

'What we really need,' I said firmly, 'is a sponsor.'

'Of course we do,' Richard agreed, 'but would you mind telling me where we can find one in this sport? Oh, I know one or two of the really big names in the team drivers have them but that's all. Have you ever heard of a pair that's commercially sponsored?'

'No, but has a world medallist ever looked for a sponsor before?'

Richard shook his head fatalistically which made me quite cross.

'It's no use doing that. Look, I think it's our only chance and I'm going to work on it. I shall draw up a profile about us and take it from there.' I stumped back to the house feeling determined and glad of something to do, but in truth I didn't think we had a great deal of chance. Perhaps Richard was right, perhaps we had come to the end of the line. We had achieved what we had set out to do and there was nothing else, nothing to aim for any more.

The letter arrived the next week and read:

'I am writing to invite you to appear in the parade of medallists at the Gala performance of the Horse of the Year Show on Monday evening, 7th October. Looking forward to seeing you at Wembley. Well done and many congratulations!' It was signed John Stevens M.B.E., Show Director.

Sonia was hastily summoned and joyfully she took over the task of keeping Bear and Blizzard moderately fit and looking well for just one more month. They were swaddled up to their ears in blankets in an attempt to persuade them not to grow their winter coats, not just for a few more weeks anyway.

I'll never know where we found the money for the diesel but it came from somewhere. But that was all we had to find. For once we were guests and so were the horses; hotel accommodation was provided for us nearby and stables, hay and bedding provided for them. I had to pinch myself into believing it was really true. The Horse of the Year Show was something I would sit glued to watching on the telly. The Horse of the Year Show was something I'd always dreamed of being able to go and watch someday. But in my wildest, wildest dreams I'd never considered actually appearing there. My horses at the Horse of the Year Show, in the Wembley arena, guests of the Gala performance. I had to pinch myself again.

The Sunday passed in a blur of rehearsals and soaking in the atmosphere and imagery of Wembley. The arena was so much smaller than I'd imagined, the noise and the ranks and ranks of tiered seats so much greater. I tried (and failed) to prevent my jaw dropping when jostling in the collecting ring with legendary show jumpers like Harvey Smith and David Broome. I thoroughly enjoyed flashing my welded-on plastic identity bracelet, which to my astonishment afforded me unhindered access to just about anywhere.

After a day of exercising and grooming the horses and polishing the harness with Sonia, I wallowed up to my neck in bubbles in the hotel before changing for the evening performance, still not convinced any of it was truly happening.

I was not actually to go into the arena with Richard in the carriage and I was not in the least bit disappointed because I had a different role to play. For once, in fact, my real role. Because at the Horse of the Year Show they acknowledge an often totally over-looked group of people — the owners. Not only acknowledge them but actually present them with an award.

So I sat at the upper end of the arena in my new posh frock facing the famous red velvet curtains, above which a military band played suitable interlude music. Waiting. Behind the curtain I could imagine Richard, Paul Gregory and Fred Pendlebury assembled to lead the parade of the country's most honoured horses and riders into the arena: eventers and show jumpers, dressage horses and long-distance riders. All the horses that had achieved national and international honours that year.

In that vast, packed arena which buzzed with excited chatter, the lights gently dimmed then faded to total darkness. The thirty-eighth Horse of the Year Show was about to begin.

In the darkness a voice said, 'Your Royal Highness, Ladies and Gentlemen, we now present a parade of British, European and World medallists, led in by the Trumpeters and Drum

Horse of the Household Cavalry.'

The red velvet curtains slowly parted and the spotlight fell on to the magnificent coloured Clydesdale horse surmounted by his rider in gold and scarlet and two glittering kettle drums. In the now-hushed space of the arena they boomed and echoed like thunder and then the pool of spotlights grew and six grey horses stood quite motionless while their riders pealed a fanfare on their long silver trumpets. Then together the seven horses moved into the arena and their glorious noise reverberated all around. The band above took up the theme and the horses parted and moved to either side of the arena. One final mighty roll on the drums and all was silent again.

Uncontrollable shivers were running up and down the whole length of my body, my eyes were straining for a first glimpse.

Once more the curtains parted and in the darkness I could hear a familiar jingling noise but could see only pin-points of lights, then two more behind, then two more still. These tiny lights spread out into a row and as the spotlights came up, there, abreast in the arena, their candles lit in their lamps, were three carriages.

'We start, Ladies and Gentlemen, with the World Pairs Bronze Medal Team: Paul Gregory, Fred Pendlebury and Richard Smith. Very well done indeed!'

Whistles and cheers rang to the roof as the carriages moved forward, then halted while the drivers saluted the Royal box, then moved on again. In the background the band was gently playing the theme from *Chariots of Fire*, but it was more than *Chariots of Fire* to me. It was the *1812*, the 'Hallelujah Chorus' and 'Land of Hope and Glory' all rolled into one, with the emphasis on the Hope and the Glory.

On legs that felt quite out of contact with the ground I quietly left my seat as directed and joined the carriage at the top end of the arena to walk down behind it back to the far end. As we walked, the next Gold medallists were now making their entrance into the spotlight. At the far end the carriages lined up and grooms jumped out the the horses' heads. Long minutes passed while wave after wave of horses entered the arena, each one to its own separate roar of applause. Long minutes during which I stood quietly beside my husband and my horses. I was totally satiated with happiness and pride and standing there my mind raced quickly back over nearly ten years.

To Bear, a gangly young cob who went on to hunt, and to jump and to drive; who so nearly died a horrifying death but recovered from his injuries against all the odds, and later recovered his nerve where a lesser horse would have given up the fight. To my own personal stormy decade of passage through emotional pain and physical pain, to finding new hope, new faith, new reasons for going on; to Richard and Blizzard; to our new path together, to our Better Way. To the incredible problems and the dizzy heights the four of us had scaled together — to the long path that had led us all to this arena, to this one night of glory.

Surely, dear Lord surely, that path would not, could not, end at this point? There must be a way forward, there must be a way to go on together. 'And, indeed,' a firm voice inside reassured me 'there will be a way, though it surely won't be easy, there will be a way.'

And I knew in that moment without a shadow of doubt that we would find it when the time was right.

As we always had.

And then, as slowly as they had dimmed, the lights came back on in the Wembley arena to reveal row upon row of horses and riders — and of course three carriages and drivers.

'Ladies and Gentlemen, the parade of medallists is complete.'

Blinking a little in the renewed light, Bear and Blizzard, gleaming copper and glorious, stood arrogantly accepting the wave upon wave of applause as it it were all totally, unreservedly, their own. They acted and looked every inch exactly what they were: world-class horses.

As the applause was dying away, the announcer said simply, 'Owners, would you please join your horses.'

I moved as did all the other owners to their horses' heads and from the Royal box end a gentleman approached. It was John Stevens, the Show Director. At each owner he stopped, shook hands and presented a small memento.

When he reached me, he took my hand and said, 'Thank you so much for bringing your beautiful horses here tonight.'

And I answered with what was the simple truth, 'It is my very great pleasure.'

When he moved on I gazed out at the mass of people packing the stands and imagined fleetingly I saw familiar faces among them. That couldn't be Janice, or Alison Cowley, nor Carol Herbert? And yet . . . no, it couldn't be Lizzie, Brian Patterson and surely not John and Joan Sykes? And yet somehow they were there. They were all there: all those who had kept faith.

In the rise and fall of the crowd's chatter I thought I could discern familiar voices, familiar words: 'That horse should be 'tween shafts . . .', 'You must be prepared for the worst . . .',

'No promises, no promises . . . ', 'What appears to be the end could really be a new beginning . . . ', 'Ride? Young woman, be thankful to walk!', 'Don't ever trust him again . . . ', 'Sorry I'm a vet, not a psychiatrist . . . ', 'Flag horses in front please!'

And then with absolute certainty I heard behind me a low chuckle, a dry, low chuckle I had not heard for many years. Had I turned I knew I would have seen her: the woman who coloured, and perhaps still colours, my life more than any other individual in my family; seen the tiny figure with bent arthritic hands and shaggy eyebrows, the figure who was saying to me: 'Aye, hinny, he's a grand hoss. They're both grand bonny horses; and I'm proud of ye.'

And very deep inside a voice was telling me that the legacy had been well spent.

Epilogue

IN LATE 1985 a sponsor came forward for the cobs: Alan Robson, chairman of Montan-Lago Ltd, an international shopfitting group. The 'Montan-Lago Carriage-Driving Team', (by now consisting of three horses), went on to win the 1986 National Championships.

In 1987, Richard was once again selected for the World Pairs Driving Championship in Germany, where, sadly, the official British Team came to grief (only the individual entry, Gordon Henderson, finished). However, in September 1987 Richard regained national glory at Windsor by winning the National Championships once more.

In 1988, Bear and Blizzard, together with two additional chestnut cobs, are to be sponsored for their third year by Montan-Lago. Who knows? Could the driving force that's brought us so far be about to develop into a team spirit?

Time will tell.